INTERNATIONAL
POLITICS

INTERNATIONAL POLITICS

Balance of power

Balance of productivity

Balance of ideologies

RALPH PETTMAN

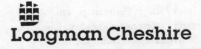

Longman Cheshire

Lynne Rienner Publishers, Inc.

Longman Cheshire Pty Limited
Longman House
Kings Gardens
95 Coventry Street
Melbourne 3205 Australia

Offices in Sydney, Brisbane, Adelaide and Perth. Associated companies, branches and representatives throughout the world.

Published in the USA by
Lynne Rienner Publishers, Inc.
1800 30th Street, Boulder
Colorado 80301

Copyright © Longman Cheshire 1991
First published 1991

Edited by Adrienne Linley
Designed by Nadia Graziotto
Set in 10/12 pt Times
Printed in Malaysia
by Vinlin Press Sdn. Bhd., Seri Petaling, Kuala Lumpur.

National Library of Australia
Cataloguing-in-Publication data

Pettman, Ralph.
International politics.

Bibliography.
Includes index.
ISBN 0 582 86899 8.

1. International relations. I. Title.

327

Library of Congress Cataloging-in-Publication Data
Pettman. Ralph.
International politics / Ralph Pettman. p. cm.
Includes bibliography reference and index.
ISBN 1-55587-281-6 : $16.95 (U.S. : est.)
1. International relations. I. Title
JX1395.P44 1991
327-dc20

Contents

Preface

x International politics

This book is an introduction to international politics and as such assumes
no prior knowledge of the subject. It looks in turn at state-making, wealth-
making, and social movements. In that sense it is not only an *intro*duction.
It is an *extra*duction as well. It leads in to the subject. It also leads out.

By leading out I mean going beyond the conventional boundaries of the
discipline. To account for the complexity of global affairs, as well as the
richness of the human experience of it, I argue that three approaches are
required, namely, a political, a political–economic, and a social one. It is
the first that receives the most detailed treatment in traditional studies of
the subject. I argue here for an analysis, in at least equivalent detail, of the
other two.

State-making and the interstate system are obviously important. There is
more to world politics than this, however. There is wealth-making and the
global political economy, and there are acculturation patterns and people's
responses to what international politics means to them. Each aspect relates
closely to the others and each has its own philosophical and historical
context that also deserves close scrutiny.

Such a book covers a lot of ground. It makes many trade-offs between
breadth and depth. To anchor the analytic narrative somewhat, and to help
show how some of the basic ideas work in practice, three case studies
(keyed to the text) have been included as appendices. Effecting such trade-
offs is no simple matter. Hopefully the case studies help in this regard. The
balance struck can only remain contentious, however, which is the nature
of the beast at best.

A number of colleagues read the whole or parts of the first draft and
offered helpful advice on how to improve it. In this regard I would like to

thank Alastair Davidson, Patricia Springborg, John Ravenhill, Barbara Leigh and Sharon Caldwell (University of Sydney); Nancy Viviani (Australian National University); Rob Walker (University of Victoria, BC); Morag Fraser (intellectual itinerant); and the publishers themselves.

I asked Deborah Snow to read the first draft but she didn't get past the first few pages. However, if she'd been home more often this book would never have been written. So it is dedicated, with love, to her.

Introduction

The study of international politics, like the practice of it, typically centres on the state. The state is a catch-all concept covering the efforts made by state-makers to keep particular kinds of order, both within their borders and between the peoples these borders contain.

The latter attempt, that is, the ordering of international relationships, is most commonly described and explained in terms of balances of power. The power referred to is mostly military and strategic. Force or the threat of force is never far away. This is 'high politics' (as conventionally understood). It includes all aspects of conventional diplomacy, alliance-making and alliance-breaking, and all the practices meant to promote and protect territorial integrity, sovereign autonomy, the legitimacy of state-making, and the authority of the state-makers themselves. This is International Politics, with a capital 'I' and a capital 'P'.

You do not, strictly speaking, ever have states. Rather, they are made on an ongoing basis from the human material to hand, which is often very imperfect for the purpose. It may, for example, consist of recalcitrant ethnic groups, or rural peoples with little interest in anything larger than the family, or business executives of transnational corporations. These are people who may not want to be made into members of states. State-makers seek to assert their sovereign singularity regardless, and those who are good at it will usually have considerable resources at their disposal for doing so. Those who fail must often suffer that fate because the country they are trying to define or defend is poor.

International politicking takes place, in other words, in the context of the international political economy. This is the domain of 'low politics' so-called, where the entrepreneurs of the world marketplace manufacture goods and services, exchange them, and invest. The global struggle to out-produce, out-trade, and out-consume is as dynamic as diplomatics. It radically conditions the state-makers' world, where it does not — directly or indirectly — determine it. The ordering of the commercial relationships involved is not just a traditional state-centric concern, however. It entails what is called here the balance of productivity.

Wealth-making on a world scale is arguably nothing but state-making by other means. The argument for seeing it this way is made by those traditionally called mercantilists. Those entrepreneurs, however, who like to see politics and economics as separate realms, and who regard prosperity and peace as a result of the universal pursuit of profit, tend to see state-making as more of a hindrance than a help. A perspective of this sort denotes, in classical parlance, a liberal.

There are those, on the other hand, who see the world political economy in terms of what capitalists do, and in terms of the class contradictions between those who own and control the means of production, and those who sell their labour for a wage. Such an approach is basically Marxist. To Marxists the state serves capital in general, or fractions of capital in particular. Marxists highlight the inequalities that result from world development and, in classical parlance, they anticipate the bid the impoverished and the exploited are historically supposed to make for their emancipation.

We can also, however, look at international politics from the perspective not only of exploited wage-workers but also of all those disadvantaged by all the state-making and wealth-making that goes on in the world. By doing so we draw attention to the social practices that define the domain we might dub 'even lower politics'. We highlight the plight of those marginalised by or alienated from both political institution-building and political economics. We draw attention to all those social groups and movements who, in the name of justice or freedom or equity or basic needs, question whether the state, the interstate system and the world political economy serve any more than the minority interests of dominant classes, or particular ethnic groups, or men. The ordering of the relationships involved — between the world's topdogs and the world's underdogs — is also not a matter of traditional state-centric concern. It entails a complex and uneven balance of ideologies.

This book covers all the above. This is a great deal to attempt, but then a great deal goes on in world affairs, and any discussion that claims to be comprehensive is going to have to range far and wide. Since what happens in the world is intimately associated with what we think is happening there, such a discussion will have to account for more than just current affairs. It will have to account for the different perspectives that have been brought to bear upon the subject. To a radical political economist, for example, there is no such thing as international politics. To choose such a label is already to suggest that politics and economics can be discussed separately, which is a conclusion she or he would resist from the start.

The diversity of world affairs does not mean we cannot approach the subject in a disciplined and discriminating way. What I shall do is start with international politics as it is conventionally understood. I shall discuss state-making, the concept of the balance of power, and the importance placed upon order as the core value. In this realist conception of the subject, power is primarily construed in terms of the brute force wielded by the military and the police, and the state is the key unit of analysis.

I shall then take a second cut into the welter of world events to consider international political economy in three guises — neo-mercantilist, liberal and Marxist. I shall discuss the entrepreneurial activities of the world's wealth-makers, and the class-forming effects of the world market. I shall conceptualise this as a balance of productivity. Such an approach is usually called structuralist. I shall discuss it in terms of the value placed by those concerned upon wealth, upon human emancipation by material means, and upon power as primarily a matter of production, distribution and exchange.

I shall then take a third cut to consider how all this appears from the people's perspective. I shall discuss the significance of various social groups and movements and the role they play as keepers of the moral flame. I shall conceptualise this in terms of a balance of ideologies. This is conventionally known as the pluralist approach. It covers a wide range of preferred values, like freedom, equity, community and well-being. Without force or wealth, the power to articulate such ideas comes from a belief in the ideas themselves.

Rather than visualising this as three cuts into the subject, each one deeper than the last, it can also be thought of in terms of degrees of embeddedness. State-making takes place in the context of world wealth-making, which takes place within world society as a whole. Each dimension, in other words, is embedded in a larger and more comprehensive one, that must in turn be understood adequately to describe and explain what goes on within it.

Though inferior dimensions condition, or even determine, what happens in superior ones, superior dimensions condition, even determine, what goes below them. It may not be sufficient but it is certainly necessary to know the nature of lower politics to describe and explain higher ones. Likewise, higher politics define the parameters, where they are not even the direct cause, of what happens in lower domains.

We are familiar with the notion that states affect markets and productive chains, as well as what people think. We are less familiar, however, with the equally plausible attempt to identify how wealth-makers affect state-makers and ideologies at large, or how ordinary people can influence markets and productive capacities and even foreign policy.

Yet another way to visualise the approach taken here is in terms of a process of spiralling out. Starting with the familiar concept of the state and of interstate politicking, I spiral out to consider the political-economy of world affairs. In doing this I encounter the state again, only this time it looks rather different. It is not just the locus of a web of diplomatic and strategic activity, as high politics would have it be. It looks more like a source of autarkic strength (the mercantilist view), or a side-play to the world's commercial activities (the classical liberal view), or a fraction of world capital (the classical Marxist view).

Spiralling out further I encounter the state again, only this time it looks like a large number of political/productive practices that have the effect of marginalising or alienating many of the world's population. Technically such people may live within states, but in practice they live largely outside them where they must fend for themselves.

Most of what is written about international politics falls within the first domain. It is about high politics, sovereignty, anarchy, spheres of influence, alliances, intervention, clientelism, strategic hierarchies, international organisations, peace and war. This is a great deal to discuss. It is also only a fraction of the subject. It says very little about the second domain of low politics and the international political economy. It says even less about the even lower politics of the world society beyond the state.

The importance of the first domain is self-evident. There is also growing acknowledgement now of the need to understand international political economy (though this still consists in the main of ideologically liberal writings on the politics of international economics or the economics of international politics).

There is very little recognition still of the relevance to world affairs of those who live 'beyond the pale'. While not wishing to detract from the significance of more traditional concerns, or the discussion of the first or second domains (indeed, I talk about them here at length), this book seeks to extend as far as possible the circle of such concerns. Though many of those marginalised by the state-making and wealth-making practices of the world's movers and shakers may have little immediate impact on world affairs, they are not to be ignored. Indeed, they have the capacity to revolutionise world affairs, which is not to say they will, but they have the competence and the capacity to do so. They are not likely to go away, and meanwhile they have much to say about conventional versions of global politics.

The feminist re-conceptualisation of power, for example, as a process of competence and not just dominance/subordinance, leads to a radically different understanding of the traditional concept of the balance of power. Likewise, the environmentalist concern with sustainable development questions the commitment of most contemporary state- and wealth-makers to economic growth and consumerism. Furthermore, the persistence or the resurgence of a host of religious beliefs puts the rationalism of the modern world in a metaphysical context it has never, despite a long and valiant attempt to do so, finally escaped.

It is the aim of this book, then, to provide a skeleton key with which to unlock the complex conundrums of world affairs. If a conscientious attempt is made to consider any particular global issue in the light of the three domains sketched above, and in the light of the many and varied relationships between them, I can imagine no more comprehensive account that can be given of it.

I contend, therefore, that it is not enough to talk about international politics in terms of the state and its foreign and defence policies, or the interstate system. International politics is now world affairs or world studies. The subject requires a detailed knowledge of the international political economy. It also requires a detailed knowledge of the social consequences of world state- and wealth-making, and a detailed knowledge of the sentiments of those ordinary men and women who are normally seen as the passive consumers of international politics rather than its producers.

We live in the most materially productive era in human history. It would seem sensible, therefore, to begin by looking at the patterns of world productivity — primary, secondary and tertiary. State-making so dominates the global scene, however, that it is more convenient to start with 'the state' in its conventional setting — the system of states.

This state system is an industrialising and a capitalist one. Capitalist industrialisation has had mixed benefits. It has immeasurably augmented our capacity for state-making. It has immeasurably augmented the human capacity to support many more people, many of them at a very high standard of living indeed. Against this, however, has to be put a commensurate increase in human (and particularly female) poverty, in mental stress and despair, and in damage to the natural environment. There is ample scope for pessimism. It is heartening therefore to see how often people refuse to succumb to despair, and how often they refuse in constructive and affirmative ways.

Indeed, an outstanding feature of contemporary world affairs is the way ordinary men and women continue to mount humanistic alternatives to state-making and wealth-making practices that in the name of security or growth-and-development fail to provide either. It may yet be the case that the political communities ordinary people forge at the bottom of the world political pile prove more durable in human terms than any of the initiatives we see taken at the top.

International politics

What is international politics? Who are the international politicians? How is sense to be made of questions like these?

1 What is international politics? Who are the international politicians?

Most of us would say we have a common-sense idea of what international politics involves. Most of us could say something about what an international politician is and what he or she might do. Our common-sense in this regard we get from what we see on television, from the conversations we have with family and friends, from what we learn in more formal settings like schools, from the experiences we have in our travels, from periodicals and newspapers, and from what we think ourselves.

Because newspapers are so widely shared and so readily available I shall begin by looking briefly at how the world is described and explained in one fairly typical sample of this medium. I shall take as my text a copy of the *Canberra Times*, chosen at random, dated Saturday, 25 February 1989. The *Canberra Times* appears daily in the capital city of a medium size power in the South Pacific, namely, Australia. It is read by many of the country's policy-makers. It is not a mass circulation tabloid, nor is it like one of the major dailies that circulate in the two big cities on Australia's south-east coast, Sydney and Melbourne. It is merely a large-town morning paper, self-conscious about its capital-city status, somewhat pretentious as a consequence, and serving a well-educated and relatively powerful population of administrators, politicians and academics.

One section of this paper is devoted specifically to world politics. Indeed, like most such dailies it has a foreign affairs editor whose job it is to compile world news and to make sure such news is current, relevant, interesting and helps sells copies. Most people want to know these things, and those who read the *Canberra Times* pay a modest sum in local currency to gain the information.

The first and most obvious observation I can make of the world affairs section of the *Canberra Times* on 25 February 1989 is how small it is compared to what went on around the globe on that day. All the politicking everywhere, all the to-ing and fro-ing, all the incidents and the institutional outcomes are put before us in two pages. This limited coverage is quite normal for the *Canberra Times*. Occasionally world affairs spill over onto other pages, and even onto the front page, but usually a smorgasbord of snippets is meant to summarise in less than 250 column centimetres all that is happening around the world.

Newspapers are meant to be portable; to be held in the hand. They are meant to be disposable. They are meant to be a summary. To achieve the miracle of compression that is required their foreign news editors must, among other things, be highly selective. Out of the welter of reported world events he or she must choose a handful of items for print. The daily choice can cover only a few issues, and only a few aspects of those issues chosen, a fact that quickly becomes apparent to anyone using newspapers for research purposes. No matter how good the newspaper may be, as a source of sustained information it will invariably prove infuriating. Tantalising glimpses will be given of events and ideas. The newspaper will be repetitive. It will not provide a cumulative account of any issue over any period of time. It will be highly selective and more than a little incomplete.

Newspapers are also biased. There are three dimensions to the question of bias — a commercial, an ideological and an epistemological one. The first two dimensions are obvious. Newspapers have their own political agendas, typically set by their senior personnel and their journalists. These people are often conservative, sometimes progressive, sometimes radical. They do not just provide information. They provide information more or less pertinent to the larger causes they believe to be important.

Ideally, of course, a newspaper's political perspective should show only in its editorial. There the paper's editors draw conclusions about what is good or bad or right or wrong in the world. In practice papers have (in capitalist societies) to sell, which encourages editors, subeditors and journalists to look for the angle which will catch a reader's attention and induce him or her to want to buy a copy and read it. The political predilections of newsworkers will inevitably influence the selection of what is newsworthy and what is to be emphasised in the items selected for print.

'Serious' newspapers will give their reporters considerable leeway to tell their stories as they see them. But in market-based societies in particular they do not escape the commercial temptation to look for what will attract attention. Nor can they escape the ideological bias they bring to the news as they believe it to be.

This problem is exacerbated by the fact that many papers are secondary as well as primary producers of news. The cost of keeping foreign correspondents at posts overseas is very high. Where these are not borne by governments, as in the case of papers run by and for particular statemakers, they will often rely on syndicated services such as Reuters, Agence France Presse and Associated Press. This puts a double filter and a double interpretative screen, namely, that of the press agency and of the newpaper itself, between the world and the reader.

What is 'news'

There is more to bias than these commercial or ideological questions, however. There is an even more subtle epistemological question to do with the nature of news knowledge itself. What is news? A newspaper, whether its makers know it or not, will necessarily articulate theories of international politics. It will impart these theories to its readers who, in a democracy, are voters as well as policy-makers. It has no choice in the matter. Without a theoretical framework in which to gather and place them, news facts would be meaningless. Similarly, without criteria for selection, newspaper workers who tried to document every event in the world would signify everything in particular and nothing in general.

This then leads to another question. What theoretical framework does any particular newspaper seem to be using? If we can clearly answer that, further questions follow. Is the framework adequate? What are our indices of adequacy? For example, does the paper describe and explain what is going on in the world as well as it might? What would be a good or a bad description or explanation? What is the paper not saying, or not saying very clearly? What voice, for instance, does it give to those who live on the margins; to those who live in the vast slums and ghettos of the great cities; to women's affairs; or to indigenous peoples whose ways of living may be daily jeopardised by the state?

I am reminded at this point of John Mabbot's account of our attempts to make sense of the world as something akin to climbing the tower of a great cathedral.[1] Up the spiral stairway we go, and as we ascend 'the common and particular details of life ... shrink to invisibility and the big landmarks shake themselves clear'. Little windows open at our elbows, with ever wider views. We look in our newspaper as if through a window and we see nation-states like Iran, the USA or New Zealand. Over there is a multinational corporation. There is the nation-state again, looking quite different from a new level — as a member of a region perhaps, like the Middle East or Central America; as part of a balance of power; or as part of a balance of productivity. Now we are high enough to see the balance of power and the balance of productivity together.

What keeps us going? The vision of the summit, Mabbot says, where there is a little room with windows all round, where we can catch our breath and see the view as a whole and where that gargoyle (Karl Marx was it, all hairy and grim?) which loomed in on us so menacingly at one stage in our climb has taken its rightful place in the larger scheme of things. We shall be told, Mabbot warns, that no one reaches the top. Theorists who cease to climb do so because they get tired. They crouch against some staircase window, with its dusty and one-sided view, obstinately telling the crowds below (who do not listen) that they are at the summit and can see the whole city.

Mabbot's metaphor is very evocative. It is also very misleading. It assumes, for example, that reality is 'out there' and that the big landmarks shake themselves clear. But reality is not only out there to be discovered by changing one's perspective. It is also to do with what is 'in here', that we think is out there. It is something we not only discover, but that we impose on the world in the very act of looking at it. A more appropriate and accurate image than climbing a tower might be that of digging a garden. We turn over our ideas like garden loam. We plant all sorts of ornamental and fruitful notions that we protect from bugs and weeds. What we reap is directly related to what we sow.

We participate very actively, in other words, in what we do as newspaper readers, even when we think we do not. In this sense reading a paper is not just finding out something (climbing Mabbot's tower). It is also taking part in designing a culture, our culture (cultivating the mind).[2]

What has this to do with our text? On Saturday, 25 February 1989, the *Canberra Times* index refers us to pages 10–12 for its version of world affairs. Turning to these pages we find eight separate items. The first is entitled 'Woman jailed for running over "Mickey Mouse"'. This was a human interest story from Associated Press about someone in Hauppage, New York, who killed her husband by repeatedly running over him with a car. She had apparently become convinced that he was possessed by the spirit of Mickey Mouse. Somehow Disney's cartoon character had taken over the poor man's body. The second item was more serious. It was a Reuter's report on how Yugoslav leaders had hinted that they might send in troops to put down ethnic Albanian unrest and strikes in one of

Yugoslavia's provinces. There was a picture of striking miners. The third item returned to Associated Press and another human interest piece. A pair of human legs, wearing different socks, had been found in the garbage behind a grocery store in Salt Lake City, Utah. 'We have no idea what we have here', Sheriff's Captain Robert Jack is quoted as saying. 'It might be something from the university'. The fourth item was a Reuter's account of the funeral of Emperor Hirohito of Japan. Item five was about Winnie Mandela and her associates in South Africa. Item six was about government plans in Helsinki for sex holidays to help people relieve the stress of everyday life in Finland. Item seven was about general elections in the Solomon Islands. Item eight was about a United States Navy captain, before the courts for abandoning at sea a boatload of Vietnamese refugees.

These items suggest that the foreign editor of the *Canberra Times* chose the news almost at random. Elsewhere in the same edition, however, there was a feature article from the English daily, the *Independent*, called 'Soviets seek to redefine friendship with Egypt'. This talked about the Russian attempt to reestablish a presence in the Middle East after fifteen years outside the diplomatic process there. It was a very serious piece and definitely not a contingent choice. Most revealing, then, is the way it used the language of power politics: countries allying and re-allying, jockeying for advantage, applying pressure, intriguing, heightening conflict, establishing detente. It was all about suspicious state players pursuing their interests in a deadly earnest, and often just plain deadly, game.

As a feature article this was something those who control the content of the *Canberra Times* clearly considered important. From the page place-ment and the size of the piece, this was serious news. Doubly significant, then, is the conventional geopolitical character of the picture it paints. 'Historically', the article says, 'the Soviet Union has considered the Middle East a natural and legitimate area of interest. Geographically so much closer to the region than the United States, it [has] resented the fact that the diplomatic running ...[is] made by its rival superpower'. There is mention also of a plan for an international conference to solve the region's main problems: the Arab–Israeli conflict and what to do about the displaced Palestinians.

Coaching the reader

The point to note here is that an article like this is shot through with theoretical assumptions about how the world works and what world politics might be. It coaches the reader in a world view that most would probably agree is the common sense one. Listen to the language: superpower, conference, interest, history, geography. How familiar it is. The terms are certainly common enough, but what sense is to be made of them? What kind of a world is this newspaper describing and explaining? What does it prescribe?

First and most obviously it is a world of states. We sit on the sidelines and watch while, like a lot of boxers in a ring, 'they' spar and parry. Some win and some lose. Some are midgets and some are giants. They gang up. They fall out. The metaphor could be extended with ease before it became unduly strained.

Unlike most boxers, however, they don't just use brute force (though it is another common sense assumption that brute force matters, and matters a great deal). They use bribery and persuasion to score points. They each have a name like the Soviet Union or Israel. We are meant to imagine separate entities. We are supposed to assume discrete, corporate bodies, persisting no matter who runs or inhabits them. Where those involved don't have such a corporate identity, like the Palestinians, we are shown them trying hard to achieve one.

Secondly, we notice a distinction between the outside and the inside of these states. Much world news is about the domestic doings of others (hence the news about internal affairs in the Solomon Islands, Japan, South Africa and Yugoslavia). At the same time we are reinforced in our feeling of 'us' in our state and 'them' in theirs. (The us–them dichotomy is the most basic sociological discriminator, and the systematic definition and endorsement of it in this way is of considerable analytic interest.)

At one point in the major article cited, however, there is mention of a new Soviet political priority being given to trade and commerce. The mention is brief, but it tokens a view of the world somewhat different from that of boxers in a ring. We glimpse the Soviet state as a trader, and of course, to trade you have to have products and be a producer. There must be a market, and in this case an international market. Markets are typically busy places, and the world market is no exception. Given the amount of modern global production, and how efficient and far-reaching contemporary means of communications and transport have become, participation in it is intense. Should it not feature in our reading of world affairs?

The state-based view of the world reflected in the *Canberra Times* feature piece could be readily extended, of course, to include the politics of international economics. The frame would simply be pushed back to take in trade, aid and investment as part of foreign policy, along with more traditional matters of strategy and diplomacy. The view would remain essentially the same. It would merely be a bit broader.

Some states, like the Soviet Union, trade as a corporate entity in this market. Most do not. It is not the Japanese government, for example, which

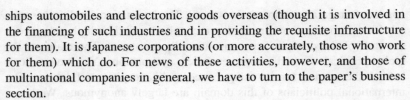

ships automobiles and electronic goods overseas (though it is involved in the financing of such industries and in providing the requisite infrastructure for them). It is Japanese corporations (or more accurately, those who work for them) which do. For news of these activities, however, and those of multinational companies in general, we have to turn to the paper's business section.

Corporations don't sign international treaties or put armies in the field. They sign contracts and send out salespeople. Like a crowd of boxers' managers, they lurk in the half-light, egging on the men in the ring. They make deals that often have little to do with their state-based affiliations. It is in this half-light, however, that we begin to see the dim outlines of another picture of world politics, and one the *Canberra Times* does not systematically describe or explain — at least, not in the context of its world news.

Of course, the paper has plenty to say from time to time on how Australia has to battle to make a living in the world. Its primary producers must sell their goods on glutted markets. Its people buy manufactured goods from overseas in greater quantities than they can collectively afford. The Federal Treasurer must try to balance the public books. All this consolidates the concept of the state, though it is an expanded concept, where state-makers promote and protect public welfare as well as territorial security. Since the mundane life-chances and life-choices of most ordinary people now have as much if not more to do with trade balances and investment portfolios as they have with the threat of invasion or war, the picture of what international politics involves must necessarily be enlarged to include these processes.

International political economy

Not so obvious, however, is the power of those who own and manage the means of producing goods and services in the world. It is their prime purpose to make a profit. They use their industrial and financial capital to do so, and the system they serve is called, not surprisingly, capitalism. Capitalists couldn't make profits if they didn't have people to work for them — to sell their labour for a wage. The worth of what these workers do is usually greater than what they get paid for, and it is this difference that the capitalist gets to cover his or her costs, to consume personally, and to re-invest.

This is a different domain from that of alliances, state interests and foreign affairs. It is a world of money and goods and the human relations that make and remake the global patterns of production, distribution, consumption and exchange. It is a world you will glimpse only obliquely in the *Canberra Times*.

The state administrations and foreign relations departments which conduct foreign affairs are obvious to all. The international politicians who inhabit these institutions are readily recognised, and their high policies are the stuff of the discipline as conventionally construed. The realm of the global political economy, however, is less conspicuous. You have to look behind the scenes for it, using concepts like capital and labour. The international politicians of this domain are largely anonymous. We know many of the names of the leaders of states, but how many leaders of large transnational corporations can we name, though they command more resources than most states?

Indeed, if capital and labour are taken seriously enough, they can be used to describe international political events as contingent upon a battle to out-produce, out-trade and out-consume. This is rather different from the notion of international politics as causing the events that we summarise as world affairs. 'International politics' may well be the wrong term. 'International political economy' may be more appropriate, and not just in the sense that we should look nowadays at world economy as well as world politics, but in the sense that world politics and world economics are one. They are two aspects of a profound revolution in human affairs, namely, the advent of industrial capitalism.

'Politics' and 'economics' are apart, in this view, because they have been pulled apart by those with vested interests in denying their integrated nature. Many seek to disguise the complex interplay between wealth-making and state-making. They are routinely taken to task, however, by those who see states in terms of competing fractions of world capital. An integrated view of this sort highlights the opportunistic pursuit, by wealth-makers, of as much profit as possible. Wealth-makers, such theorists argue, constitute a global class of private and state-capitalist entrepreneurs. The state nature of the bases from which these entrepreneurs operate are to them of secondary, not primary, concern.

Theorists of this type also see labouring as an international process. Workers migrate to centres of productive power — Yugoslavs to West Germany, Indians to Saudi Arabia, Thais to Singapore. Capitalists locate industries where labour can be bought cheaply, in the process drawing the whole world into a single productive web that continues, in its highly uneven fashion, to grow and grow.

Living on the margins

Can growth of this sort be sustained indefinitely? The world capitalist political economy has been likened to a running man leaning forward, having to run faster and faster to keep from falling flat on his face. Has the system stumbled already in the marginalised zones where growing numbers of people now have to live? Can the ecosphere on which we ultimately depend be preserved short of collapse?

The *Canberra Times*, like its counterparts in other cities, reports regularly on planetary warming, the greenhouse effect, and the depletion of the ozone layer. It shows pictures of environmental activists pushing their rubber dinghies into the white teeth of superpower warships, or publicising the spread of industrial pollutants. It reports on African famines and the destruction of the Amazon rainforests. These are issues that only the narrowest of definitions would fail to recognise as international and political, and yet we are not coached in how to read their significance. The steady din of state affairs drowns them out. Nor are we likely to recognise any of the names of the international politicians involved in these activities.

Think, for example, of the slum-dwellers of Lima, Lagos or Los Angeles, who the world market includes in only the most tenuous fashion, as the last link in a long chain of exploitative practices. They live in dire poverty, with their traditional cultural routines seriously dislocated, little or no educational or medical care, and only the stamp of the government's heel if they revolt. Many millions of people live this way. How many of their leaders would we recognise by name?

Think of the environmentalists trying to build a social movement that makes disparate peoples in diverse places aware of their ecological interconnectedness (and having to do so without falling into the trap Western cultures set of assuming that reasonable action necessarily means 'progress' and a more desirable ecological order). Do we know the names of the leaders of movements like these?

Think of the many Islamic fundamentalists manifesting their faith in a transcendental eternity rather than a mundane present, and having to deal nonetheless with the organised profanity of markets and states. Who represents them 'abroad'? What does abroad mean in this context?

We don't have to think very long to find examples of people who practise world politics without using the conventional words and the traditional means. They live beside, behind and beyond the pale, and they may well be the majority of the earth's population. Their international politicians are largely unknown.

Reflections of this sort take us outside the often narrow and quite rigid confines set by the daily news. They ask us to look at aspects of world affairs that may be unfamiliar from the regular reporting of papers like the *Canberra Times*. Most newspapers relegate accounts of these other dimensions to supplementary sections, if they report them at all. This inhibits our capacity to place international events in their larger contexts. The same applies to the other media as well, and this is clearly problematic, since we need to know as much as we can about how the world works if we are to live in it happily, or indeed, if we are to go on living in it at all.

What do I mean by the larger contexts in which we should place international events? Given the theme of this study it might be worthwhile briefly exploring a number of ways in which the conventional reading of current world affairs can be readily extended beyond the usual range of the daily newspaper.

Conceptualising 'world society'

To begin with, try this simple thought experiment. Imagine the world's population as a single entity: 5 billion people. Think of how many ways they can be organised conceptually; how many sociological sets they can be placed in — cultural, ideological, religious, political or economic. The relationships that define these sets will be clumped, more or less intensely, into what we call states. However, a lot of them will not. To get them all to fit into the one category, the state, is like stuffing jelly-fish into pigeon-holes.[3]

World society is divided by this thought experiment into many specific networks — global, regional and local — that reach down to the level of the family. While we can separate particular networks for analytic purposes, any particular individual will belong to a number of them. An oil producer, for example, may be a company executive, a Muslim, an amateur astronomer, a mother, and an Armenian. She may have different allegiances depending on what identity or identities we choose to highlight.

World society appears in this view like 'millions of cobwebs superimposed one upon another covering the whole globe ... Each separate cobweb ... represent[s] a separate system — trade flows, letters exchanged, tourist movements, aircraft flights, population movements and transactions in ideas, cultures, languages and religions, traffic flows within towns and social interactions within village communities'.[4]

The problem with this thought experiment is that it ends up unduly downplaying the state. It takes politics without states as the norm of politics, which is legitimate and proper. It fails to do justice, however, to the contemporary significance of state-making. To go from politicking in general to the special case of politics as state politics in particular may be interesting as an intellectual exercise, but in practical terms the current importance of states and state-making is too great not to acknowledge their contemporary significance.

The cobweb metaphor is a good antidote nonetheless to the conceptual tyranny that state-making tends to impose, and that newspapers typically foster. It can be a useful reminder of the plurality of human experience, and the way human beings do many things other than those sanctioned by states.

A second way of enlarging our awareness of world society is to start with states and with the familiar geopolitical map they provide, and then to redraw this map to represent, schematically, information other than that of land mass or surface area. A map that represents relative industrial capacity, for example, will show a huge North America above a tiny Central and South America. Europe will include a disproportionately large UK, while Africa will be hardly perceptible at all. Japan will be enormous.

Given that industrial capacity is the most important measure of productive power, and given that productivity and sustained strategic might are synonymous for practical purposes, a map like this will be a good way of representing the relative power of modern states, and a reminder of the analytically limited nature of the geographic representations we normally go by. (Similar redrafting can be done with regard to a wide range of issues. The world will look different every time. This tells us much we may already know verbally or statistically. We may not fully appreciate it, however, until we see it displayed in this way. [5])

A third way of challenging our conventionally conditioned view of world affairs is to reflect on the compass model of it. I refer here to the notion that there is a first world, a second world, a third world, and (though people mean different things by it) a fourth world. The first world is the West and the second world is the East. Together they make up the global North. The third world is the poor South, and the fourth world is the very poor South, or the poor everywhere. This model is a basic part of the common sense of how the world should be categorised.

Common sense is not necessarily good sense, however. Robert Walker, for example, suggests a compelling alternative to the compass model. This alternative describes the life experiences of earth's people as a whole. In doing so Walker highlights some interesting features of world affairs that statism obscures.

What he does is sketch two scenarios. His first is what he calls a 'no world' one. It entails large-scale nuclear war. Variations on this theme also point to 'fundamental social forces that, whether through a reliance on ecologically destructive practices or through the encouragement of militarization and institutionalized violence, threaten to bring about a general civilizational collapse'. The second scenario he calls a 'two worlds' one. This promises a beneficial outcome 'but only for some ... It comes with a widely advertised tale of progress and an unadvertised tale of woe'. In the process of making two worlds, interstate relations are regulated and order prevails. Whose order is it, however? What is it for? It certainly has little to do with peace or justice. As Walker argues:

It simply implies a different kind of violence.

It promises economic recovery and technological miracles; but only for those who are able to participate in the world economy ...

It promises better management of environmental resources, but not beyond limits prescribed by profitablility ...

It promises a reduction in the abuse of human rights, but only as defined in the narrowest terms ...

It promises a happier, more meaningful existence for all, but only through the commodification of desire. [6]

How much of Walker's underworld makes the news? How much of it seems common sense to those reading the world affairs that newspapers, for example, report ?

There is a certain circularity about taking newspapers. They provide a version of the world that is overwhelmingly statist. Readers recognise this version of the world and it reinforces the conceptual perspectives they have been coached to see in the first place. A world news section, organised by country, can't help but perpetuate the importance of the state. Of course the state richly deserves much of this significance. Should it get it, however, at the expense of reporting on events and practices that fail to fit a state-centric view of the world? Does it make these other views that much harder to see and understand?

2. How is sense to be made of questions like these?

As the discussion above about newspaper reporting indicates, any description of world affairs will make assumptions about what is important and what is not. However factual our interest, these assumptions will sieve for the facts we seek. They will also manifest the values we, wittingly or unwittingly, promote and protect.

Take a discussion of something as seemingly obvious as terrorism, for example. Defining the concept is not just a matter of naming particular terrorists. It is a matter of deciding who is a 'terrorist' as opposed to who is a 'freedom fighter'. This requires a theory of government that defines what constitutes political legitimacy, and the difference (in this context) between private and public gain, which leads directly back to what we think about state-making and state-unmaking and social change.

Take, as another example, something as seemingly straightforward as a reference to the rise of the market economy in China or the Soviet Union. The meaning of such a reference would seem self-evident, yet 'market economy' implies a wide range of issues. These include the making of labour into something that is bought and sold (commodification), the sanctioning by state-makers of the activities of individual entrepreneurs, the supply of the appropriate financial and intelligence services and, ultimately, whether or not these are good things.[7]

Knowing a lot about little

The simplest concept can be the starting point for a branching tree of theoretical propositions. This makes 'reality' very difficult to describe and explain. Without the capacity to perceive all there is at once, we explore the world piecemeal, and what we see is coloured and framed by what we think we already know and by our intentions. There are no simple or plain facts in international politics, or anywhere else for that matter. All facts are problematic because they are all selected from a large array, and we make as well as choose them.

Why are some facts made or chosen rather than others? Because they are thought to be important. What says they are important? Some concept we have, which is derived from a theory we have, which articulates a fundamental view of the world and gives our concepts their coherence and meaning.

How can we cope with the host of branching conceptual trees that make up world affairs? One common way is to opt to learn a lot about subjects that seem small in scope. This gives us the sense of being somehow closer to the facts, but any such sense of security will ultimately be a delusion. If facts make no sense alone, but require a patterned array with theoretical referents to make them sensible, then knowing what is real, however specific, will require all sorts of general propositions which, because they are general, will be open to further scrutiny and to test. They can't be protected from prying minds except by arbitrary and reductionist means.

Knowing little about a lot

This being so, it is tempting to go to the other extreme. Rather than concentrate on something seemingly small in scope (agricultural development policies in Chad, for example) we might decide to tackle broad theoretical questions first (the development strategies of post-colonial rulers in a time of world recession, perhaps, or the long cycles apparent in the global political economy and their influence on peripheral countries). There is the danger, however, that not only do we get to know very little about a lot, but just when that little seems about to describe and explain something, everything changes, and has to be described and explained again.

It is for this reason that Heraclitus, the Greek philosopher, said we can never step into the same stream twice. His student, Cratylus, impressed by one implication of this idea — that no true thing can ever be said —

reputedly spoke no more and henceforth only wagged his finger. This seems an eminently sensible response, though Cratylus has few followers.

All this suggests that the description and explanation of world affairs can only be tentative at best. It is a cautionary reminder that we can only ever claim a partial and temporary understanding of what is going on.

The contemporary tradition

Not only is what we know contingent, most of it is quite recent as well. It derives from the last 300 years when the state-making and wealth-making practices familiar to us today became common.

The study of international politics has a long history. There are descriptions and explanations of political relationships between independent communities that are considerably older than the European Renaissance. They are of more than antiquarian interest. Thucydides, the Greek historian, or Kautilya, the Chief Minister to Chandragupta (who was the founder, in about 300 BC, of the Mauryan Empire in what is modern-day India) were just as concerned as we are with what to make of the way large, territorially based populations interact.

The novelty of living in a world entirely consisting of states, set in a single global market and one world society, however, means that the most relevant thinking will be comparatively recent. The 'traditional' literature, therefore, consists of works no older than those of Machiavelli, Hobbes, Rousseau, Grotius, Kant, Marx, Weber and Clausewitz. Each has made significant contributions to the philosophic corpus from which contemporary theorists draw, and several modern-day schools of thought have been identified in terms of the main ideas of one or another of these theorists.

It is not my purpose to provide a schema of traditional approaches.[8] Rather, I wish to draw attention to an important problem that attends any account of international politics that is at all abstract, namely, the way abstraction obscures any sense of human beings doing things. By its very general and impersonal nature, analytical activity of this sort loses the sense of international politics as lived lives.

Abstraction is a radical act. It seems to have been a Greek invention. At least, it was the early Greek philosophers who first explored systematically the concept of a personal intellectual vantage point from which to view the world. They were the first to arrive at a sustained sense of the significance of experimental reason.

The full force of their discovery was not felt until the European Renaissance. The revival at that time of Greek thinking led theorists to seek, as they have ever since, for singular, coherent explanations in materialist terms. 'Every culture lives within its dream',[9] and the cosmopolitan cul-

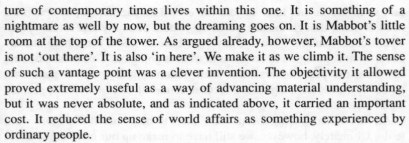

ture of contemporary times lives within this one. It is something of a nightmare as well by now, but the dreaming goes on. It is Mabbot's little room at the top of the tower. As argued already, however, Mabbot's tower is not 'out there'. It is also 'in here'. We make it as we climb it. The sense of such a vantage point was a clever invention. The objectivity it allowed proved extremely useful as a way of advancing material understanding, but it was never absolute, and as indicated above, it carried an important cost. It reduced the sense of world affairs as something experienced by ordinary people.

This is no reason, of course, to go away and wallow in prejudice, bias or subjective imaginings. My awareness that I am sometimes dishonest doesn't prompt me to go out and rob a bank. My awareness of the limits of objectivity doesn't prompt me to surrender objectivity altogether. How is a thoughtful person to proceed, then, in the certain knowledge of endless uncertainty? How are we to set our face? One solution to the dilemma, though by no means the only one, is to use our 'critical understanding'.[10]

Critical understanding

'Understanding' is the basis of an interpretative or humanist approach to social science. This means looking at the actions of everyone involved not only from our own standpoint or from that of a (relatively) objective observer, but from the various points of view of the participants themselves. Though it is ultimately impossible to use other people's perspectives, with all the experiences and meanings implicit in them, this would still seem the obvious thing to try to do. It is astonishing how rarely it is done, however.[11]

Mervyn Frost describes the significance of doing so, that is, the significance of participant understanding, using the example of a summit meeting between heads of state.

> An external observer with no knowledge of the practice of high level diplomacy with its elaborate rules of protocol, but restricted to the observation of the physical event, would be able to record the arrival of a large aircraft, which was met by crowds assembled beside a strip of red carpet. He would record that when a man emerged from the aircraft, lights popped and bands played and that then the man walked up and down rows of men all uniformly dressed in unusual clothes ... To make sense of the proceedings [however] he would need to understand the practice of international summitry from the internal point of view. He would need some understanding of what a state is, he would need to know what a head of state is, he would need to know how states conduct their relations with one another, he would need to know what a guard of honour is, what press photographers are, what red carpets symbolize and so on. [12]

To make sense of international politics, in other words, we have to take part in it. We do not have to join the crowd on the tarmac, or become a head of state, though those experiences would certainly add to our 'participant understanding'. We do, however, have to know something already about what is going on to understand what is going on. This means finding out what the practitioners think their actions signify, and in their own terms. It means an imaginative reconstruction of what may have seemed significant at the time.

All this understanding means more facts to be gathered and more work to do. Ultimately, however, we still have to make up our own minds about it all. Whatever the understanding of the participants may be, we must remain critical of that understanding, if only because the participants may be wrong. Despite our respect for their points of view, what the participants understand as having gone on may be a misunderstanding. We have to retain the right to judge for ourselves.

Our judgement is not infallible. It involves our own values, which means asking value questions from the start. We can't wait until the information-gathering is over to determine what values are involved, and this includes our own. Frost provides another example that makes this clear.

> Imagine a social scientist in international relations studying the Soviet invasion of Afghanistan. She seeks to answer the question: 'Why did the Soviets do it?'… [I]n seeking to penetrate the practice of Soviet foreign policy-making [she] finds that there is no one clear understanding of the act, but rather several competing understandings [e.g. that it was meant to distract ethnic groups at home from coming into conflict, or that it was necessary to secure the Soviet sphere of influence]. Her own preferred understanding is simply one of the competing understandings. It follows, and this is the crux of the matter, that our social scientist, in seeking a proper understanding of the invasion, has to join the argument.[13]

However judicious we think our amalgam of arguments may be, we have to take sides. Saying what happened (as in the case of the Soviet invasion) involves evaluating why it happened. Being objective, in other words, entails a subjective stand. Absolute objectivity is impossible. Therefore getting the facts straight means asking what the facts mean, whose facts they are, who they are for, and what we believe ourselves. Not to ask these questions is not to know what is going on.

Again, this may seem obvious, but it bears testimony to the power of the notion that fact and value are separate that so many still assume we must get the facts straight before we ask why we want to do so. Questions about values, about methods and their inseparability are not second order questions that we can put off until we've found out what is happening in the world. They are built into us, and therefore they are built into the

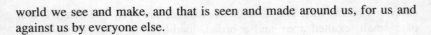

world we see and make, and that is seen and made around us, for us and against us by everyone else.

Metaphorical understanding

As one last example of how important ways of knowing are, and how directly they bear on how we make sense of international politics, let us consider the metaphor. I have used a number of metaphors already, exploiting their graphic potential to make particular points. I have talked of pyramids and towers and gardens, for example, and this is common practice. It is worth asking, however, why we do this. Why are metaphors so common?

Perhaps we can't help ourselves. As primates we rely very heavily on our sense of sight, and evocative images may have inordinate appeal because they help us 'see' what is meant. Metaphors are also powerful persuaders. They accent an aspect of what it is we wish to say, and in doing so cast other, perhaps equally important but undesired, aspects in the shade. They certainly simplify. In doing so, of course, they select, perhaps distort, and even falsify the subject concerned. (This will become apparent in chapter 3, on the balance of power, where the metaphor of the beam balance or the bank balance is used to create an image of the power political relationship between states that it purports only to describe or explain.)

The simplification can be relatively benign. The power of much poetry relies on this capacity. It can be quite useful, allowing us to picture things we don't know or understand in terms familiar to us. The danger comes in losing sight of the limitations or biases inherent in any particular metaphor. Meanings can be implied without our knowing it or without our realising the consequences.

Murray Edelman illustrates this danger by citing a couple of metaphors to do with war. When we speak of war in terms of a competition to resolve a dispute about strike capacity, for example, we encourage a view of war as a game. The metaphor becomes a euphemism. When we speak of war as legalised murder, however, we heighten our sense of the slaughter of human beings. Both metaphors make strong, and very different, conceptual and moral cases.[14]

Our capacity to think in images — our imagination — is our most extraordinary trait. We don't imagine at random, however. We have a repertoire drawn from our culture, and all that it contains. Think, for example, of the use of the image of a potter crafting clay as a metaphor for making foreign policy. Implicit is the sense of 'policy objects' as inert, lacking in purpose or volition, passive and compliant in the hands of a superior being (the policy maker).[15] Think of the pyramid — its rigidity, its stability, how hard it is to overturn — and how often society is described in this way. The metaphor is loaded, however. The image is that of a small, exalted apex and a broad, load-bearing base. Think of the wheel — of fate, of fortune, of cycles of civilisation — lifting up and letting down each part of itself in turn in a predictable sequence. Think of the thread — of fate, of an argument — and the web (of relationships) that several threads can make together. Think of the beam-balance, the image implicit in it of equipoise, and the sense that the more this position is upset, the stronger the strain to restore the natural position will be.

Karl Deutsch, from whom these examples are drawn, provides a number of others. Historically, he argues, we took the image of our own society, where we live and talk and seek to influence each other by verbal means, and we used this as a way of understanding the cosmos at large. We depicted the world as a 'society of animated objects that could be magically influenced by talking to them through the right kind of incantations'.[16]

As our technology became more complex our images and metaphors became more complex too.

> The impersonal plan or law of the city ... [came] to serve as a model for an assumed impersonal plan or law of nature, and the structure of this impersonal law or architecture appear[ed] to remain effective regardless of the subsequent activities of any invisible architect or lawgiver who might have originated it.[17]

With the invention of the clock, a new and extremely pervasive metaphor became available. The clockwork mechanism became a very evocative image for society. We can see it in Isaac Newton's mathematics of motion, for example, or the prescriptions of Thomas Hobbes on how to control human competition.

The image came at a price, however.

> Classic mechanism implied the notion of a whole that was completely equal to the sum of its parts, that could be run in reverse, and that would behave in exactly identical fashion no matter how often those parts were disassembled and put together again, and irrespective of the sequence in which the disassembling or reassembling would take place. It thus implied the notion that the parts were never significantly modified by each other, nor by their own past, and that each part once placed into its appropriate position, with its appropriate momentum, would remain in place and continue to fulfill its completely and uniquely determined function.
>
> As this model implied certain assumptions, so it excluded others. The notions of irreversible change, of growth, of evolution, of novelty, and of purpose all had no place in it.[18]

In more recent times the metaphor of the mechanism has had to contend with that of the organism. In many ways a more sophisticated idea, an organism can't be disassembled and reassembled without destroying it.

Each part is integral. Such an image can be applied to the state, for example, to stress the interdependence of all the parts in a global system. Again, the image is compelling but the bias profound. 'Models of classic organisms permit ... greater complexity and some very limited development, but they ... [leave] no room for consciousness or will, which [are] assumed powerless to change the organism's inner laws'.[19] No room for consciousness or will, however, would seem to leave out most of what is interesting about any political practice.

What are the metaphors used in international politics? The thread, the web, the wheel, the balance, the mechanism and the organism are all very common. They are all useful heuristic tools. They all have important and not readily recognised limitations, however, that prompt us to see the world in self-serving ways.

Social scientists are not the only ones who have to be wary in this regard. Even the 'hardest' of sciences is finding it problematic. It seems that at the moment physical scientists can find no single metaphor with which to describe and explain what goes on in the world. Instead they have eight.[20] Each predicts the same set of observed experimental events, yet each is also consistent with all the known facts.

Given that physicists are so confused, students of world affairs would seem to have every right to be so too.

Notes

1 J. Mabbot, *The State and the Citizen*, Arrow Books, London, 1958, pp. 9-10.
2 J. Carse, *Finite and Infinite Games*, Penguin, Harmondsworth, 1986, p. 118.
3 A metaphor first used to my knowledge by Hans Morgenthau.
4 J. Burton, *Systems, States, Diplomacy and Rules*, Cambridge University Press, Cambridge, 1968, p. 8.
5 See M. Kidron & R. Segal, *The New State of the World Atlas*, Pan Books, London, 1987; also J. Seager & A. Olson, *Women in the World: an international atlas*, Simon & Schuster, New York, 1986.
6 R. Walker, *One World/Many Worlds: struggles for a just world peace*, Lynne Rienner Publishers, Boulder, 1988, pp. 19-20.
7 M. Banks, 'The Inter-Paradigm Debate' in M. Light & A. Groom (eds), *International Relations*, Frances Pinter, London, 1985, p. 7.
8 M. Wight, 'Western Values in International Relations' in H. Butterfield & M. Wight (eds), *Diplomatic Investigations*, Allen & Unwin, London, 1967; or H. Bull, *The Anarchical Society*, Macmillan, London, 1977, pp. 24-7. Also more generally M. Banks, 'The Evolution of International Relations Theory' in M. Banks (ed.), *Conflict in Society*, St Martin's Press, New York, 1984.
9 L. Mumford, *Technics and Civilisation*, George Routledge & Sons, London, 1934, p. 28. Walker argues that the contribution of Hebrew monotheism to this dream has been at least as important as that of the Greeks, and that the convergence of the two in the work of St Augustine was crucial too (personal

communication).

10 This is just one part of the book where the trade-off between breadth and depth has been very difficult to make. For a stimulating overview of the debates involved in how to interpret politics in general, see M. Gibbons (ed.), *Interpreting Politics,* Basil Blackwell, Oxford, 1987. Note especially the introductory chapter, and the one by R. Rorty, 'Method, Social Science and Social Hope'.

11 M. Frost, *Towards a Normative Theory of International Relations,* Cambridge University Press, Cambridge, 1986, p. 17.

12 ibid., pp. 20-1.

13 ibid., pp. 28-9.

14 M. Edelman, *Politics as Symbolic Vision,* Markham Publishing Co., Chicago, 1971, p. 67.

15 K. Deutsch, *The Nerves of Government,* The Free Press of Glencoe, New York, 1963, p. 24.

16 loc. cit.

17 ibid., p. 25.

18 ibid., p. 27.

19 ibid., p. 38.

20 N. Herbert, *Quantum Reality,* Rider, London, 1988, ch. 2, 'Physicists Losing Their Grip'.

Polity

2

The state and the state system

What are states? Where did they come from? Where are they going to? Why are state-makers mostly men? What is the interstate system?

1. What are states? Where did they come from? Where are they going to? Why are state-makers mostly men?

The concept of the state is common currency in international politics. We take states more or less for granted now, but what are they? Where did they come from? Where might they be going to?

The idea of the state

States are very curious. We are coached to think of them as things, as reifications, as abstract and generalised catch-alls, as independent countries and governmental institutions. But they are not things. They are particular human practices sufficiently important and sufficiently regular to warrant their own (most problematic) conceptual label.

Thinking of states as things and giving them a corporate personality is part of the attempt to make sure they play their part in keeping the whole system of states going. This way they can be held accountable, regardless of who rules them. But mostly we take states for granted because for most of us, in our own lifetimes, they have always been there. They have presence. They are familiar. They seem natural. With the arrogance of our own immediacy we assume something like this must always have been so, although of course it hasn't. The practices that go to make up the institutional routines and the habits of command, compliance and consent, and the many and varied relationships involved, are highly contrived. They have to occur continually or what they embody — the state — would disappear. This hasn't always been the case and it won't always be the case but at the moment it is. So what are these practices? Who makes this one world of citizens, exiles and refugees? And why?

State-making

State-making refers to those boundary-drawing (territorially specific), centralising (institution-building), secular and singularly authoritative practices that define the sovereign domains into which the world is now divided. The key components of any one such domain are its geographic area (the spatial representation of the state), its government (the institutional embodiment of the state), and the governed (more or less cohesive, more or less part of the governing process, more or less provided for).

There are around 180 of these units at this time, and highly diverse behaviour patterns assert and maintain them. The rubber-stamping officials at any point of immigration or emigration, the file-swapping clerks who levy and disburse taxes, the politicians and party personnel who argue about what practices are the most appropriate, the industrialist seeking higher tariffs or tax exemptions or greater worker discipline, and the teacher telling stories of how the country came to be — all articulate and animate whatever state they inhabit. By state-making, then, I mean state-maintenance as well as the historical construction of the state from scratch.

A complete list of state-specifying practices would be very long. Think of the myriad relationships that make up one, even tiny, country. Think of all that must happen at a global, capital city and local level to create and sustain the state. Think of what must be taught to every generation for the government, law, administration, religion, science, literature and art of any particular state to persist. Everything we are in this regard we learn to be. It is an awesome amount to have to inculcate, and whoever does the inculcating obviously has an important say in determining what a particular state is for, and for whom.

Sovereignty

All state-specifying practices assert the primacy or sovereignty of state-makers themselves. Sovereignty summarises in one word the claims state-makers make to the kind of authority single rulers, like kings and queens, once possessed. It has an inward-looking and an outward-looking aspect, and it can be described in political, politico-economic, or legal terms. The concept can also be regarded in terms of the three parts to the state described above: territoriality, centralised institution-building, and the authority conferred by popular support.

In the light of these latter categories, sovereignty is firstly a statement about formal independence and equality. It gives territoriality its special significance. It is made on behalf of a state which is part of a system of states.

Modern state-makers, unlike their predecessors, have to contend with being part of a global network of peers, formally equal, independent, and entitled — in theory at least — to the same rights and privileges. They look to each other to validate their legitimacy and in reciprocation they can usually expect to get it. The equality, the independence and the legitimacy are invented, but because enough state-makers behave as if their expectations were well-founded, they are discernible social facts.

So popular is the whole fiction that it is only necessary to demonstrate physical control over the capital city (the centralisation typical of modern state-making invariably creates a capital city) for a particular elite to be considered legitimate, and hence representative of the collective sovereignty of the people at large, and hence internationally entitled to the rights and privileges of state rule.

After a coup, for example, a new regime will wait for peer recognition. International recognition is the key to systemic legitimacy and it will be inevitable if strategic sites like airstrips, radio or television stations, the army or police barracks, and the previous state-maker can be held long enough. With the previous leader or leaders safely dispossessed of their power, the affirmation of governments elsewhere will only be a matter of time, but recognition of the new regime by all the world's other state-makers is not necessary. Indeed, given the ungoverned nature of the whole system, a pariah regime can persist with very little peer recognition at all, although it will not find international relations easy.

Sovereignty in the modern context is not only a statement about the formal equality and independence that make a geographic domain possible. It is also about singular authority, and the centralised institution-building that typically attends the claim to have the authority to state-make. When no other group or person can make more claims that seem more authoritative within the territorial limits of the state concerned, the ascendant regime is deemed to be sovereign.

This is an elaborate way of saying that sovereignty means being boss within the borders either drawn around the state by other governments or taken and held by putative state-makers themselves. It is, of course, the domestic dimension of the international claims discussed above. In formal terms sovereignty means domestic preponderance. It means the absence of effective rivals able to exercise public power on a continuous basis. Sovereignty is what can be enforced as such.[1]

There will be many who contest such control. If they cannot compel compliance, however, the contest will remain marginal. State-making means having a monopoly over the means of violence. The collaboration of those on the receiving end is clearly preferred to coercing them by force, however, and a key characteristic of the modern state is the degree to which it rests upon general consensus rather than elite compulsion.

This is the third aspect of sovereignty in its contemporary context. State-making is carried on by those who staff particular political, judicial and cultural institutions. It is done in the modern state, however, in the name of all who live within its physical domain. Contemporary state-making proceeds on the assumption that it is, in principle at least, democratic. Contemporary state-makers seek legitimacy not only from each other, but also from those over whom they rule. Diehard exceptions, like the white state-makers of South Africa (who used apartheid and the fiction of Bantu homelands to maintain minority control) were politically ostracised as a result.

While state-makers throughout history have sought to concentrate power in a few hands, it is a relatively recent development to seek to justify this behaviour by claiming a mandate from most if not all of those ruled. This has meant an intensified conception of citizenship, and of popular participation. Citizens of city-states traditionally thought of themselves as such, and they often participated actively in their own governance, but state-making is now so broad and deep that it incorporates the inhabitants of much larger domains, and in ever more intensive ways. We are all, in a sense, state-makers now, since it is ultimately mass consensus that makes possible the power to compel mass compliance.

There is undeniable tension between models of sovereignty that highlight the capacity to enforce authority and those which see such authority as bestowed by popular compliance and consent rather than brute force. This tension remains evident today, though the latter model is currently the more popular, in declaratory terms if not in practice. The tension is not resolvable, reflecting two different conceptions of power, the one as the capacity to dominate regardless ('might makes right'), and the other as the competence that comes from general acceptance or acclaim ('consensual democracy').

Whatever the quality of its sovereignty, the state itself is a marked feature of modern times. The success of the very idea of a statist way of doing things, and the pervasiveness of the identity it provides, has been overwhelming. The ideology of statism, and the sense of being a law-

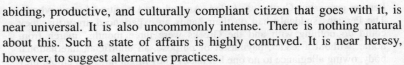

abiding, productive, and culturally compliant citizen that goes with it, is near universal. It is also uncommonly intense. There is nothing natural about this. Such a state of affairs is highly contrived. It is near heresy, however, to suggest alternative practices.

I say near heresy since the further development of arrangements like the European Common Market may well represent a kind of compromised statism that ultimately undermines the ideology as a whole. Indeed, from the great empires of the last several millennia, through the religious regimes determined to maintain secular control in the name of the divine good, to the smallest commune struggling with its conflict resolution techniques, we find ways of behaving politically at odds with those of state-makers. These ways are currently anomalous, however. It is state-making that prevails, and those not prepared or not able to comply with the reasoning involved — politico-economic, legal or ideological — are faced with the choice of actively fighting back, or passively disappearing into prisons or hospitals or any one of a number of other social cysts.

The idea of the nation

Civic identity raises not only the question of state-making, but that of nation-making too. The idea of the nation is that of a self-consciously imagined community. This community is likely to be described by its members in terms of the language they speak, the traditions they observe, the general culture they bear, and the sense they have of where they come from. It will have a history of struggle and change, out of which will have come the principles of exclusion and inclusion, and the principles of difference, that nationhood considers socially significant.

The idea of nationhood and the practices that animate it are very old. In contemporary times, however, they have been grafted onto the state as something synonymous with it. Nations without a state, or states enclosing many nations, make civic consensus harder to achieve, and state-makers therefore generally disapprove of them.

Some would like to dispense with the idea of the nation altogether. Most would acknowledge, however, that 'nation' does capture a feeling of solidarity that the concept of the state does not. A graphic example of this feeling is provided by H.D. Kitto in his book on the ancient Greeks.

> It concerns an incident in the march of the Ten Thousand through the awful mountains of Armenia towards the Black Sea. These men were mercenary soldiers who had been enlisted by Cyrus the Younger to help him drive his half-brother from the Persian throne — not that Cyrus told them this, for he knew very well that no Greek army would willingly march three months from the sea. However, by deceit and cajolery he got them into Mesopotamia. The disciplined and well-armed Greeks easily defeated the

Persian army, but Cyrus was killed. An awkward position for everybody. The Persians suddenly had on their hands an experienced army that they could do nothing with and the Greeks were three months' march from home, without a leader, paymaster or purpose, an unofficial, international body, owing allegiance to no one but itself. They might have run amok; they might have degenerated into robber-bands to be destroyed piecemeal; they might have been incorporated into the Persian army and empire.

None of these things happened. They wanted to go home — but not through the length of Asia Minor, of which they had seen quite enough. They decided to strike north, in the hope of reaching the Black Sea. They elected a general, Xenophon … an Athenian country-gentleman, and he was as much Chairman as he was General, for they decided policy in concert. With the self-discipline that these turbulent Greeks often displayed, they held together, week after week, and made their way through these unknown mountains, conciliating the natives when they could, and fighting them when conciliation failed.

Some perished, but not many; they survived as an organized force. One day, as we read in Xenophon's quite unheroic 'Anabasis', Xenophon was commanding the rearguard while the leading troops were climbing to the head of a pass. When they got to the top they suddenly began to shout and to gesticulate to those behind. These hurried up, imagining that it was yet another hostile tribe in front. They, on reaching the ridge, began to shout too, and so did each successive company after them — all shouting, and pointing excitedly to the north. At last the anxious rearguard could hear what they were all shouting: it was 'Thalassa, thalassa'. The long nightmare was over, for 'thalassa' is the Greek for 'sea'. There it was, shimmering in the distance — salt water; and where there was salt water, Greek was understood, and the way home was open. As one of the Ten Thousand said, 'We can finish our journey like Odysseus, lying on our backs'.[2]

Thus, a nation is a people and it has two main (ideologically loaded and politically contested) characteristics: common heritage (a composite quality, made up of the shared experiences already mentioned, such as language, culture and a sense of a shared history); and territory (a nation is typically associated with a particular geographic area, though the gypsies are only one exception that qualifies this rule).

Nation-making

Nations, like states, don't drop out of the sky. They are made. Nation-making means actively promoting the attributes identified above. It means promoting or protecting the sense of a unified group that is larger than the family, village or local community, but smaller than the species as a whole. This means fostering or consolidating the use of the same tongue, the same cultural traditions, the same awareness of what the members of the group have been through together, and the same awareness of the challenges they currently face. There are gender differences in how this is

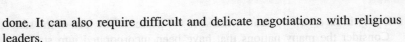

done. It can also require difficult and delicate negotiations with religious leaders.

Nation-making usually means establishing and defending specific geographic boundaries and reinforcing a people's sense of their common significance in geographic terms. Since the idea of a territory is crucial to state-making too, this helps explain the feeling that nation-making and state-making are intimately related. This relationship has been used to create a hybrid entity, the nation–state, and it is this entity that nominally partitions earth's peoples into countries. The overlap between them, in other words, has helped pull the concepts of nation and state together in many people's minds, and not least, those of self-interested state-makers.

Nations and states

The range of modern states and nations, while all now cast in the same general mould, remains very wide, as befits their varying origins. As earth's peoples try to make sense of the diverse territorial domains they have inherited or been bequeathed, they must contend with many, often quite bizarre, anomalies. Consider, for example, the sovereign state of Tuvalu, once part of the British colony called the Gilbert and Ellice Islands. Its population of 10 000 or so live on nine populated islands spread over more than 1 000 000 km^2 of ocean. Its entire land mass is no more than 50 km^2, yet it has the same formal standing internationally as the modern state of China, where one in five of all of the world's people lives. Both make claims that are regularly met by fellow state-makers around the globe — the right to a seat in the General Assembly of the UN for example, the right to exchange ambassadors, or the right to levy tariffs and customs duties. These are claims that would be ignored if they came from New South Wales or Texas, despite the fact that Texas earns more money than all of Australia, of which New South Wales is one part. New South Wales can't sit in the UN, like Australia can. And for Texas to declare war on Mexico would signal a radical un-making of the whole USA.

Curiosities abound. Consider China, which consists of two countries, one on the mainland and one on the island of Taiwan. Both are widely recognised as sovereign states. They have separate governments, yet both insists the other is part of itself. The Ukraine and Byelorussia sit in the UN, and yet they are not considered sovereign by fellow state-makers. The South African government insists that the Bantu homelands are states, though it is the only one to do so. Greenland behaves as a separate state though in formal terms, given its rather odd relationship with Denmark, it is not. Equally odd is Puerto Rico's relationship with the USA. Each anomaly in its own way bears witness to the power of the idea of the state.

Consider the many nations that have been incorporated into states, or divided arbitrarily between them. Consider the nations which clamour loud and long for the restoration of the sovereign statehood they have lost in the vagaries of world affairs. Given the hundreds of nations there are in the world, it is no wonder that getting them to fit into a much smaller number of territorially expanded states has been very difficult indeed.

Some state-makers have had more success in consolidating their realms than others. All typically use governmental control to foster a sense of nationhood, as well as generally endorsing the ideology of statism itself. Needless to say many people have prospered in the process, and many more have been impoverished. The whole process has been and still is highly problematic.

The story of the state

From the idea of the state I shall turn to the story of it as traditionally told. State-making of the modern sort began in pre-Renaissance Europe. It had at that time to compete with a wide range of other political practices. Given formal status by the Treaty of Westphalia at the end of the Thirty Years' War, state-making was extended by successful alliances and further wars over most of the continent, and then over most of the globe. All of this sounds very straightforward, but in practice, it was not. What did happen? What did bring states about?

Charles Tilly suggests that the whole process was for the most part unintended. States, in his view, are what happened when self-aggrandising European monarchs began building large armies. They had at the same time to build the institutional and bureaucratic capacity to sustain such armies. They had, for example, to raise regular taxes.[3] The state was the result. As an institutional outcome it was an accident, the unplanned consequence of the self-aggrandising practices of a bunch of greedy plotters in pursuit of short-term advantage and local gain: '... small groups of power-hungry men' fighting off 'numerous rivals and great popular resistance in the pursuit of their own ends', who 'almost inadvertently promoted the formation of national states and wide-spread popular involvement in them'.[4]

The outcome was not entirely accidental, however. There were compelling precedents for the state-making involved. The end of Roman rule in Britain in 410 AD, for example, saw the emergence of a mosaic of tiny proto-states, each no more than a few kilometres across, and each containing no more than a few hundred people. Several generations later, however, the stronger of these tiny domains had taken over the weaker to make mini-countries up to 1000 km² in extent. The process of dog eating dog went on, so that within 200 years, by about 620 AD, there were 250 or so. Within sixty more this number was down to about forty. It took only 400 years, in fact, for the original 1000 independently governed territories to become only seven. A hundred years later there were only four, and these, in the tenth century, became the component parts of the kingdom of England.[5]

We know that the story of history is typically told by the victors, not the vanquished, and that every generation of scholars researches and rewrites history in ways relevant to the present. As a consequence the story of ambition and accident told above may merely reflect the contemporary predominance of the state itself. A more objective and comprehensive account of what went on would probably not rely so much on statist thought and practices, and as a consequence the story of the state itself would not emerge so clearly.

It is a sobering thought, however, that the nation–state is not the outcome of some intended design, but the chance resolution of a complex equation of interests and opportunities that happened to have this particular organisational outcome. Moreover, as we learn more about how violent is the cosmos, we are also learning, perhaps not coincidentally, how violent have been the human practices involved in state-making. However we look at it, the first European states were forged on the anvil of war, and war, both interstate and civil, remains immanent throughout.

An appreciation of the violence involved in state-making is not new. Writing in the early days of the rise of the modern state and state-system, the English philosopher Thomas Hobbes described the primary desire of all humankind in terms of a perpetual and restless pursuit of power. A sense of secure possession over what influence and wealth one already enjoyed might only be had, he argued, by striving for more.

> Hereby it is manifest, that during the time men live without a common Power to keep them all in awe, they are in that condition which is called Warre; and such a warre, as is of every man, against every man. For WARRE, consisteth not in Battell onely, or the act of fighting; but ... in the known disposition thereto ... in all times, Kings, and Persons of Soveraigne authority, because of their Independency, are in continuall jealousies, and in the state and posture of Gladiators; having their weapons pointing, and their eyes fixed on one another; that is, their Forts, Garrisons, and Guns, upon the Frontiers of their Kingdomes; and continuall Spyes upon their neighbours ... Where there is no common Power, there is no Law: where no Law, no Injustice. Force, and Fraud are in warre the two Cardinall vertues.[6]

By including in his definition not just overt violence but cold war too, Hobbes was able to emphasise the precarious nature of human security. He was also making a powerful argument for state-making, and the role state-makers play in protecting those under their territorial jurisdiction, since wars, he said, strengthen states. This argument is still heard today.

What these 'Kings and Persons of Soveraigne authority' found out about raising armies and keeping them in the field was carried over into the routines of peace. The point that Tilly emphasises is that states were human machines built first and foremost for battle. 'War made the state' he says 'and the state made war'.[7] Indeed, war-making and state-making could even be seen as our largest examples of organised crimes, since '...[b]anditry, piracy, gangland rivalry, policing, and war-making all belong on the same continuum ...'. This makes it easier to see, Tilly concludes, why state-making can revert so quickly to the cruder forms of coercion.

Consider the definition of a racketeer as someone who creates a threat and then charges for its reduction:

> To the extent [then] that the threats against which a given government protects its citizens are imaginary or are [the] consequences of its own activities, the government has organised a protection racket. Since governments themselves commonly simulate, stimulate, or even fabricate threats of external war and since the repressive and extractive activities of governments often constitute the largest threats to the livelihoods of their own citizens, many governments operate in essentially the same way as racketeers.[8]

Granting Tilly even part of the argument prompts us to ask how state-makers get the authority to behave in this way? Why does it seem legitimate for them to monopolise the capacity to use brute force within their domains? Is it because of the strength of the abstract principle itself? Is it a shared norm or an expectation on the part of the governed that is too strong to resist? No, says Tilly. The legitimacy of a government is 'the probability that other authorities will act to confirm ... [it]'.[9]

We are back to sovereignty and the way the system works as long as the stake-holders keep the game going. If all the state-makers — the power monopolisers — agree to acknowledge each other's legitimacy, then legitimate they will be. Of course, you have to show you have the local monopoly of the means of coercion, and control of at least the capital city. But once this minimum qualification is met, legitimacy is mostly automatic. The odd exception — a pariah state like apartheid-centred South Africa, for example — is instructive because it heightens the significance of recognition. White South Africans built a state by self-assertion. Its credentials were not accepted by many of its peers because it flouted the modern commitment to the principle that the citizens themselves should rule. As such it was given marginal status only.

Tilly's analysis is compelling. It has a healthy Hobbesian respect for the importance of military power, and it tells us how state domains were made and how the laws within them were originally enforced. Those who wanted to monopolise the means of coercion had to eliminate local rivals, destroy their power bases, co-operate with each other, and construct a direct rule that ran over the whole territory claimed. In this way 500 more or less autonomous European political entities were reduced to twenty-five or so over a 400 year period from 1500 to 1900 AD. There were many losers, all rendered subject rather than remaining sovereign.

Local leaders monopolising the means of coercion and extending their domains has not been a process peculiar to Europe. So why were the processes of political aggregation and integration carried to such a pitch there?

Religious fervour played a part in it. The crusades set important precedents for general taxation and specialised institution-building as the basis on which to wage sustained war and organise large numbers of people. Other factors were room to grow in the region, the relative absence of strong opposing peoples, and the growth in cities and trade and thus in merchant capitalism and manufacturing.

The last were particularly important. The evolution of capitalist productive and exchange practices were closely linked to state-making ones. Capitalism generated resources which state-makers were able to use to their own ends, where the state-makers were not capitalists already. (In classical Marxist parlance the state is the institutional aspect of bourgeois rule. Class formation determines the nature of the state, both in part and in whole system terms.) Capitalism also generated new markets, bigger cities, a class of wage-earning, landless proletarians, gender-referenced domains of public and private endeavour, and a political ideology of liberal self-aggrandisement.

Capitalist practices did occur independently of state-making ones, and state-making did proceed without large-scale capitalist involvement, unthinkable as it seems today. In the main, however, their relationship has been both intimate and complex.

The puzzle resists definitive solution. Whatever it was that caused such an intense process, we know that it happened because we live with the consequences. They were revolutionary, and the costs were tremendous in death, suffering, loss of land, loss of goods, and labour. Getting countless rural communities to aggregate and integrate on this scale, and getting the means to do it, meant widespread repression. A huge variety of long-established institutional structures and systems of political rule had to be ignored. Single religions had to be imposed, minority peoples persecuted or expelled, and the use of national languages made mandatory. Cultural unification practices were intense.

Resistance was endemic, and popular rebellions against the dislocating effects of centralised change were legion. There were tax rebellions, food riots, movements against conscription and cultural repression. All, in the main, were to no avail. A succession of state-makers continued to develop their key practices in a ruthless way, building large and loyal staffs, coercing and co-opting the more reluctant sectors of the populace, gathering information about what resources the state-makers had at their command, promoting the economic activities necessary to provide the goods and services they required, and even fomenting rebellion where it served to defeat recalcitrant local authorities. A 'tough, complicated and well-set web of political relations' had to be completely rewoven.[10] No wonder state-making became synonymous with conflict, domination and expropriation.

Once begun, practices like these generated their own momentum. They came to seem habitual and a matter of course. The mirror-play of mutual recognition we now call sovereign legitimacy was used to undermine all opposition. War, in the name of the formal equality that the state-makers claimed to possess, was used to fight off those who might try to carry state-making through to its natural conclusion — a single system to rival or to surpass that built by the Romans over a thousand years before. In the process a number of likely alternatives never came to pass.

Europe did not, for example, become a theocratic conglomerate run by the Catholic Church. It did not, as it might have done, remain a feudally organised society of manors, merchant towns and provincial magnates, trading with each other but resisting any temptation to form a political federation or confederation. It became a place of states, and we are still not sure why.[11]

Having consolidated their domestic domains the leading European state-makers pushed out into the world to make empires, both for profit and for pure self-aggrandisement. However, they eventually ran out of room. Once the world had been divided among the major expansionist regimes, they turned their imperialism back on themselves. The heartland imploded. Two disastrous wars followed, the first fought largely in Europe, and the second accompanied by a war in the Pacific. (It is a typical European conceit to have called these conflicts the First and the Second World Wars.)

One result of these wars was to create the political space for non-colonial national self-determination, as it was called, and a rash of state-making and state remaking by local, non-European elites. Unlike their European predecessors, these elites had to pursue their state-making in a world not of their own devising. At the same time, having come late to the practices concerned, they devised many variations on the European theme. Whereas state-making in Europe led to civilian control of military power

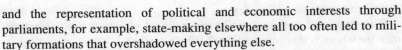

and the representation of political and economic interests through parliaments, for example, state-making elsewhere all too often led to military formations that overshadowed everything else.

The remnants of Europe's empires have now largely been remaindered. The result is a patchwork quilt of human allegiance of more or less random geopolitical design. For the first time nearly everyone in the world can be identified in terms of his or her residence within a sovereign state. Those without such an identity are either anomalous, like the European gypsies or the nomadic East African Masai, or refugees. State-making practices have been intensified everywhere to eliminate such anomalies, and to consolidate the current pattern of civil allegiance.

The outlook for the state

All of this is extraordinary enough, but the story goes on. Other developments, in the world political economy for example, and in the use of new technologies of communication and transportation, have begun to compromise the whole state-making process. Consolidating civil allegiance and monopolising the means of civil violence have also become more difficult. Curiously, we seem to have a situation in which both state-making (the way states divide up the world) and interstate interconnectedness (the way they collude) are becoming more important at the same time. It is impossible to say which set of practices will prevail in the long run, or what the outcome might be in terms of a mixture or synthesis of the two. They both exist, however, and the contradictions they cause are often acute.

Regimes

One feature of this contemporary paradox is the growing significance of international governmental and non-governmental arrangements that deal with matters of common concern. These arrangements are currently called regimes.[12] They have proliferated at a great rate, as have multinational institutions and multinational corporations. Indeed, people organise and are organised across state boundaries today in a wide variety of ways that actively belie the dotted lines between them on geopolitical maps. At the same time, by contrast, state-making tasks continue to grow, pre-empting private realms that were once well outside the civic domain.

Perhaps, as the Europeans themselves are demonstrating, it is possible to have economic integration and greater freedom to move from one country to another without notably detracting from the political independence and cultural autonomy state-makers promote and protect. Centralised economic unity and a decentralised political pluralism may be compatible to a quite surprising degree.

If international economic unity and political pluralism are compatible, then for whom is this compatibility? Who benefits?

From a global perspective it is said that as the wealth-making activities of industrial capitalists have become progressively more international, those of the world's waged and unwaged workers have not. International practices are coming to impinge on more local ones in ways that create new tensions between economics and politics. The waged, in their struggles to hold or improve their living standards, do so now knowing that their success will be as much dependent on the standing of the state as a whole in world markets as on the capacity of workers to confound the power of their capitalist employers:

> On a world level we now have exactly the opposite of the pre-capitalist cellular feudal societies ... in which political integration extended beyond and outstripped economic integration ... Since 1945 ... economic integration has outstripped political integration at the national level and is also incorporating the Third World into a new international division of labour. Paradoxically, this both benefits and threatens nationally-organised unions in the advanced countries. On the one hand ... internationally mobile capital establishes a two-tier system of exploitation, which is to the advantage of workers in the advanced countries. On the other hand, it also shifts the balance of power away from national labour (and nation states) and towards internationally mobile capital ...[13]

Capitalism grew up in the context of a politically pluralistic world. There was always a global market but capitalists, until relatively recently, have worked largely within the framework that state-making provides. They are now doing so less and less. The result is a growing gap between how the world is organised for production and exchange, and how it works to diplomatic and strategic effect. Capitalists would argue that this all to the good. The waged and unwaged are not so sanguine.

It is possible, of course, that we have found a lasting and desirable compromise between world government (whether a world federation, confederation or empire of some sort) and localised rule. Though states vary enormously, from tiny Tuvalu to mainland China, perhaps this organisational unit really can provide more for more people more successfully than any conceivable alternative.

The problem remains that there are many more nations than there are states. Can statist loyalties be made to transcend nationalist ones? What of the many cases where the fit between nation and state is a bad one? Can demands for autonomy be contained within the current set of territorial limits? Questions like these seem to become more relevant, not less, as the newer states age.

Gender

The problem also remains that the state was evolved by men, largely for men, and as a consequence does not serve feminist concerns anywhere near as effectively as masculine ones. This is readily documented in terms of the fact that women, though half the world's population, live in a psychological and social world separate from that of men. It is a world that is also often spatially separate, too.[14] Even in those cases where sex-based divisions of labour have been seriously questioned, and where the inclusion of women in state-making affairs has been conscious and sustained, they represent no more than a quarter of all elected state officials.

The number of males present in the absence of females is striking. This is the case wherever we care to look — in cabinet and party rooms, in corporate boardrooms, in church and university synods, in bureaucratic senior services, among the ranks of union leaders, among the ranks of senior military personnel, in professional associations — in every upper echelon of every pyramid of social power that constitutes the state. Though they are 50 per cent of the world's enfranchised population women hold no more than 10 per cent of the seats in state-making legislatures. 'In one government in three there are no women in the executive council which represents the highest decision-making body of the country; in those cabinets where women are included, there is usually only one woman'.[15] That one post, furthermore, is much more likely to be education or social welfare than a job as defence minister, attorney-general, finance minister or head of state. The exceptions to this rule are also very instructive in terms of the sort of co-option and conditioning required to make it to the top.

None of this is surprising if we accept the extent to which state-making is bound up with war-making and the extent to which war-making has been a masculine monopoly. Revolutionary armies offer some exceptions in this regard, but stereotyped gender roles are invariably reasserted once victory is achieved.

State-making has fostered personal and social aggrandisement and a great deal of violence. Whether this is an expression of universal masculine values, or of one cultural version of them, the result has been 'a lack of connection with the conditions of life (human and biospheric) so profound as to mystify the material limits of it'.[16]

Provision

Despite all this, the general popularity of the idea of the state is high, and so are the expectations state-makers must meet. Besides the question of

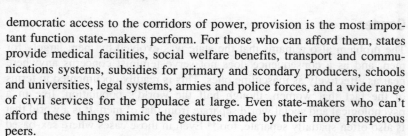

democratic access to the corridors of power, provision is the most important function state-makers perform. For those who can afford them, states provide medical facilities, social welfare benefits, transport and communications systems, subsidies for primary and scondary producers, schools and universities, legal systems, armies and police forces, and a wide range of civil services for the populace at large. Even state-makers who can't afford these things mimic the gestures made by their more prosperous peers.

J.D.B. Miller concludes that:

> [T]he effect of provision is to bind groups of people more closely to the state, and to the need for its preservation; without it (or, rather, without it in the particular form of regime which benefits them) their source of livelihood would be lost ... The situation of the sovereign state is rather like that of the family, which is subject to the strongest criticisms, but continues to reproduce itself. Both are human forms which suit people. They may not suit everyone, but they suffice for most.[17]

Miller's analysis is plausible, but it is a defence of the status quo which, at least in the case of the state, is becoming progressively less defensible. Consider Walker's much more sceptical comments.

> For most of this century, and for the most influential political ideologies the state has been treated as an instrument capable of redressing at least the worst aspects of economic inequality and alienation ... [however] with the increasingly internationalized and capital-intensive nature of contemporary economic life ... [t]he welfare state has been seriously eroded. Inequality has become increasingly respectable. Demands for law and order have become louder than demands for social justice. The poor and marginalized are more and more likely to be castigated as social deviants and subjected to surveillance and control ... The claim that it is possible to do something about poverty and inequality by taking over state power becomes more and more illusory.[18]

Walker's comments can be applied to rich and poor states alike. However, in countries where the state-machinery is still rudimentary, the situation is typically worse. State-makers under such conditions provide little more for most of their citizens than physical and judicial repression and systematic underdevelopment. To say that this is what most people want seems callous at best, and at worst it is simply cruel.

Whether those marginalised or dispossessed by state-making practices have much alternative is harder to say. Certainly alternatives can be envisaged, but realising them in a world as state-bound as the current one would be highly problematic. It would not be difficult to convince perhaps the majority of people in poor states, and a sizeable minority in rich ones, that alternatives are desirable. However, the false promises of much civic

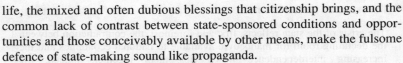

life, the mixed and often dubious blessings that citizenship brings, and the common lack of contrast between state-sponsored conditions and opportunities and those conceivably available by other means, make the fulsome defence of state-making sound like propaganda.

It remains to be seen how long the promises of this particular institutional form can be sustained before they are generally deemed to be broken. The prospect of their being more fully met is not great. The fact that most people don't have to be coerced into staying where they are is as much of a statement about their inertia, and the other ties that bind them, as it is an argument for the benefits of the state.

The promise of the state is also compromised by another dilemma for state-makers. On the one hand, as indicated already, they must provide for the growing expectations of their citizens. On the other hand they must foster productivity. To provide for the public welfare they must control the national means of production. Too much control of these means, however, can stifle those who animate them, with potentially self-defeating effect (see appendix 1).

A crisis in legitimacy?

In liberal capitalist countries this dilemma is said to have resulted in a legitimation crisis. State-makers try to provide what most of the voters seem to want. At the same time they must meet the needs of state-based wealth-makers. Where they fail to satisfy either we find governments having, on the one hand, to regulate the market and its entrepreneurs and, on the other, to meet a demand to free markets from intervention to allow productive investment flows and capitalist accumulation. 'This leads ultimately to crises of inflation, public finances and rational administration.' [19]

Such crises are made worse by moves to open domestic markets to global wealth-makers. Deregulation that leads to unproductive speculation, further inflation and an economy more compromised than before, feeds only avarice and despair. It does so, furthermore, at cost to the values of probity and integrity upon which capitalist entrepreneurs ultimately depend. The alternative is more control and less liberal capitalism.

Command socialist state-makers confront a similar dilemma. Having opted for a planned economy to provide for public welfare, they have found the results far from those anticipated. Stagnation, shortages, shoddy goods, an active black market and an unwieldy bureaucracy have made public altruism difficult to sustain. Apathy and alienation are endemic. One alternative is to allow for greater individual enterprise and economic openness, though this must to some extent undermine the socialistic ideals for which the state-makers ostensibly stand.

To restate an earlier theme:

> The crisis of the state reflects, first and foremost, the contradiction between
> the declining room for manoeuvre available to national economies and the
> increasing interdependence which ties them together. Indeed, the
> accelerating expansion of trade and capital flows, characteristic of the most
> recent phase in the process of internationalization, narrows the range of
> national policy options, while at the same time magnifying the need for state
> intervention in the economy. Increasing economic interdependence
> enhances the economic and political functions of the state while at the same
> time diminishing the efficacy of its intervention. [20]

2. What is the interstate system?

State-making practices not only seek to establish singular authority over a
particular territory, they also promote and protect a measure of civility
among the state-makers themselves. An ill-assorted lot, they must pursue
their diverse policies in a system that is formally ungoverned. An index of
their success is given by the fact that this system is not chaotic. No one set
of state-makers has a monopoly of the means of coercion, yet neither has
the most Hobbesian prediction come to pass. There has not, in other
words, been unbridled passion, brutish incivility and a world where all
must face only lives that are mean, nasty and short.

The result has been a system and even, in some respects, a society of
sorts. From our analytical and historical heights we look down on a plain
of more or less heavily armed camps, the biggest ones mostly battling by
proxy, the smaller ones fighting over matters of more local note. There is
conflict aplenty, but there is co-operation as well.

The arrangements that regulate the conduct of state-makers towards
each other evolved as state-making did, and these ordering practices have
helped sustain the coexistence of the separate governments. They have not
led to the acceptance of a common government, but neither does any one
government or coalition of governments dominate.

There is a great deal invested now, both materially and mentally, in
state-making practices. Third world state-makers want the boundaries
state-making provides, ostensibly to promote the welfare of the peoples
they govern, though all too often to exploit the entrepreneurial opportunities of state-making to make personal fortunes. Second world state-
makers of the Eastern bloc for many years used their frontiers to confine
their people, many of whom would rather have moved to or have had
greater commerce with the West. They also used their borders to control
the influence of liberal capitalist enterprise upon their economies and
societies. First world state-makers of the Western bloc are the heirs to

those who originated modern state-making practices. These practices have been used ever since to draw lines to first world advantage — selectively to keep people out, and to keep the profits of capitalist enterprise coming in.

This is the sort of investment that lies behind the diplomatic routines that make it possible for nation–states to co-exist and not to come to grief. Many things get done in the world, and agreed rules make possible more than the perpetual war of everyone against everyone else. Hobbes himself acknowledged this possibility. He argued that sentiments such as 'Feare of Death', the desire for 'such things as are necessary to commodious living' and the hope of having such necessities prompt people to subscribe to 'Articles of Peace' that allow them to regulate their collective affairs in a co-operative way.[21] Hugo Grotius documented these articles in detail and found the outlook they provided a reasonably hopeful one.[22] Contemporary analysts have done the same, carefully identifying, and describing in great detail, the proto-society that the rules of international concourse define and defend.

The story of this society is typically told in such a way as to convince us of its merits. It is an argument, in other words, for the status quo. It highlights the convergent, solidarist characteristics of world society, and does so largely in terms of nation–states. It pays little attention to what happens apart from, because of, and usually despite, state-making practices.

Hedley Bull, for example, who subscribed to a definition of international society like that above,[23] knew very well that this society was built, as states themselves were built, using force and fraud. The rules and institutions most common today were not established by dialogue and consent. They were made by monologue, and what consent we find was not freely given but coerced.

Whatever reading of events we choose, however, it is clear that when the European state-makers of the fifteenth century began their extraordinary burst of politico-economic activity, the world was not organised into one system. There were several. There was the empire of Arab–Islam. There was that of the Indians, of the Mongol–Tartars, and of the Chinese. There were the New World empires of the Incas and the Aztecs, and those of West and East Africa. All these empires had a centre, surrounded by zones of diminishing control.

This being the case, the system that the Europeans evolved had few historical precedents since it was, as Bull and Watson observe, 'non-hegemonial'. There were earlier instances of societies of political entities without a central government, such as the city–state system of ancient Greece, but they were few.

The evolution of the European system was uncertain. The Roman empire still figured largely in European thinking, not only for the Church of Rome and 'medieval Latin Christendom' but also for a number of lay imitators like:

> Charles V, Louis XIV, Napoleon, and Hitler, who were restrained only by coalitions seeking to maintain a balance of power. Only in the eighteenth century was the idea firmly implanted among European states that an attempt by any one of them to establish hegemony over the others was a violation of the rules of their international society.

Bull and Watson also argue that:

> European international society ... did not first evolve its own rules and institutions and then export them to the rest of the world. The evolution of the European system of interstate relations and the expansion of Europe across the globe were simultaneous processes, which influenced and affected each other. Both began at the end of the fifteenth century, and both were concluded by the end of the Second World War, by which time European dominance was clearly at an end and the global international system, while still evolving, was being shaped less by Europeans than by others.[24]

The end of formal European dominance involved a series of anti-imperial claims: claims by the colonised for independence and for self-determination; claims (once nominal autonomy had been achieved) for fairer treatment in developmental terms; claims by captive nations and captive faiths for greater respect for other ways of living and alternative systems of belief. However, the channels down which these claims have run are state-making ones. Even the most revolutionary and universal of these claimants, secular or spiritual, have been forced to work within the constraints that state-making practices represent. They have used the same language as those who built the world system to justify their assertion of sovereign equality, to initiate diplomatic relations, to join international organisations, to resist intervention in their domestic affairs, and to rail against other state-makers who collude to dictatorial or exploitative effect.

The consequence has been the extension and consolidation of the contemporary state-system. The new crop of state-makers, far from undermining the ideological handiwork of their European mentors, have furthered it. While many are well aware of the handicap they carry as latecomers to the game, they have chosen to play rather than sit out. Exceptions like Albania are conspicuous by their disdain, but they have reinforced the system anyway by deciding to eschew it. The choice to play has been heavily constrained by inheritance, but all attempts to rewrite the rules (to create a coherent movement of the ostensibly non-aligned, for

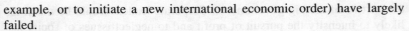

example, or to initiate a new international economic order) have largely failed.

Along with the consolidation of the interstate system has gone the continued evolution of the global political economy and the further development of fighting and weapons systems. The result has highlighted the difference between how state-makers organise the world we live in and how we actually do live in the world. We have the fiction of sovereign equality and the fact that this sovereign equality is heavily compromised by contemporary patterns of production and labour use. We have the strident defence of territorial autonomy and at the same time the advent of weapons potentially so devastating that any defence of such autonomy could be utterly self-defeating. We have all the pluralistic endeavours sanctioned by the state and serious threats that transcend state borders, like those of ecological deterioration, the internationalisation of crime syndicates, or disrespect for humane values.

In sum, while state-makers continue to guard their formal autonomy, they can hardly be said to be independent of each other, if indeed they ever were. This has made boundary maintenance and the policing of distinctions between the inside of the state and the outside of it much harder. State-makers find themselves compromised economically, strategically or culturally, some to the point where it is impossible to say that they are sovereign in any meaningful respect.

State-makers continue to practise the high politics of strategic power and diplomacy. The international nature of the issues raised by nuclear weaponry, environmental degradation and human rights, however, prompts us to ask whether state-making can provide adequate solutions to these problems. This is especially so when state-making may be in no small part a cause of such problems. The discourse within international society about peace and war may have become too limited, too conventional and too ritualised to provide an adequate response to these sorts of issues. In those cases where it is the state-makers themselves who may be the main threat to people's security and well-being it would seem perverse to ask for more of the same.

Given the universal nature of such problems, it would seem appropriate to advocate universal solutions. If international society is too decentralised to co-ordinate an adequate response, then greater integration would seem called for. Institutions like the UN are often cited as a possible starting-point. When we turn to such organisations, however, we find confederalism rampant. They are a microcosm of international society, and do little more, except in specialised and largely technical areas, than represent the diverse concerns of various state-makers. Nor would there seem to be much solace in the prospect of a world run by world business leaders or by one or two of the big governments. Corporate leaders would be much too likely to intensify the pursuit of profit and to neglect issues of social justice. Hegemonic power-brokers would soon be ruling in their own interests, not those of the common weal.

Perhaps more local initiatives would be better, though this flies in the face of all state-making practices and, as we have seen, it is these practices, albeit somewhat compromised, that currently prevail. The danger is that these practices may obscure the potential of possible alternatives. Articulating any particular alternative and trying to bring it about is invariably seen as an attack on state-making practices and on the whole system they define and defend. In the current context this is tantamount to revolution and, though revolution may be warranted, those who would raise it are fragmented and unresolved. So the state persists, by default as well as by design.

Notes

1 A. Vincent, *Theories of the State,* Basil Blackwell, Oxford, 1987, pp. 32-7. In international law this is the position normally associated with John Austin. The contrasting, consensual approach is that of Hugo Grotius, *De Jure Belli ac Paris,* Clarendon Press, Oxford, 1925.
2 H.D. Kitto, *The Greeks,* Penguin, Harmondsworth, 1951, pp. 12-13.
3 C. Tilly (ed.), *The Formation of National States in Western Europe,* Princeton University Press, Princeton, 1975, p. 633.
4 ibid., p. 635.
5 S. Bassett (ed.), *The Origins of Anglo-Saxon Kingdoms,* Leicester University Press, Leicester, 1989.
6 T. Hobbes, *Leviathan,* J.M. Dent, London, 1914, p. 64-6.
7 C. Tilly, op. cit., p. 42.
8 C. Tilly,'War Making and State Making as Organized Crime' in P. Evans et al. (eds), *Bringing the State Back In,* Cambridge University Press, Cambridge, 1985, p. 170-1.
9 loc. cit.
10 C. Tilly (ed.) (1985), op. cit., pp. 25, 72-3.
11 ibid., p. 26.
12 S. Krasner, *International Regimes,* Cornell University Press, Ithaca, 1983.
13 C. Vogler, *The Nation State: the neglected dimension of class,* Gower, Aldershot, 1985, p. 154.
14 J. Bernard, *The Female World from a Global Perspective,* Indiana University Press, Bloomington, 1987, p. 2. See also N. Yuval-Davis & F. Anthias (eds), *Woman–Nation–State,* Macmillan, London, 1988:

Women's link to the state is complex. On the one hand, they are acted upon as members of collectivities, institutions or groupings, and as participants in the social forces that give the state its given political projects in any particular social and historical context. On the other hand, they are a special focus of state concerns as a social category with a specific role (particularly human reproduction) ... A number of attempts ... to conceptualise the link between women and the state have focused on the central dimension of citizenship and how, far from being gender-neutral, it constructs men and women differently. Thus the feminist and socialist feminist critique of the state and state theorisation has advanced from one which points to the way the state treats women unequally in relation to men. There now exists a theoretical critique of the way the very project of the welfare state itself has constituted the 'state subject' in a gendered way, that is, as essentially male in its capacities and needs'. (p. 6)

15 R. Sivard, *Women: a world survey,* World Priorities, Washington, 1985, p. 5. See also J. Seager & A. Olson, *Women in the World: an international atlas,* Simon & Schuster, New York, 1986, p. 115; V. Randall, *Women and Politics: an international perspective,* Macmillan, London,1987, 2nd edn, esp. ch. 3, 'Women in political elites'.
16 V. Burstyn,'Masculine Dominance and the State' in R. Miliband & J. Saville (eds), *The Socialist Register 1983,* Merlin Press, London, 1983, p. 78. See also C. Enloe, *Bananas, Beaches and Bases: making feminist sense of international politics,* Pandora, London, 1989.
17 J.D.B. Miller, *The World of States,* St Martin's Press, New York, 1981,   pp. 21-5.
18 R. Walker, *One World, Many Worlds: struggles for a just world peace,* Lynne Rienner Publishers, Boulder, 1988, p. 42.
19 A. Vincent, op. cit., pp. 38, 176-7.
20 J. Camilleri,'The Advanced Capitalist State and the Contemporary World Crisis' in R. Walker (ed.), *Culture, Ideology and World Order,* Westview Press, Boulder, 1984, p. 91.
21 T. Hobbes, op. cit., p. 66.
22 H. Grotius, op. cit.
23 H. Bull, *The Anarchical Society*, Macmillan, London, 1977, p. 13.
24 H. Bull & A. Watson (eds), *The Expansion of International Society,* Clarendon Press, Oxford, 1984, pp. 2-3, 6-7.

3

The balance of power

What is power in the context of international politics? What is the balance of power? What pattern of relationships does this concept describe? What reading of world historical events is used to explain it? What happens if, instead of reading the balance of power in terms of power as dominance or subordinance, we do so in terms of power as competence?

1. What is power in the context of international politics?

In conventional terms, states are Good Things. The idea of them is used to push people together and to provide them with a basic framework within which to lead decent lives. That the result has not always been very successful has not stopped its supporters universalising it.

State-makers invariably claim to act for all. They do so to justify their efforts, to represent their behaviour as legitimate, and to distinguish between what is done for private gain and what is done for the public good. Whether they do act in the public good is highly contentious, but that is their claim. It is this (often tenuous) claim that distinguishes state-makers from robber barons and buccaneers.

The ideology of modern statism, in other words, commits its adherents to civil and consensual practices of a relatively responsible kind. Hypocrites abound, of course, but they must mouth the sentiments of civic duty or stand condemned by their state-making peers.

The expectation that state-makers will behave in a civil and consensual way toward their client populations does not obtain toward each other. In drawing borders, either territorially on the ground or notionally in people's heads, state-makers create a host of hazards that are the substance of much of international politics.

The failure so far by any one set of state-makers to universalise their own particular domain by creating a world state, and the failure by all of them to accede to any overarching authority that would amount to a world government means they must work on their own. For state-makers it is a self-help system, which presents them with a security dilemma or, in the words of Kenneth Waltz, '[b]ecause some states may at any time use force, all states must be prepared to do so — or live at the mercy of their militarily more vigorous neighbors'. [1]

Such a system sanctions selfishness. It fosters suspicion and competitiveness and makes human altruism hard to sustain. However sympathetic people may feel toward each other, and however considerate they would like to be to each other, their sense of vulnerability as a group will make self-regarding behaviour the more rational choice. Altruism is only possible under such circumstances when it serves a collective purpose that is also self-referential. International efforts to deal with the greenhouse effect and the depletion of the ozone layer, for example, are clearly self-serving, and it is the self-referential component that makes co-operation possible in dealing with problems like these. Even here, however, conflicting interests are common.

Since self-regarding behaviour all too readily becomes self-aggrandising behaviour, such a system affirms the more selfish aspects of human nature. Hence the conclusion by analysts like Reinhold Niebuhr, that 'Every group, as every individual, has expansive desires which are rooted in the instinct of survival ... The will-to-live [inevitably?] becomes the will-to-power.' [2]

What credence are we to give this concept of a will to power? We know that the desire to determine events and to structure relationships in ways that we want them to be is an important motive for much human behaviour. These desires denote an autonomous urge to get one's way. Perhaps this urge is biologically based, though even so it will be clearly subject to individual variation, and it will be amplified or reduced by particular cultures and subcultures in ways specific to them. (The will to power, whatever its cause, is not the only one. Equally important is the desire to reproduce, as well as the desire to find in life a meaning and a purpose.) [3]

Where the will to power, such as it is, gets frustrated, either apathy or sublimation may ensue. Sublimation refers to anything from simmering resentment to the use of brute force. In an ungoverned system or society of states it can mean state-makers resorting to violence to try to get their way. In other words, it can mean war.

Is this picture of cause and effect credible? Some analysts, like Niebuhr, are extremely pessimistic about people in groups being able to meet high moral standards in their behaviour towards each other. They are pessimistic about human nature and about the prospect of improving it. They live in a world where national (self) interests conflict and brute force is the most important way to prevail. They think of themselves as tough-minded, hard-headed, dry-eyed people who face facts, which suggest to them that state-makers, in a world where state-making practices predominate, will be more concerned with their survival than with issues of equity or justice.

This was very much the ideological tone of the discipline of international relations after the Second World War. In the USA its most eminent exponent was Hans Morgenthau. His major work, *Politics Among Nations*, described international politics as a struggle for power between state-makers in the pursuit of their national interests.[4] It was written as a primer of European statecraft, cast in analytic terms that confirmed the importance of the state and the perils of the interstate system. It is a profoundly pessimistic work. Morgenthau wore his cosmic despair like a crown, and with thorns taken from this carefully woven headpiece he prodded away at all the idealistic balloons, all the highly-coloured optimisms of contemporary foreign policy. Utopian assumptions like those that have regularly seized key United States state-makers, prompting them to promise the practical realisation of universal moral principles, were his prime target.

Morgenthau posited six principles of 'political realism' as an antidote to idealism and as a guide to good policy. These were:

1. that 'politics, like society in general, is governed by objective laws that have their roots in human nature';
2. that international politics is best characterised by, and foreign policy can best be predicted in terms of, the 'concept of interest defined in terms of power' (a concept that 'sets politics as an autonomous sphere of action and understanding apart from other spheres, such as economics' which is 'interest defined as wealth');
3. that

   interest defined as power ... may comprise anything that establishes and maintains the control of man over man. Thus power covers all social relationships which serve that end, from physical violence to the most subtle of psychological ties by which one mind controls another. Power covers the domination of man by man, both when it is disciplined by moral ends ... and when it is that untamed and barbaric force which finds its laws in nothing but its own strength and its sole justification in its aggrandisement;

4. that

   while the individual has a moral right to sacrifice himself in defense of ... a moral principle, the state has no right to let its moral [principles] ... get in the way of successful political action, itself inspired by the moral principle of national survival';

5 that the

> lighthearted equation between a particular nationalism and the counsels of Providence is morally indefensible ... for it is liable to engender the distortion in judgment which, in the blindness of crusading frenzy, destroys nations and civilizations — in the name of moral principle, ideal, or God himself; and

6 that the 'autonomy of the political sphere' is best maintained by asking always and only '[h]ow does this policy affect the power of the nation?' [5]

Morgenthau's six principles have been widely discussed and criticised. Numbers 2 and 3 seem somewhat inconsistent, for example, since in the former 'interest' defined in terms of 'power' is supposed to set politics apart from other disciplines, and yet power ostensibly includes any controlling social relationship, which rather than setting politics apart would suggest that it is ubiquitous. Though Morgenthau may well be positing a distinction here between the instruments of power and the purposes towards which power is put, a definition of power so broad does blur the distinction he is trying to make between (say) politics and economics, or politics and psychology.

Though he wrote in the main about states and state-making, it is important to note that Morgenthau did not deny the possibility of the state system ultimately being transformed. He said:

> Nothing in the realist position militates against the assumption that the present division of the political world into nation states will be replaced by larger units of a quite different character, more in keeping with the technical potentialities and the moral requirements of the contemporary world.

He did not think this would happen by moral exhortation. Rather — and this was the essence of his 'realism' — it would come about through the 'workmanlike manipulation of the perennial forces that have shaped the past as they will the future'. [6]

In England, the role of realist iconoclast was played by E.H. Carr. Carr wrote on the eve of the last European war:

> with the deliberate aim of counteracting the glaring and dangerous defect of nearly all thinking, both academic and popular, about international politics in English-speaking countries from 1919 to 1939 — the almost total neglect of the factor of power. [7]

His approach was to point out how our political beliefs and behaviour combine the linked but incompatible strands of idealism and realism. Either alone is ultimately ineffective. Idealism is too unrealistic ever to

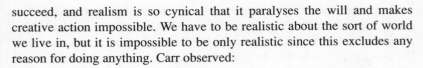

succeed, and realism is so cynical that it paralyses the will and makes creative action impossible. We have to be realistic about the sort of world we live in, but it is impossible to be only realistic since this excludes any reason for doing anything. Carr observed:

> The impossibility of being a consistent and thorough-going realist is one of the most certain and most curious lessons of political science. Consistent realism excludes four things which appear to be essential ingredients of all effective political thinking: a finite goal, an emotional appeal, a right of moral judgment and a ground for action. [8]

Human beings do have visions of better ways of being, despite the fact that their visions are soon tarnished by self-interest and hypocrisy, and they become fitting targets for a realist attack.

Power is all-pervasive in Carr's world. It is a 'necessary ingredient of every political order' [9] though, as he is quick to point out, power — even in the form of brute force — can never be enough to achieve other values. Nor can it be an end in itself. '[I]n the long run' people will undermine or overthrow those who wield such power in the name of other values. Idealism and realism must therefore, in Carr's view, be combined. Neither power nor morality can ultimately dominate. They must be co-ordinated in political action. [10]

> We shall never arrive at a political order in which the grievances of the weak and the few receive the same prompt attention as the grievances of the strong and the many. Power goes far to create the morality convenient to itself, and coercion is a fruitful source of consent. But ... it remains true that ... international order and ... international harmony can be built up only on the basis of an ascendancy which is generally accepted as tolerant and unoppressive or, at any rate, as preferable to any practicable alternative. [11]

As with Morgenthau, it is important to note that Carr had no particular commitment to state-making or the state. He considered sovereignty as a concept 'blurred and indistinct', and likely to become more so. He didn't see the 'effective group unit of the future' as being, in all probability, that of the state. Indeed, it was his specific prediction that an international order based on states was likely to prove 'unreal'. Small states, he argued, were obsolete,[12] and though scientific progress and the growth in productive capacity had made much bigger states possible, he considered these political units might have an optimum size, beyond which they would break up again. Indeed, it was this issue that he considered 'likely to be more decisive than any other for the course of world history in the next few generations'.[13] He could also envisage a world in which political power was not territorially organised, but built on other bases, such as race, creed or class.

Morgenthau and Carr represent an important tradition of thought and practice in international politics. They, and others, have attached great significance to power. This prompts us to ask what is meant by the word. We use it freely, assuming we know what we are talking about and that we all mean the same thing. In a commonsense way, we generally do know what we are talking about, and we make enough sense to each other most of the time to share ideas and co-ordinate our actions. When we try to arrive at a comprehensive definition of the term, however, it proves very slippery indeed. Just how slippery is clearly shown by Steven Lukes. In a recent exploration of a number of familiar academic definitions of the concept he concluded that any comprehensive statement would be 'too thin and formal' to be very meaningful. [14]

Therefore, let us begin with the commonplace. Whenever we talk of the practice of politics, from the local tennis club to the UN, we think of people politicking. They bargain, they buy support, and they coerce. They do so to 'make a difference in the world'. [15] Power is the extended ego at work. To be powerful is to have an effect. It is to get away with something. It is to determine events and to structure relationships in ways we desire.

Power capacities can be conceptualised in more and less tangible terms. State-makers, for example, consider themselves powerful if they command relatively numerous and efficient military resources, and a relatively productive and efficient economy. They will also seek to foster high national morale. Thus state-making practices will include maintaining military and police forces and the country's productive capacity, as well as maintaining morale and fostering the ideological commitment by the populace to the state-makers' aims. [16]

League tables of strategic might, and of secondary and tertiary industrial strength, provide a quantitative measure of comparative material capacity. [17] However, the mental dimension is a qualitative one and its moral and spiritual components make the ranking of human groups in this respect highly subjective.

Power to do what? Any of the material or mental powers mentioned above could become an end in itself. However, power is usually considered a means to other ends, such as prosperity, security, peace or the desire to dominate (for any one of many rational and irrational, moral or immoral reasons). Capacity does not translate directly into power in international politics. The complexity of the practices involved, that is, do not always provide the expected outcomes. The failure of the state-makers of the USA to prevail in their war over the revolutionary forces of Vietnam is an example. Despite enormous military and economic resources and, initially at least, the will to win, the erosion of United States resolve in the face of sustained Vietnamese resistance ultimately rendered those resources useless.

The failure of the USA in this case, or the Soviets in Afghanistan in another, does not negate the tendency to see considerable military or productive or ideological might as an index of 'great power' status. The strategic size, the wealth and the cultural nerve of the USA or the Soviet Union, as collective entities, are all impressive, although not everyone looking on is favourably impressed. Nor do lesser powers necessarily have less to offer. In general, however, the great powers can deploy substantial resources on any front, whether diplomatic, military, material or ideological.

One danger with constructing ladders of relative power, however, is the propensity for those designated powerful to presume that this is not only 'how it is' but 'how it should be'. But is it? Consider (some) contemporary feminists' trenchant critique of those who think in this way, and the cult of power to which they subscribe.

In their analysis of what 'power-over' means, these thinkers posit an alternative version of what is possible, namely the 'power-to'. Clearly power-over can denote the power-to. What these theorists are reaching for, however, is a conception of power which is more personalised and, in this context, less state-centric. They portray power less as a capacity and more as a process, a dynamic interaction. In this sense to have power means

> to have entry to a network of relationships in which one can influence, persuade, threaten or cajole others to do what one wants or needs them to do. Although no other syntax is available to us, it is in fact false to speak of 'having power'. One does not possess power: it is granted to the dominator by hosts of other people, and that grant is not unretractable ... It is always true that those whom we control control us. [18]

One alternative to power as dominance is therefore power as competence. The shift in perspective involved is not a simple one, conditioned as we are by the value-universe of the topdogs. We all too readily assume that to be dominated is to be helpless. However, the assumption is not warranted.

In a landmark analysis Berenice Carroll points out why, and explores a number of the dimensions of the underdog view. She points out how this perspective has been downplayed, in no small part because of our preoccupation with the state. There is a cult of power, she claims, that promotes '(1) un-critical acceptance of prevailing conceptions of power; (2) preoccupation with institutions, groups, and persons conceived to be powerful; [and] (3) identification with institutions, groups, or persons conceived to be powerful'. [19] She then outlines what we find when we escape this preoccupation with the powerful to explore the 'powers of the allegedly powerless' and their 'potentialities for autonomous action'. [20]

Carroll begins by noting the preoccupation in the study of international politics with power as dominance, conquest, and control. She notes the close and relatively recent link in Western culture between this particular conception and notions of manliness and virility. She also notes the negative associations that being powerless (in this sense) has with being incapable, weak, inadequate and effeminate. What is required, in this regard, is an awareness on the part of analysts and ordinary people of power as competence. We need, that is, to know power as 'independent strength, ability, autonomy, self-determination, control over one's own life rather than the lives of others, [and the] competence to deal with one's environment out of one's own energies and resources, rather than on the basis of dependence'. [21]

As her own contribution Carroll first draws attention to Kenneth Boulding's distinction between 'threat' power, 'exchange' power and 'integrative' power. Threat power refers to the familiar 'I win, you lose' relationship we find in a football match, for example. Exchange power refers to those situations where everyone wins. (Imagine a football match played for the pleasure of the game alone, and where no score is kept. Or one where every player has his own ball to kick as he pleases. These would hardly make 'matches', but that is because of the emphasis conventionally placed upon winning as an indicator of individual or collective enjoyment.)

Integrative power, by contrast, is more solidarist. It is the capacity children have, for example, despite their relative helplessness, to evoke self-sacrificing behaviour in their parents. It denotes the sense of communal identity that kept Kitto's Greeks together in their long march to the Black Sea.

Most impressed by this notion of integrative power, Carroll goes on to discern nine ways in which the ostensibly powerless can assert themselves. The competences concerned are mostly diffuse and unorganised. They are harder to see than those of threat or exchange. They deal with intangibles; with people's thoughts and behaviour rather than with 'defined group[s] or institution[s]'. Intangibility makes them difficult to mobilise around, and difficult to define in terms of conscious policy. At the same time, however, it is probably upon 'just these forms of power that all major, long-term social change ... depends'. [22]

The nine capacities Carroll identifies are disintegrative power; inertial power; innovative power (norm-creating); legitimising power (integrative, socialising); expressive power; explosive power; the power of resistance; collective power (co-operative); and migratory power (population). To some extent these capacities overlap, but each does denote a different dimension of the power-to people have despite the subordinate status they may otherwise possess.

The attempt to specify so many dimensions of the power of the weak is very rare. To my knowledge no attempt has ever been made to build upon Carroll's work (which raises serious questions about who sets research agendas, why such work hardly ever appears on them, and why?).

Let us look more closely at each category in turn. By disintegrative power Carroll means the power of large numbers of people to dismantle or break down large social, economic and political structures. As examples she cites urban decay, failing service industries, the

> overloading and burgeoning deficiencies and injustices of the legal system; the defiance of 'law and order' not only by 'organized crime' ... but increasingly by disaffected or alienated individuals, gangs and political groups, not only in the ghettos of poverty, but now also throughout the class structure.

It is power of this sort, she claims, which over time can bring down whole empires, however highly developed, and has done so in the past. [23]

Disintegrative power may be little better than apathy. Dissociative strategies are used intentionally, however, though the more self-conscious and the better organised the dissociating movement, the more tangible and visible it becomes and the easier it is to repress. Solidarity in Poland would be one example of a dissociative strategy that succeeded.

Inertial power is even more privatised and diffuse. It refers to the 'resistance of the ... masses, who are well aware that they would rather not work or fight for other people's profit, and must therefore either be persuaded to do so by manipulation or coerced into doing so by physical or economic force'. [24] In sum this self-serving and common-sense conservatism can be a hard brake riding on rapid change. (Given the right demagogue, however, and adverse social circumstances, it can make change inevitable.)

Innovative power is used to refer to the inventiveness and creativeness of the masses:

> it appears not only possible but quite likely that, in the social arena, ideas and proposals for radical change ... come from below — from those who suffer from 'things as they are' and would benefit from changing them — rather than from above — from those who benefit from things as they are and have a stake in preserving them.

Indeed 'the most innovative demands and proposals, those that seem most extreme and unrealistic because they depart furthest from accepted norms, [can] come from the underdogs and the alienated, not from their middle-class sympathizers nor from the topdog groups struggling to keep up with the demands'. Such demands may seem 'extreme' or 'irrational', and the form they take may seem 'inchoate' and 'violent' (like ghetto riots or street-gang warfare). [25] They may be rational and pacific as well, though. The form they take may be quite structured, such as the norm-setting activities of peace movements, or of human rights groups.

Legitimising power is Boulding's integrative power, the power to craft the ideas and the behaviour of the people that constitute society, and without whose collaboration or compliance government could not occur. Carroll is well aware of the socialising power of all the conventional sociopolitical institutions like schools or the media. These must reckon, however, with all that goes on outside them. A government cannot control all the people all the time, no matter how hard it tries to train and restrain them. Control and legitimisation fail most clearly at that moment when no-one will do what their governors tell them to; when troops refuse to fire, for example, upon those deemed insurgent. [26]

By expressive and explosive power Carroll means the expression of discontent or anger in ways that go beyond the social, legal, and moral norms which keep a community together. At one end we find riots, mob violence, bombings, assassinations, and spontaneous mass demonstrations and at the other 'ways in which discontent may be dramatically, but less violently, displayed (including art, literature, theatre, "extremist" political speeches and demands, organized nonviolent protests, etc.)'. The power here is a warning power. It is also in some degree an educative power. It is not usually able to evoke much of a response from the powers that be, or bring about much of a change in the status quo, but in the long run it may grow in breadth and depth, either of its own accord or in response to attempts to suppress it. [27]

The power of resistance and of collective or co-operative power refers to more organised or more self-conscious ways of offering opposition. It is something more than individuals who come together in apparently spontaneous congress. [28] Gandhi's passive campaign in support of Indian self-determination is an obvious example. So are partisan or guerrilla activities in times of war. As noted in the discussion of disintegrative power, however, the more institutionalised and routinised resistance becomes the more readily it can be opposed. The more vulnerable it becomes, in other words, to the conventional use of the power to repress.

Finally, Carroll draws attention to the capacity of those ostensibly powerless to 'move or to reproduce themselves'. [29]   State-makers may legislate limits on family size to control this capacity. They may also supervise the emigration and immigration process. To what extent people are able to remain largely independent of such governmental initiatives, as Carroll claims they can, is debatable. Nonetheless, the population of China continued to grow despite government directives and incentives to limit family size, and Indochinese boat people continued to leave for points east and south despite governmental restrictions and the lack of a welcome at their destination. Again, there are overlaps with other categories of power as competence, since these are powers which can have disintegrative or integrative effects.

The implications are profound. Many and varied are the studies of the human desire to dominate and win. Much more scarce are studies of ordinary people making do and getting by, concerned with the quality of their lives rather than doing others down. Of course, improving or maintaining the quality of one's life may involve domination and coercion, but is the game inevitably zero-sum? It may be an ideological choice to craft human affairs in such an 'I win, you lose' way. In which case, why choose the control strategy rather than the mutually liberating one? The state-maker would remind us at this point of the security dilemma, and the need for power-political prudence in an ungoverned world. But what does this sort of prudence cost? What is the price of security under such circumstances?

From global experience it is high. It is paid in fear and suspicion; in arms races and a hierarchy of military and material might that over-shadows all else. Prudence and security mean dominance and subordination on a global scale.

The question then becomes, as Elizabeth Converse points out, 'how extensive, how sustained, how nonreciprocating, and how self-perpetuating these dominance relationships [are] ... and which party benefits most from them over time? [30] Are these relationships inevitable?

2. What is the balance of power? What pattern of relationships does this concept describe? What reading of world historical events is used to explain it?

The balance of power is the key concept in the conventional state theory of international politics. It is implicit in media analyses of world affairs, and explicit in most academic ones. The concept is ancient, but the phrase is of relatively recent origin, having been developed, as the state and the state system were, as a way of describing patterns of late second millenium European power politics. These patterns have become so persistent that the phrase has taken on a life of its own. It is used not only to describe such patterns but to explain them, and to provide policy prescriptions for state-makers having to decide what to do in the world. The idea, in other words, is an ideology, creating those very conditions it is supposed to describe and explain.

How does this happen? The balance of power typically starts off as a description of state-making practices designed to prevent an undue concentration of power in the state system as a whole. It quickly becomes clear, however, that the pluralistic nature of that system constrains the choices any state-maker might have. State-makers may choose to exercise the balance of power option. They rarely reject it, however, since the security dilemma seems too compelling, which is close to saying that state-makers have no choice but to practise balance of power tactics if they are to survive.

By this logic a description becomes an explanation that becomes a prescriptive ideology that closes the circle so that what we see is what has been put there. Closed systems of logic like this are based on the prior belief in their first premise. In the case of the balance of power the belief is based in part on the metaphor of the balance itself, of weights in equipoise. The image is a pervasive one. Sometimes we find analysts using a cognate idea, that of states as pieces on a chessboard. Sometimes we find the Newtonian analogy of bodies in space. As they move their influence on each other is relative to their size and weight. Should one unit undergo a change, becoming larger or smaller, heavier or lighter, the result is a new gravitational arrangement and a new set of systemic relationships. Neither of these notions is as popular as that of the grocer's scales, however, or the banker's balance.

Why do such images feel so apt? Largely because of the nature of European state-making these images have helped to describe and explain. After hundreds of years of the violent aggregation of local peoples into increasingly larger territorial domains, it is almost as if Europeans were not to be compressed any further. A sort of limit, perhaps nation-based, was reached. They wouldn't fit into fewer than the twenty or so groups that we now call France, Germany, and so on. Any set of state-makers who tried to consolidate further found the rest, or strategic numbers of them, allied in opposition. The result has been a kind of dynamic equilibrium, or balance.

Change, in other words, served only to maintain the balance of the system and the dispersal of power as a whole. David Hume, reviewing this process in the middle of the eighteenth century, thought the whole thing commonsense, noting how revisionist powers invariably found themselves facing a confederacy of their peers, whether or not they were former friends and allies. [31]

The turning outwards of the self-aggrandising energies involved are what we know as European imperialism and the capitalist world-economy. European state-makers not only globalised the state, but the state-system as a whole, and the balancing mechanism built into it.

What is the balance of power mechanism? There is no one answer to this question because the concept has been used in a number of different ways, and attempts to systematise such usage also differ. [32] I propose here to follow the common convention, introduced above, of discriminating between its descriptive, explanatory and prescriptive dimensions.

Balance of power as a description

The concept is most commonly used to describe the distribution of power between states. Hedley Bull makes a distinction between the objective fact of no one state being preponderant militarily (presumably a 'real' balance), and the subjective belief in this state of affairs (one that is somehow 'false'). He also discriminates between a 'fortuitous' balance (one that just happens) and a 'contrived' one (that has to be made to happen, in which case the idea has already become a policy prescription).[33] Neither of these distinctions seems particularly interesting, but I have included them here for the sake of completeness.

What sort of distribution of power do we mean? There can obviously be more than one. Indeed, there are three about which analysts typically talk. There is the balance of power as the distribution of power as it is; there is the balance of power specified as an even distribution of power; and there is the balance of power as an uneven distribution of power.

The first usage — the balance of power as a way of describing the distribution of power as it is — seems to be the most common understanding of the term. It refers to the pattern of international power evident at any particular time. This pattern is dynamic, not static, so that when it is said that the balance of power has changed, it is assumed that the power relationships in the world have also changed. It can be a simple pattern (like a see-saw or a beam balance), or a complex one (like a chandelier). There may, in other words, be two sets of state-makers involved (a bipolar system), or three or more (making the pattern a multipolar one). In the latter case the balancing act is more complicated and there is considerable debate as to whether such a system is preferable, and whether it is better at preserving peace and preventing war.

The simple balance is typically 'even'. The alliance-making required to sustain a simple balance is a dynamic process of judging how best to prevent being overwhelmed, or how best to take advantage of weakness.

Let there be three powers [for example] of which the first attacks the second. The third power cannot afford to see the second so decisively crushed that it becomes threatened itself; therefore if it is far-sighted it 'throws its weight into the lighter scale of the balance' by supporting the second power. This is the balance of power at its simplest. More generally, when one power grows dangerously strong the others combine against it. [34]

By this logic everything is reduced to a series of bipolar duels.

The balance might be uneven, however, which is typical of a multipolar and more complex situation. Balance under these circumstances implies a margin of superiority, or even the direct opposite of balance, namely, preponderance or hegemony — imbalance in fact. As state-makers seek to secure their territory, they may push up the odds step-wise or ratchet-fashion. One party looks for the edge, others are forced to counter, and the tension in the system as a whole escalates as the power-chandelier soars towards the ceiling, which is war.

Bull says that escalation can be a very general process. Where this is the case the main policy-makers involved are working to preserve the pluralistic character of the system as a whole, even if it means damage to some of the lesser participants.

This [for example] was the normal state of Europe in the eighteenth century. ... In 1718 Britain, France and Austria were allied against Spain; in 1725 Spain and Austria were allied against France and Britain; in 1733 Spain and France were allied against Austria; in 1740 Britain and Austria were allied against France and Prussia; and in 1756 Britain and Prussia were allied against France and Austria. [35]

It may also be a local process only. If so, it describes the way state-makers in a particular region will try to avoid being absorbed or dominated by each other or by a locally dominant power. This can go on quite independently of the general balance, or it may be linked to it as part of a competition between great powers that is being conducted by proxy.

Great power state-makers tend to justify their dominance of their own backyards — their spheres of influence — in the light of what is required to keep the global balance intact. Thus the Soviet Union for a generation after the last European war asserted a sphere of influence over Eastern Europe. The USA has long claimed the same sort of hegemony over Central and South America and the Caribbean. In one respect this is cynical self-interest. In another it is one of the costs of maintaining a general balance between the Soviet Union and the USA, and one of the costs of having a hierarchy of strategic power.

There is no guarantee that the balance of power will work. The collapse of every alliance system upon which a balance is built will always be immanent. The balance of power doctrine, in other words, does not promise peace. It does no more than mitigate the effects of an ungoverned global polity. State-makers can always decide to defend a particular order by opting for disorder, that is, war.

The problem today is that the collapse of the balance of power (at worst war) could entail the collapse of the balance of terror (at worst war of a uniquely destructive kind). At the end of the war of Spanish succession in the early eighteenth century, Alexander Pope proclaimed 'Europe balanced, neither side prevails; For nothing's left in either of the Scales'.[36] The modern-day equivalent hardly bears thinking about.

However abstract the analysis seems, therefore, many human lives depend upon state-making power-brokers continuing to make the balance of power work, whether automatically (where balance is the larger outcome of many lesser decisions that serve self-interest but also the commonweal, like Adam Smith's 'hidden hand'); semi-automatically (where one set of state-makers does the equilibrating); or manually (where they all manage policy with the idea of an equilibrium clearly in mind).

Balance of power as an explanation

How are we to explain the balance of power in the terms described above? Firstly, it may need no explanation. A detailed description of all the state-making and manoeuvring that has gone on in international politics, and continues to go on, may be all we can truly provide. Secondly, however, most analysts would argue that there is an inescapable logic to the balance of power, and that this is the commonsense law of self-preservation. Such a law is hardly unique to the modern state system. It has prevailed throughout human history.

The reasoning is simple. Power politics are neither chaotic nor arbitrary. As state-makers negotiate among themselves, patterns emerge that we call the balance of power. 'It is the general rule' for example 'that when powers are territorial neighbours they are hostile'. [37] Neighbours are 'natural enemies', given the competitive character of state-making practices and the human propensity for 'us–them' thinking. As a consequence, 'If your neighbour is your "natural enemy", the power on the other side of your neighbour is your natural ally. And what natural allies regard as a defensive alliance is likely to appear to the power between them as "encirclement".' [38]

Because state-makers often have more than one territorial border to defend, and have only finite defence resources, the power plays can become quite complex. Typically, however, 'local rivalries are largely ironed out by the pressure of greater rivalries; the small powers are reduced to a buffer zone between great powers; and the sandwich system is reproduced on a wider scale in the alignments of the great powers themselves'. [39]

Buffer states have been divided by Martin Wight into three types: trimmers, neutrals and satellites. [40] In modern times, Prince Sihanouk of Cambodia was famous for his trimming, playing his mightier neighbours off against each other in his bid to preserve Cambodia's autonomy. The fact that he finally failed does not detract from the skill with which he played the power political game in his nation's cause.

Satellites are states whose foreign policy is controlled by another set of state-makers. Australian state-makers are regularly accused of accepting the status of satellite to the USA. Neutrals lie low and try not to be noticed. Switzerland is the most famous case in this category.

If we read the story of Europe since the last war there in these power-political terms, it sounds like a board-game. Germany, France, Great Britain and Italy ceased to be great powers. The whole region became a buffer zone between the Soviet Union and the USA, but a buffer zone with two parts, an Eastern one for many years under Soviet domination, and a Western one allied with the USA. The line between the parts cut Germany in half.

Strategic and state-centric narratives like these can be constructed for the whole world. The policy calculations they predispose are a sort of algebra, full of unknowns. State-making, in the senses of state-creation and state-maintenance, is a complex task. It is little wonder state-makers reach for such seemingly serviceable concepts as the balance of power. 'They reach for control' in Robert Ashley's words, though they may have to 'surrender their humanity' to do so. 'They strive for mastery and b-ecome the slaves of fear'. [41]

What creates or maintains what? Does the balance of power explain interstate relations, or does it rather make for particular sorts of political units, namely states, whose makers must practise the doctrine to remain independent? Is it merely a matter of observing power politics at play? Or is the doctrine '[s]o deeply ... bound within the identities of the participant states that their observations of its rules and expectations become acts not of conscious obedience to something external but of self-realization, of survival as what they have become'?[42]

Balance of power as a prescription

As already suggested, it is a short step from explaining the balance of power to putting such explanations to work as policy prescriptions. It is not far from an account of what is and why, to recommending what ought to be. United States state-makers after the Second World War, for exam-ple, saw the world in balance of power terms. They also saw a need to restore that balance they felt would contain communism. They assumed the Soviets were expansionists (a not unreasonable assumption at the time), and had in mind a preferred distribution of power that they felt would counter their opponents. Such a balance could have been even or uneven. In the event the state-makers chose the latter. Their attempt to achieve a strategic margin in favour of the USA was an important factor in the subsequent arms race.

A critique

The map of the concept drawn above is the conventional reading of it in analytical and historical terms. The map is not as serviceable as it appears, however. Firstly, the doctrine is overly rationalistic. It places great faith in foreign policies and the human capacity to plan and change them. However, this faith may be misplaced. It assumes a regularity to world affairs of a sort that may not exist, no matter how hard state-makers try to impose it.

A balance of power is the outcome of many small and large decisions that are supposed to arrive, in aggregate, at equipoise. These decisions are not taken at random. In trying to control or to make more predictable and seemingly safe their political environment, state-makers would like to have happen what they plan. They seize upon ideas like those of the balance of power because they promise a degree of predictability and control. The idea is logical and precise, complex yet comprehensible. It appeals to a desire for order.

The problem with the world, however, is that it seems always a little more regular and logical than it is. It is not chaotic or anarchic in any stereotypic sense, yet it has a wildness that, in G.K. Chesterton's words, 'lies in wait'. In its rationalistic way, the balance of power doctrine promises control of a sort that can mislead, by promising too much. Given that wildness includes the collapse of the nuclear balance of terror, we face at least one potentially disastrous consequence of using the balance of power to keep order in the world.

A second and associated criticism of the balance of power doctrine is the extent to which it is an ideological defence of the idea of the state. The doctrine emerged in the form of particular state-relating practices, such as alliances, diplomacy and treaties. It was the systemic side of the state-making coin. As a consequence the doctrine has always assumed that states are the most important players in international politics and that the state-system is the main framework for world politics. It has always assumed that state-makers look both inside and outside; that there is an inside and an outside to what they do; that the two realms are distinct; and that international politics are different from domestic politics, or at least conceptually separable from them (because of their ungoverned nature).

What this assumption obscures is the extent to which balance of power thinking perpetuates itself, and the conservative outcome of this process of perpetuation. In Ashley's words:

> the balance-of-power scheme, far from being a logical relation deduced from a prior structure of states in anarchy, is the constitutive principle of a pluralistic states system ... For statesmen, this simple dialectical scheme has a genuine economy of logic (though it is not the logic of economy) that will make their own practices comprehensible in the eyes of other competent statesmen, and thanks to which they can understand their practices as well. More importantly, as judiciously applied by artful participants, the scheme orients the comprehension of interests and the undertaking of practices that promise to optimize power.[43]

Inevitably, a statist perspective makes it harder to see other assumptions; that the state, for example, may be only one of a number of important actors in international politics; that domestic and international politics may be much more closely linked than is commonly supposed; that there may be order other than that of the balance of power and equally deserving of our concern; that there are permissive contexts, like that of the political economy, in which balance of powering takes place, and which are just as important in their own right.

While state-making in a state system may be the main or the most readily apparent ordering practice in the world, international reality does consist of a 'multiplicity of mutually interpenetrating and opposed world orders ... totalitarian communist [for example] ... Muslim transnationalist ... corporatist authoritarian'.[44] Each contains alternative structuring possibilities, and the potential to receive much greater recognition than it does today.

Regarding permissive contexts, particularly the economic one, Ashley posits a

> deep consensus granting control over production to a sphere of 'private' decisions that are themselves immunized from public responsibility — a practical consensus that thereby produces a sphere of 'economy' operating according to technical rational logics of action. In turn, such a consensus, together with the worldwide power bloc whose dominance it signifies and secures, might be called the modern global hegemony. The balance-of-power regime is its public political face.[45]

The third and most regrettable feature of the balance of power doctrine is its implicit endorsement of war as a way of pursuing preferred sorts of peace. There is more than a hint of conventional masculinity here. Inis Claude draws attention to the symbolic significance of the balance of power and the perceived need for its explicit acceptance as a test of a state-maker's 'intellectual virility'.[46] State-makers who understand what military power can do in world affairs do not necessarily approve of what it can do, but most (and most are men) certainly seem to. Attaching masculinist egos to such a doctrine, that is, to the notion that war is a necessary and legitimate means to some other end (like the preservation of the independence of the state), would seem only to reinforce such approval.

This is hardly desirable when the war we are talking about could be a thermonuclear one capable of destroying most if not all of us. It might be more hard-headed, sensible and realistic under such circumstances to confront the common need for restraint and co-operation. In balance of power parlance, however, that would seem more like craven appeasement than resolute prudence. Why? Largely, it is suggested here, because of the doctrine's masculinist presumptions.

Militaristic machismo is a long-standing phenomenon, to which the story of world weaponry is a long eulogy. Though the story is complex and unclear, Schuman's attempted summary makes wonderfully light work of a very heavy subject.

> Since the advent of metallurgy it has been evident to all that the most effective means of inflicting injury is to hurl bits of metal, preferably hot, into the tissues of the victim and that the best way of avoiding injury is to wear metallic garb, acquire speed through the use of horse, wagon, car, or plane, or to take refuge behind stone walls, in vehicles of wood or iron, or in holes in the ground. The belated adaptation of gunpowder (long used by heathen Chinese for fireworks) to the arts of war as practised by Christians did not alter these essential characteristics ... nor did the more recent invention of internal-combustion engines ... The prime objective, even as in the days of Lagash and Ur, is still to put the enemy to flight or render him hors de combat by dissecting nerves, muscles, viscera, and bones through the subcutaneous introduction of pieces of metal into his body. All technological progress in warfare has consisted in devising more efficient means of producing and delivering to the ultimate consumer more metal, more swiftly, more cheaply, over greater distances, and at less risk to the producer and the middleman. Not until the invention of the atomic bomb was a truly novel means hit upon to end enemy resistance by ending enemy existence.[47]

With the mass deployment of nuclear weapons we have potentially hit upon an even more novel means of ending enemy resistance, that is, by ending everybody's existence.

As the above would suggest, the history of warfare is one of constant innovation. Dynamic campaigns and states of siege mean little, however, in the face of large nuclear weapons that can destroy the moving and the static alike with fireballs kilometres across and hotter than the sun, and with blast effects to match. The history of the state and of the doctrine of the balance of power is entwined with that of war. The collapse of the central balance, as conventionally construed, could now be the collapse of the balance of terror. Between the world and a war like this one is only an idea — the doctrine of the balance of power — and it is not an idea that inspires great confidence.

3. What happens if, instead of reading the balance of power in terms of power as dominance or subordinance, we do so in terms of power as competence?

The final feature of the doctrine worth noting critically is the concept of power its protagonists use. Essentially, it is military power they have in mind. While they may admit that the prevention of dominance can apply to other dimensions of power as well, they do not usually explore the consequences of their own admission, except as these bear upon military capacity.[48] They also tend to take a quantitative approach to power capacity, comparing tank battalions and the like in some detail, but little else.

These are unwarranted restrictions, as already noted above in the discussion of the politico–economic context in which balance of power practices take place. Furthermore, the quantitative bias tends to obscure the unquantifiable aspects of power. It tells us nothing, for example, about how well trained battalions are, or the state of their morale.

The theory of power politics cannot, therefore, be tested empirically to see how close states come to the behaviour the model describes. State-makers may seem to be building up the military strength of the state overall, but because of these less tangible factors it can never be said with confidence that they have succeeded. By the same token state-makers who appear not to be particularly concerned with their military power status may merely be building up the infrastructure required to manifest such force in the future. Japanese state-makers are often cited in this regard. Thus 'not only is it impossible to discern whether a government is maximizing its state's power, it is also impossible to discern whether it is trying (or not trying) to do so', with the consequence that 'power-politics theory can be used to justify almost any policy'. [49]

Obviously there are broad limits to this critique. The point is well taken, however, and it turns on the multidimensional nature of power, that is, on power as manifest in human relationships rather than or as well as in numbers of armaments and machineries of dominance and war.

The notion that power must be understood in more than a quantitative way leads to another point of equal importance, which is the bias in the balance of power doctrine towards the definition of power in terms of preponderance or dominance alone. The balance of power as conventionally construed is about attempts to prevent particular state-makers dominating the state system, or particular parts of it. Might this not, however, be an example of what Carroll calls 'looking where the light is, versus looking where the key was lost'?

How would the doctrine appear if we replaced the preoccupation with power as dominance with Carroll's various dimensions of power as competence as outlined earlier? Take, for example, the first of her categories, disintegrative power. What does the balance of power look like if we describe or explain it using this capacity? What policies would it prescribe? For whom?

Disintegrative power is the relatively diffuse capability of masses of people to undermine and erode the political, productive and social institutions and structures that massify them. Carroll identifies the disaffected and alienated poor as the most competent and the most powerful in this regard. This is not to ignore the way the alienated poor are moved on, or out, or left to die. It is rather to draw attention to their capacity to fight back using demonstrations, crime and many other less conventional tactics.

Their power is presumably counterbalanced by those who are not disaffected and alienated. The balancers have the capacity to imprison and punish; to segregate and gentrify. However, the balancers also want to see their cities and states and their main ways of making wealth maintained in good repair. To do so they may need to appease those they would otherwise merely oppress. Not to do so may ultimately mean their own demise.

The balance of power in this more radical perspective is the distribution of power between Walker's two worlds of the overdogs and the underdogs. It is the relationship between those marginalised by the way state-makers and the world's wealth-makers behave, and those who do the marginalising.

This version of the balance of power has all the attributes of its power as dominance counterpart — it can be fortuitous or contrived; it can be objective or subjective; it can be even or uneven; it can be general or local.

To explain the balance of power from this perspective we need to look beyond the state-making practices of anxious or ambitious politicans, though their division of the earth's peoples into territorial domains would be part of the story. We also need to look beyond the pursuit of profit and the dynamic interplay between capitalists and waged (and unwaged) workers, though their activities would also be part of the story.

Beyond the desire for political self-preservation and for material self-aggrandisement we find something else. We find apathy and acquiescence and we also find outrage of the sort that feeds upon and fuels mass grievance. We find people with a sense of injustice questioning in a wide range of informal ways the work of the well-placed and the well-to-do. The potential for social change of people's feelings of this sort cannot be ignored, though the balance of power, as conventionally understood, does not acknowledge their significance at all.

The other forms of power as competence Carroll identifies can also be seen as dimensions of this two-worlds view of the balance of power. If we take these dimensions all together they amount to a serious indictment of the usual preoccupation with powers and their governments, with states and state-makers, with war-fighting skills and whatever other ways state-makers impose their will on their citizens and each other. State-makers, however, have a near monopoly on the concept of the balance of power. Indeed, it may be the state 'un-makers' who ultimately show us how partial and incomplete the conventional reading of that concept can be.

Notes

1 K. Waltz, *Theory of International Politics*, Addison-Wesley, Reading, 1979, p. 102. Among many such summaries the following by one of Waltz's critics complements his picture of 'a politically fragmented world of pervasive insecurity, recurring violence, generalized expectations of war, and self-animating strategic logic against strategic logic'. See R. Ashley, 'Political Realism and Human Interests', *International Studies Quarterly* vol. 25 no. 2 June 1981, p. 205.

2 R. Niebuhr, *Moral Man and Immoral Society: a study in ethics and politics,* Charles Scribners' Sons, New York, 1936, p. 18.

3 Not coincidentally these are the bases of the three Viennese schools of psychotherapy, as represented in the works of Sigmund Freud, Alfred Adler and Viktor Frankl.

4 H. Morgenthau, *Politics Among Nations*, 5th edn, Alfred A. Knopf, New York, 1978.

5 ibid., pp. 4-15.

6 ibid., p. 10.

7 E.H. Carr, *The Twenty Years' Crisis 1919-1939: an introduction to the study of international relations*, 2nd edn, Macmillan, London, 1962, p. vii.

8 ibid., p. 89.

9 ibid., p. 232.

10 ibid., p. 97.

11 ibid., p. 236.

12 ibid., p. viii.

13 ibid., p. 230.

14 See the 'Introduction' to S. Lukes (ed.), *Power,* Basil Blackwell, Oxford, 1986.

15 ibid., p. 5.

16 M. Mann, *The Sources of Social Power* vol.1, Cambridge University Press, Cambridge, 1986, pp. 22-7.

17 The International Institute for Strategic Studies, The Military Balance (annual).

18 M. French, *Beyond Power: on women, men, and morals*, Jonathon Cape, London, 1985, pp. 505, 509.
19 B. Carroll, 'Peace Research: The Cult of Power', *Journal of Conflict Resolution* vol. 16 no. 4, 1972, p. 585.
20 ibid., p. 607.
21 loc. cit. See more recently Hartsock's

two accounts of power — the one a description of relations of domination ... the other an indication of the possibilities inherent in human activity. This second account of power points beyond relations of domination and allows for a reformulation of power (both in theory and in fact) as not simply power over others but as competence and effective action in dealing with both the natural and social worlds.

This should be read in conjunction with Hartsock's discussion of 'agonal politics, a politics based on struggle and competition' which she sees as a 'specifically masculine social experience, a masculine attempt to solve the riddle of community. If these are the power relations that both construct and are reinforced by masculine sexuality, can one envisage alternative possibilities for community present in women's sexuality?' N. Hartsock, *Money, Sex and Power,* Longman, New York, 1983 pp. 7, 137.

22 ibid., p. 608.
23 ibid., p. 609.
24 ibid., p. 610.
25 ibid., p. 611.
26 ibid.., p. 611, 613.
27 ibid., p. 613.
28 ibid., p. 614.
29 loc. cit.
30 ibid., p. 618.
31 D. Hume, 'The Balance of Power' in F. Watkins (ed.), *Hume: Theory of Politics*, Nelson, Edinburgh, 1951, p. 186.
32 See for example M. Wight, 'The Pattern of Power' and 'The Balance of Power' in H. Bull & C. Holbraad (eds), *Power Politics*, Leicester University Press, Leicester, 1978; H. Bull, *The Anarchical Society*, Macmillan, London, 1977, ch. 5, 'The Balance of Power and International Order'; I. Claude, *Power and International Relations,* Random House, New York, 1962, ch. 2 'Balance of Power: an ambiguous concept'; E. Haas, 'The Balance of Power: prescription, concept or propaganda?', *World Politics* vol. 5 no. 4, July 1953, pp. 442-77.
33 H. Bull, op. cit, p. 103.
34 M. Wight, op. cit., p. 169.
35 ibid., pp. 169-70.
36 A. Pope, 'The Balance of Europe' in his *Collected Poems*, Everyman's Library, London, 1974, p. 387.
37 M. Wight, op. cit., p. 157.
38 ibid., p. 158.
39 ibid., p. 160.
40 ibid., p. 169.
41 R. Ashley, *The Political Economy of War and Peace*, Frances Pinter, London,

1980, p. 289.

42 R. Ashley 'The Poverty of Neorealism', *International Organization* vol. 38 no. 2, 1984, p. 276.

43 ibid., pp. 269-70.

44 ibid., p. 278.

45 ibid., pp. 276-7.

46 I. Claude, op. cit., p. 39.

47 F. Schuman, *International Politics: The Western State System and the World Community*, 6th edn, McGraw Hill, New York, 1958, pp. 292-3.

48 For an explicit account of such an exploration see K. Knorr, *Power and Wealth: the political economy of international power*, Macmillan, London, 1973, ch. 3, 'The Bases of Military Power'. This exploration extends into his chapter 4, 'The Bases of National Economic Power'. The idea of an international balance of economic power is briefly raised on page 102.

49 T. Taylor, 'Power Politics' in T. Taylor (ed.), *Approaches and Theory in International Relations*, Longman, London, 1978, p. 136.

2

PART

Political–economy

4

The world economy

What is the international political economy? Why is the international political economy capitalist? What, in neo-mercantilist, liberal and Marxist parlance, does class mean in world affairs? What is the relationship between state formation and class formation?

1. What is the international political economy?

The conventional reading of international politics is largely in terms of states, the state system and the state-making practices from which, historically, they are derived. Emphasis is placed on patterns of power politics and, in particular, on power balances and how they are maintained. By power this reading means mostly military power, a dimension about which any self-respecting state-maker will be realistic. Military power is mostly measured in terms of military capacity, for which state-makers almost automatically account in their relations with each other. Much international relating involves co-operative ventures of mutual benefit, like the international postal service. Any conflict these engender is usually resolved without a thought of military confrontation. Other issues are not so innocuous, however, and in anticipation of having to prosecute or defend these by more than verbal means, state-makers build and maintain armed forces.

One result of this conventional reading is a preoccupation with hierarchies of dominance and subordinance in the state system. The perspective is typically top-down, though studies of the way the world looks and works for middle and small powers are not uncommon. Few attempts have been made in analysing international relations to think about the subordinated in terms of ordinary people rather than states, and fewer still describe the ways in which subordinate peoples may be insubordinate.

Another result of the conventional reading is the relative neglect of power in economic terms or, in other words, of the material bases upon which modern states have been built and which constrain, even determine, their form and function. State-making and wealth-making go hand in hand. Whether we see them as separate processes, closely related, or as two aspects of one extraordinarily successful historical phenomenon — that of industrialisation — it would seem impossible to talk of international politics without considering how production, distribution, consumption and exchange make for power in the world.

Neo-mercantilism

The early European state-makers saw wealth-making as state-making by other means. Since wealth helped make military power possible, for defensive or offensive purposes, it made sense to promote its acquisition as a way of augmenting the capacity to coerce. Greater military capacity made it possible in turn to make or keep more wealth. Building up both was seen as a legitimate policy objective, since they clearly reinforced each other. Securing the state might, on occasion, mean foregoing some degree of wealth, of course, but the eventual result — a secure state — created the conditions for further wealth-making. This sort of trade-off, between getting more military power or getting rich, was clearly warranted in state-making terms. [1]

By wealth was meant not just money, but a sufficiency, derived within the state domain, of essential goods and services. It meant securing all the key elements of state supply. The basic way to be strong, in other words, was to stimulate domestic industrial and agricultural production, buy as little as possible from abroad, and accumulate disposable income in the convenient form of precious metals. The belief in practices like these was later dubbed 'mercantilism'.[2] It emphasised the role state-makers could and should play in building a rich and resource-full country. It saw individual citizens as subordinate to that role, and promoted a vigorous nationalism to effect and to justify that subordination.

Economic nationalism like this would today be called neo-mercantilism or protectionism, and its protagonists, like the mercantilists of old, would argue that political independence and state security are best served by economic strength and productive self-sufficiency. Strength and self-sufficiency can be secured in many ways, however, in varying degrees of comprehensiveness and isolation.

Myanmar (formerly Burma) and Albania, for example, are clear contemporary examples of state-makers opting for comprehensive autarchy. The economic stagnation both countries have suffered as a result is striking. It is much more common, however, for particular sectors of a state economy or for particular industries to use economic nationalism as an argument for their protection. Sometimes this is a ploy to defend or extend special status or narrow gains. Steel-makers, for example, may convince state-makers that they need tariff shelters 'in the national interest', even when they may not. Sometimes, however, state-makers may deliberately attempt to foster 'infant' industries, taxing imports as a way of protecting the new industries and as a way of stimulating productive capacity.

Sometimes state-makers see building up their export industries as a way of remedying stagnation, particularly where it appears that domestic demand is not enough to sustain economic growth. State-makers may go further, too, and subsidise a specific manufacturing sector as part of a deliberate and strategic trade offensive elsewhere. Using state-based investment and savings strategies, their sponsorship of a particular industry may enable it to capture specific product niches in other countries. Where the manufacturers in that niche in another country are not well protected by their tariff walls, they may be forced out of business, and the sponsoring state can then monopolise the market segment concerned. The Japanese, for example, did something of this sort to the colour television set manufacturing industry in the USA.

Too many countries using such self-aggrandising tactics at the same time will lead to direct trade and tariff conflict, trade and tariff wars, or even worse. Blatant economic nationalism typically prompts retaliation in kind. If the rivalry the interstate system promotes then gets the better of it, the ring of reciprocity that holds it all together will be broken. Short of such a consequence, however, there can be notable national gains.

Contemporary mercantilism also has its roots in neo-Keynesian theories of underconsumption. Assuming that in a capitalist world system people underconsume (or, in other words, that the system as a whole overproduces), it is in the national interest to run a balance of payments surplus, that is, for a people to buy less from abroad than they collectively sell. If they don't do this they can end up paying more for what other countries make than they sell themselves, thus going into debt, which is not self-sufficiency. The aim is to corner other people's markets rather than have them corner yours. This also has the effect of generating greater economies of scale and greater facilities for home research and development, both of which enhance self-sufficiency.

From the above it is clear that state-makers (in association with wealth-makers) can build self-sufficiency in relatively unaggressive ways, reinforcing state borders to protect productive capacity, for example, or employment opportunities. They can also, however, become highly assertive. Economic nationalism can fuel imperialistic feelings that lead not to the self-contained strength that protects autonomy, but to imperialism. Greedy, anxious or chauvinistic state-makers, determined to win more for themselves in the world, may try to control foreign markets, causing acute conflict.

Not so obviously nasty, though also a mixed blessing, is the international use of capital. Securing sources of supply for important raw materials; seeking out cheap, docile labourers; setting up branch plants or joint ventures that avoid the protective tariffs meant to control economic penetration; selling loans that augment debt — all this may sound benign enough. In practice, however, it can involve extensive exploitation and much human misery. Rich state capitalists who skew the process of world development in their own favour may do so at great cost in human terms. This cost must be taken into account when assessing economic nationalism in this form.

The main problem with (neo)mercantilism, then, is the propensity its protagonists have to view the world in highly competitive terms. In a state-centred, state-bound world this fits in readily with the realist's defence of the national interest. The national interest may well be served other way. Co-operation may be more beneficial for states than competition. The urge to rely on one's own resources remains strong in the world, however, and with it the desire for self-sufficiency. This readily precludes the feeling that mutual benefits might be derived from international reciprocity. This in turn reinforces statism, and somewhat obscures the way the activities of capitalists undermine the autonomy of the state.

It also obscures the amount of competition there might be within any particular state between military-making practices, for example, and wealth-making ones. For example, if too many resources are committed for too long to the stockpiling of expensive weapons or the development and deployment of new ones, or to maintaining large standing armies, it can distort the whole economy to counterproductive effect. This was one cause of the Soviets' lagging living standards. It was what United States state-makers found with their burgeoning military–industrial complex.

Another cost of economic nationalism is inefficiency. Though the protection and promotion of industry may be necessary to get this sector off the ground, particularly in the face of the sort of competition mounted by developed firms in rich states, protectionism can lead to inefficiency and to slower development than would otherwise be the case. Rich states have all used this ploy, and many still do. [3]

Neo-mercantilism can also lead to undue emphasis on industry over agriculture. While industry can have spillover effects that can benefit a whole economy, as Gilpin points outs 'few societies have developed without a prior agricultural revolution and a high level of agriculural productivity'. [4]

Being nationalistic in economic terms does not, in the end, allow for simple policy prescriptions. Neo-mercantilists believe that interventionist economic practices will guarantee productivity and military might. But how best to intervene? And what of the argument that, given the way the world economy works, a less interventionist approach may paradoxically result in people producing more, producing more efficiently, trading to their advantage, and thereby better providing the means to secure the state?

Liberalism

The argument above was most clearly put by the radical economic liberals of the nineteenth century who, in their own interests (they were mostly entrepreneurs), saw no reason why 'economics' should be of overt political concern to state-makers. Quite the contrary. They believed in laissez-faire and a doctrine that separated economics from politics altogether. Indeed, in their view economics was not only a separate domain from the political one, but that was how it ought to be. Wealth-making worked best when state-makers let the market flourish unimpeded. Allowing the rational acts of free consumers free reign made for greater growth and greater efficiency. It was not state-makers or their attempts to intervene that enhanced prosperity and the success of the state, but the price mechanism of the market, in other words the reciprocal movement of supply against demand, and the ongoing assessments producers and consumers made of costs and benefits.

The unqualified contemporary version of this doctrine makes the same basic assumptions, namely that the market is inherently stable, and that both producers and consumers gain from it more than they lose. The stability comes from the ostensibly self-correcting character of the system and its dynamic capacity to maintain a general state of equlibrium. The benefits it provides result from the growth it promotes and the way it weeds out the inefficient and the commercially inept. Radical liberal market practices advantage everyone, its protagonists claim, albeit some more than others. They are inherently progressive, and the wealth they generate grows indefinitely regardless of the busts that might follow boom periods, wars, civil strife, or ecological collapse. Gilpin points out that:

> On the basis of these assumptions and commitments modern economists have constructed the empirical science of economics. Over the past two centuries, they have deduced the 'laws' [principles] of maximising behavior,

such as those of comparative advantage, the theory of marginal utility, and the quantity theory of money ... These 'laws' are both contingent and normative. They assume the existence of economic man — a rational, maximising creature — a variant of the species homo sapiens that has been relatively rare in human history and has existed only during peculiar periods of favorable conditions. Further, these laws are normative in that they prescribe how a society must organize itself and how people must behave if they are to maximize the growth of wealth. [5]

In radical liberal parlance commerce makes for co-operation which makes for peace, between countries as well as within them. Economics unites; politics divides. Some will inevitably do better than others, of course, but all are supposed to gain. Disparities in wealth are supposed to matter less than the absolute material returns the system provides, which is why harmony and not conflict prevails.

The tendency, then, is to separate economics from politics as much as possible, and allow state-makers to intervene only when the market fails, or when a public good or service has to be provided or performed that private marketeers don't or won't.

Radical liberals actively prefer economics to politics. Economics, in the crudest sense, clarifies. It fosters reciprocal accord. It brings people together. It caters for people's material needs and, in organising their daily lives as consumers, makes them happy. Politics, on the other hand, while it may provide a few public goods and services, fosters division and discord. Compared to markets, which are creative and good, state-makers and their governments are destructive, even evil.

This doctrine has been assiduously universalised. It was first used to any great extent to rationalise nineteenth century European, particularly British, imperialism (a set of policies that were not liberal at all, but mercantilist). With the rapid internationalisation of capital after the last European war it was used again, as it still is, to rationalise a wide range of neo-imperial policies by European state- and wealth-makers that again were largely mercantilist. Why use cannon when lines of credit from neo-imperial investors allow similar or superior control?

How does the doctrine work? The key device, already mentioned, is that of comparative advantage or laissez-faire. Taken to its logical and global (and very simplistic) extreme this would see 'all the wheat consumed by the human race in Canada, all the wool in Australia ... all the motor cars in Detroit [or Japan] and all the cotton clothing in England [or Hong Kong]'.[6] What gets in the way of such a rational division of labour and capital? Market-manipulating oligopolies do, hence the opposition to them by pure liberals who want a free market. (Oligopolies include mercantilist state-makers, of course, who protect domestic industries that by the rational criteria of the market would deserve not to survive.) Why don't oligopolists see the light? Because they are doing too well and don't want to do worse.

What is wrong with this conviction? Basically, the argument here is that while economics can be described and explained in political terms without much loss of meaning, to talk of politics in economic terms alone is to run the risk of trivialising it.[7] The science of economics, in other words, always assumes a given political order and to be relevant cannot be discussed without at least some consideration of that order and its implications for economics.[8]

This is not only an argument in theory. Radical liberals who would like state-makers not to intervene, or to accept a more marginal role, are bound to be disappointed in practice. People expect the state, where resources permit, to provide for and protect not just their territorial autonomy but their material well-being. This inevitably makes economics a highly political subject. It is for this reason that radical liberals themselves will sometimes admit the failure of the market mechanism to deal with externalities, like providing a habitable environment.

People expect state provision or protection because they know that radical liberalism is not primarily concerned with the justice and equity of the practices it recommends. Because it is an article of faith that, short of oligopoly, radical economic liberalism benefits all, its protagonists are largely unconcerned that people get more or less. For those getting less, however, this is not an article of faith, but the circumstances under which they must live. In the rich world they turn to the state-makers for reprieve. If the state is capitalist it will offer welfare benefits, more or less grudgingly. If it is socialist it commits itself to meeting such claims as a matter of course, more or less effectively. In the poor world people must fend for themselves.

Historical materialism

Radical liberalism has been a controversial doctrine since its inception. Its prominence in the nineteenth century was matched by an equally comprehensive critique of it, mounted most notably by the German theorist Karl Marx. It is not uncommon to portray Marx as subscribing to the same extreme distinction between politics and economics, though unlike radical liberals he emphasised the negative consequences of liberal market practices, rather than the positive ones. Unlike them he ostensibly saw liberal 'economics' as a source of social conflict, not as a source of social harmony. The conflict was necessary, however, to destroy the market and to replace the repressive politics of capitalism with a society that did not need politics at all.

This misrepresents both the subtlety and the relevance of Marx's analysis. Marx saw the relationship between politics and economics in highly sophisticated terms. These concepts referred, in his view, to two aspects of any mode of production, and of the social relationships characteristic of it. One could no more talk of economics as separate from politics than one could talk of human nature as separate from human nurture. They were not 'related' at all but, rather, were the same reality viewed from different angles, much as a bean tin appears round from the top but rectangular from the side. One might talk about these projections as if they were separate, but only at the risk of forgetting the singular entity they represent.

Marx was also an intensely practical thinker.

> We must begin by stating the first premise of all human existence and, therefore, of all history, the premise, namely, that men must be in a position to live in order to be able to 'make history'. But life involves before everything else eating and drinking, a habitation, clothing and many other things. The first historical act is thus the production of the means to satisfy these needs, the production of material life itself. And indeed this is an historical act, a fundamental condition of all history, which today, as thousands of years ago, must daily and hourly be fulfilled merely in order to sustain human life. [9]

The consequence, as he saw it, was clear.

> As individuals express their life, so they are. What they are, therefore, coincides with their production, both with what they produce and with how they produce. The nature of individuals thus depends on the material conditions determining their production. [10]

The same, Marx said, applied to world society. International relationships depended on how far each state had managed to develop its productive capacity.

Marx was reacting against the tendency in nineteenth century German thought to depict history in terms of ideas that somehow had a life of their own. He believed in looking at what went on in the world as directly as possible, and not, as he saw it, through fogs of philosophy or religious faith. He was convinced, not surprisingly since he lived (as we live still) in the midst of the industrial revolution, of the importance of material life in determining social structure.

Marx's time was dominated (as in many respects it is today) by those who owned the factories and the farms and all the facilities that produced what people consumed. Furthermore, 'through its exploitation of the world market' this class had given a 'cosmopolitan character' to production and consumption everywhere.

> All old-established national industries have been destroyed or are daily being destroyed. They are dislodged by new industries, whose introduction becomes a life and death question for all civilised nations, by industries that

no longer work up indigenous raw material, but raw material drawn from the remotest zones; industries whose products are consumed, not only at home, but in every quarter of the globe. In place of the old wants, satisfied by the productions of the country, we find new wants, requiring for their satisfaction the products of different lands and climes. In place of the old local and national seclusion and self-sufficiency, we have intercourse in every direction and universal inter-dependence. [11]

The rapid growth in the efficiency of production processes to which Marx alludes, the extraordinary extension of the capacity of the means of communication and the development of new, faster and more capacious modes of transport have been profound developments. No-one lives now beyond their reach. The cheap price and the novelty of the commodities the new technologies have made possible, and the entrepreneurial eagerness of their manufacturers, have drawn people world-wide into one huge net.

All states have been forced, in Marx's words, 'on pain of extinction' to adopt the less capitalist mode of production.[12] States themselves have become singular territorial and administrative domains. The countryside has come under urban dominion. Whole continents have been cleared for cultivation. 'Whole populations [have been] conjured out of the ground and ... whole countries of peasants have been made dependent on those where capitalists prevail. What earlier century', Marx says, 'had even a presentiment that such productive forces slumbered in the lap of social labour?' [13]

Just as the feudal organisation of agriculture and manufacturing was not able to cope with such dynamism, and just as the owners and managers of the modern means of production had burst the bounds of the old order to establish a new one (with free competition, and the appropriate social and political conditions), so Marx believed such a society itself was doomed. Plagued by recurrent crises that were engendered in turn by something that in all earlier epochs would have seemed extraordinary, namely overproduction, capitalist societies were — in his view — simply too limiting to contain the wealth capitalists could create.

Who would bring the system down? Wage-workers; the class of those:

who live only so long as they find work, and who find work only so long as their labour increases capital ... who must sell themselves piecemeal, as a commodity, like every other article of commerce, and are consequently exposed to all the vicissitudes of competition, to all the fluctuations of the market. [14]

Progressively pauperised by it, labourers would, in Marx's view, rebel. Their employers, according to Marx unfit to rule because incompetent to provide for their slaves in their wage-slavery, [15] would be brought down. Thus communism would ensue, where all would contribute whatever they could, and get back whatever they truly required.

The process Marx described, and the future he foresaw, was global. As industry became more and more international, as commerce and the world market and profit-making industrial production became widespread, so too did wage-working. Because of their common plight, wage-workers had 'no country', Marx argued. Once they became the dominant class, however, they would be able to replace the nationalism and the universalism of the owners and managers of industry with their own. Nationalism in the old sense would then disappear. The new universalism would be without class antagonism. It would end the exploitation of one individual by another, and the exploitation of one nation by another.[16]

Marx was, however, quite wrong on two key counts: firstly on revolutionary locale, and secondly on wage-workers' internationalism.

In those widely industrialised countries where wage-labouring was most common and the conditions Marx described were most evident, the workers did not sink deeper and deeper. Pauperism did not grow more quickly than population and wealth or, if it did, the trend was reversed in time to avert global revolution. At least some of the largesse of industrial production and of imperialism was passed on via welfare legislation and the social reforms won by workers' parties at the polls and in the parliaments. When revolution did occur it was in the most unlikely of places from a Marxist point of view — in Russia, a feudal peasant country still ruled by aristocrats, with a bourgeoisie and a proletariat which by European standards were quite small.

The Russian revolution was Marxist inspired and as such bore witness to the force of ideas. This rather detracted, however, from Marx's own emphasis on the material reasons for worker revolt. The first great Marxist revolution was, in this sense, an inspired negation of Marx's most basic premise about revolutionary social change. The second such revolution — the Chinese one — was also (though clearly not only) a veritable triumph of idealistic perseverance.

Not only did communist revolution begin in the wrong place for the wrong reasons but the European war of 1914-18 dramatically demonstrated (among many other processes) the power of patriotism. This prevailed over any transnational sentiments the wage-workers of the various countries might have been coming to share (as subnational patriotism was later to prevail over loyalty to the party in the USSR).

It fell to Lenin to explain why the Marxist law of historical progress had come up with the Russian revolution rather than one in Munich, for example, or Manchester. He did so by agreeing with Marx that the revolution was inevitable, and then arguing that therefore it was not necessary to wait for the contradictions of capitalism to become fully evident. A tightly organised party — a revolutionary vanguard — could act for the infant proletariat, in alliance with the peasants, thereby fulfilling Marx's scientific prophecy.

European capitalism had bought a reprieve by expanding. Becoming imperialistic and making colonies provided money and bought time. By building overseas dependencies, in other words, England, Germany and the other industrial powers had found new areas in which to invest and new populations to which to export their manufactured goods. The surplus capital they raised was used to further the employment prospects and to raise the living standards of the wage-working classes at home. This in turn reduced the awareness of those wage-workers of the fundamentally exploitative nature of the class situation, and defused their revolutionary resolve. National capitalism survived, Lenin argued, by becoming a global phenomenon. The contradictions were still there. They had simply become world-wide.

The process of formal decolonisation that followed the period of European wars gave the colonies their political independence. In terms of the historical materialist approach, however, capitalist exploitation persisted. The relationships of which these patterns were composed did not come to an end just because a colony had become a state. They merely changed form, the monopoly capitalism of direct rule becoming the multinational capitalism of neo-imperial proxies. The song of the overlords was over, but the 'malady' lingered on (see appendix 2).

State-makers and the state system revisited

It seems that there is not one international political economy but three. The first — the neo-mercantilist one — is hyphenated. Because polity and economy are so closely joined in the whole business of state-making, that is, we can only speak in these terms of an international 'political–economy'.

From the second perspective we find international politics plus international economics. These are two quite separate spheres of activity. We can therefore talk simply of 'international political economy'.

In the third, we find historical materialism, which considers international politics and international economics to be two aspects of whatever stage in the historical development of humankind's productive capacities we are studying. Because they are basically one, not two, we need to hyphenate international 'political–economy' as in the neo-mercantilist case. We would, however, use the hyphen for very different reasons.

What version is 'correct'? How are we to choose? The choice is important since it bears directly upon how we respond to such crises as the current level of third world debt. When we ask who is to blame for the plight of the debtor countries, our answer will depend on our view of the world political–economy.

A neo-mercantilist, for example, would see this crisis as the predictable outcome of not having pursued policies of self-reliance and self-sufficiency. A radical liberal, however, would blame state-makers for not allowing market forces to cull the weak and reward the strong. A historical materialist, by contrast, would highlight the distortions wrought by internationalising capitalists, who are all too ready, from this perspective, to sell credit for a profit regardless of the consequences.

The different concepts of cause lead to different prescriptions. What is the most constructive response to this crisis? Economic autarchy, says the neo-mercantilist. More credit, says the liberal. A radical change in the world political–economy, says the historical materialist.

Which one is correct? As was pointed out in the first chapter, this is essentially a meaningless question. We might wish nonetheless to approximate an answer that allows us to act without seeming either dogmatic or arbitrary. To attempt such an answer, however, means engaging in ideological debates that we can never hope to win to the satisfaction of all.

How do these theories bear upon our understanding of the state? From the neo-mercantilist point of view state-makers are crucial, their task being to secure their country's military and productive power, mostly by autarchic means. From the liberal perspective state-makers are a race apart. They are supposed to play as small a role as possible. From the historical materialist perspective state-makers are key components in a political superstructure that is generally determined, as all social and political processes are determined, by the prevailing mode of production. In the current era, which is a capitalist one, state-makers have to ensure that capitalists continue to profit. If they don't they face subversion or even a capital strike. In the words of the Communist Manifesto, they are an executive committee for managing the common affairs of the capitalists.

And the state system? From the neo-mercantilist perspective we find state-makers securing their domains by all the means at their disposal. This results in a conventional reading of the balance of power, though one that includes in its definition of power material and productive as well as military factors. From the radical liberal perspective we find politicians either expediting or getting in the way of world commerce. The balance of power is a military game politicians play. It is beneficial as far as it secures stable conditions for the market and for economic growth. If it impedes the rational workings of the world economy then it is a detrimental process.

From the historical materialist's perspective we find a global conflict between capital and labour. States are one set of social sites where this conflict occurs. The balance of power is the exploitation of wage-workers by those who own or manage the means of production, a balance destined to be upset because it emiserates the workers. The latter's self-emancipation, however, should ostensibly abolish capitalism, states, the state system, and the unbalanced way in which the world's wealth is distributed.

2. Why is the international political–economy capitalist? What, in neo-mercantilist, liberal and Marxist parlance, does class mean in world affairs? What is the relationship between state formation and class formation?

All three approaches to international political–economy agree that we live in a world system most appropriately called capitalism. We live in very different local worlds, materially speaking. In the world at large, however, the wealth-makers and the profit-takers, be they individual entrepreneurs or private or public corporations, behave as capitalists.

What is capitalism? The answer differs somewhat depending upon the ideology of the respondent. The difference is evident in the debate about this concept between liberals and historical materialists. (The neo-mercantilists adopt whatever view best serves their perception of the national interest.)

To the liberal, capitalism is an end in itself. The concept denotes the exchange practices of free and open markets and the profit-making that results from the efficient, cost-effective use of money, land, information, tools, ideas or skills, to garner more of any one of them. The untrammelled pursuit of private gain in this way is said to result in benefits for all, as rising productivity and greater wealth generates growth in employment opportunities and rewards for labour, as well as investment. Individual self-interest can be seen to coincide happily with that of the community as a whole, hence obviating any need for outside intervention. To love one's self is in effect to love one's neighbour. Greed becomes good, in a convenient marriage of economics and morality that not only empowers the rich but, in radical liberal parlance, is the main hope of the poor.

To the historical materialist, on the other hand, capitalism is a means to another end — socialism and communism. From a Marxist perspective, however, the pursuit of private gain is exploitative and ultimately self-defeating. Capitalism certainly empowers the rich, and does so in systematic ways that involve first the creation of goods and services that are valuable and then the appropriation of that value by whoever owns or controls the means to make it. Capitalism is not philanthropic. Those without capital do not have access to the main means of generating wealth, and without external controls and the distribution of the benefits of the processes of production and exchange, their only hope is in replacing the system with a more self-consciously humane one.

The facts about economics or political–economy never speak for themselves. In this case they speak through one or the other of these two approaches, and the optimism of the former is not readily reconciled with the pessimism of the latter. In no small measure this is because they reflect very different assumptions about human nature. Radical liberalism assumes we are essentially competitive. Not surprisingly, therefore, it sees the point of any political or economic system as the extent to which it promotes and protects individual self-interest. Historical materialism assumes that, given the appropriate material circumstances, we are essentially co-operative. Therefore, it sees the point to any political–economy as being the extent to which it promotes and protects the material interests of the community as a whole.

Why capitalism?

Why was it capitalism that came to define the working parameters of the international political economy? Bob Connell suggests that there may be an anthropological answer to this question that only a reading of human nature will reveal:

> … (if we can use that term in an unreified way to include basic features of social relations as well as of the person). … Perhaps more precisely, capitalism makes unusually efficient use of some possibilities that are permanently present in human life: more importantly, the possibility of making use of other human beings as means rather than ends; the possibility of detaching the results of labour from its cultural and social conditions. In short, capitalism institutionalizes the element of calculative ferocity in human life. [17]

Such an answer is interesting but not very useful. We need to look a little closer at what capitalism means in practice if we are to find out why it is so ubiquitous today. Perhaps we should start with capital itself, and a more historical view.

The use of capital (money, land, information, ideas, tools or skills) to make more of itself by whatever means available is certainly ages old. Usury, trade, mass production, piracy, invasion and occupation have all been used to augment wealth; to make a profit. But capitalism as the defining characteristic of the global system is relatively recent, and its early protagonists had to fight hard against deeply held convictions and conventions to have personal material aggrandisement accepted as socially and morally respectable.

In Europe, where the capitalist world economy was inaugurated, it was originally regarded as anything but respectable. In the grand tradition of Carroll's 'innovative power', where competence and capacity is manifest among the underdogs before it becomes an overdog attribute, it appears that the pioneers of this way of behaving were upstarts. In R.H. Tawney's words, these pioneers:

> elbowed their way to success in the teeth of the established aristocracy of land and commerce ... [moreover] the tonic that braced them for the conflict was a new conception of religion, which taught them to regard the pursuit of wealth as, not merely an advantage, but a duty. This conception welded into a disciplined force the still feeble bourgeoisie, heightened its energies, and cast a halo of sanctification round its convenient vices. What is significant, in short, is not the strength of the motive of economic self-interest, which is the commonplace of all ages and demands no explanation. It is the change of moral standards which converted a natural frailty into an ornament of the spirit, and canonized as ... economic virtues habits which in earlier ages had been denounced as vices. [18]

Max Weber traced this change to one particular Christian sect — Calvinism. Capitalism, he argued, was the socioeconomic counterpart of Calvinist theology, in which only a limited number of people were eligible for life after death. Evidence of divine predestination was apparent, however, in the sober and diligent mien with which one led one's daily life. This clearly encouraged the public display and the private embrace of such values. Furthermore, values like these were quite compatible with making money, as well as giving a high spiritual purpose to honest toil. Not only Calvinists, but Protestants in general and even Catholics (in Weber's view) came to accept this connection. The ethic of work and the messianic point to acquiring wealth became widespread, carrying with them the sense of sanctity Calvinists could give to the making of profits by means of rational enterprise, and to the conscientious use of one's labour.

A historical materialist would argue, of course, that these religious values were the result of a prior change in the mode of production. Marx, for example, argued that the production of 'ideas, of conceptions, of consciousness, is ... directly interwoven with ... material activity ... Men are the producers of their conceptions ... as they are conditioned by a definite development of their productive forces'.[19] Where a ruling class, made up of owners of capital, pursues profit and employs legally free workers for wages, we might well expect the 'ruling ideas' to be their ideas.[20] Perhaps the Calvinists were no exception. Perhaps their thrift and sobriety more reflected their material success and pre-eminence, rather than causing it.

Whatever the explanation for capitalism's success, it did encourage opportunism and fostered unprecedented productive and commercial activity. So productive was this free or private enterprise that the liberal desire to separate economics from politics came to seem a well warranted one. Anything that impeded opportunism, such as state-built barriers to the flow of trade and capital, was construed as literally counterproductive. Anti-capitalism was anti-growth, which could only spell, from this perspective, social harm and political instability, both between and within states.

The neo-mercantilist and the radical liberal concept of class

Growth is not, however, the same everywhere. Some capitalists get or are able to make more market opportunities for themselves. State domains are differently endowed with resources, skills and the like and, because of these advantages or lack of them, become more or less wealthy. The differences in gross national product that follow can be used to divide states into classes; rich as opposed to poor; or to neo-mercantilists, self-sufficient as opposed to non self-sufficient.

States can also be categorised in many other ways; by military budget, child mortality rates, adult longevity, numbers of literate people, even the number of diplomatic missions maintained abroad or operating in the capital city. Despite the unprecedented expansion in the human capacity to make and distribute material wealth, however, the world exhibits the one predominant pattern of the rich as opposed to the poor.

Such a static and schematic reading of the concept of class is characteristically radical liberal. It denotes little more than sets of individuals or groups of individuals performing particular functions. It suggests where to look for important explanations of the modern world, but it is much weaker when it comes to doing the explaining. Even the more subtle of such schemas, like Hayward Alker's attempt to overlay the rich/poor divide with an East/West one, entails after-the-event labelling that is heuristic, not explanatory.[21] It sees such differences as more the outcome than the cause of the uneven spread of capitalist enterprise in the world.

Radical liberals are more interested in what restricts the flow of goods, finance, labour, ideas or technology. When this is unimpeded, the tides of economic growth are supposed to lift all the socioeconomic boats together, even those stuck on sandbanks. As the market expands, no differences are supposed to long resist the universal resolving power, or the buoyancy, of open economic competition.

Even the most doctrinaire of radical liberals will admit that economic competition can never be entirely open. If the poorer class of state-maker can only co-operate with the rich one (the one prescription they will allow); if such state-makers will only remain optimistic and opportunistic and build their development out of whatever materials they have to hand; then all will be well. In practice this means encouraging foreign investment in, foreign ownership of, or foreign control over, new industries. It also means rich state state-makers not legislating to keep the goods of the poorer states out of their home markets. Only this way will the superior benefits of interdependence be ultimately realised.

The historical materialist's concept of class

How does a rich state/poor state classification look from the analytic perspective of historical materialism? Historical materialists view the market as exploitative. In the words of J.M. Keynes (who was not a historical materialist), 'decadent international but individualistic capitalism … is not a success. It is not intelligent, it is not beautiful, it is not just, it is not virtuous — and it doesn't deliver the goods'. [22]

Historical materialists find nothing benevolent about the inequalities that result from untrammelled market behaviour. Where growth occurs it gears local productive systems to the larger wheels of world enterprise, rendering them not sovereign but segmented. Rather than a rising tide of prosperity lifting all the peoples' boats regardless of their size or seaworthiness, the waters of wealth run towards the world's central quays, leaving those who live on far shores high and dry. The standard of living for the latter grows absolutely worse, not because of a lack of resources, or stupidity, or over-population, but because of expropriation and the way wealth-makers collude at local and global levels to make money for themselves rather than to meet the needs of ordinary people.

Thus when radical liberals talk of poor states a historical materialist will say they are obscuring the amount of transnational co-operation required to augment profits and to divide and rule those selling their labour for less and less. Talk of rich people or poor people obscures the importance not only of wealth, but of the control of capital, of the capacity to use it productively, and of how capitalism can prolong the plight of those without it. It obscures the significance, in other words, of capitalist production methods and their social effects. Owners and managers of capital, as a class, have different interests from those without capital. They know it, and this socioeconomic difference, and the awareness it brings, is the paramount point of the whole system.

Marx defined class not as a thing, a classification, but as a process. In a capitalist society the value of what wage-workers do is taken from them by those who can buy their labour, and who can then sell what is made or done with that labour. For the expropriating group Marx used the technical term, the bourgeoisie. Wage-workers make capital using capital, and in doing so are freely and systematically expropriated. They become what he called the proletariat.

The Marxist concept of class is much more dynamic and much more a part of a total world view than the radically liberal one. Classes of people are created in the process of producing the world's wealth, and the conflict of interests between them is not only a way of describing world affairs but a way of explaining them. The explanation will be in terms of class formation, and the classes referred to will not be mere labels. They will be, in Robert Cox's words, a whole lot of social practices 'shaped by events [that] give people the common experience of class identity and of collective action'. 23

Everything is affected thereby. Human relationships become exchange relationships (in line with the significance of money). They become threat relationships (in the light of the hire-and-fire capacity of the capitalist to control access to wages and hence the means to live). The integrative relationships that characterise political–economies where you make or do yourself what you need to survive become the defining feature of a utopia.

Marx, in his analysis of the effects of bourgeois capitalism, saw the use of mental and manual labour in such a rationalistic way as eroding human community, as robbing people of their humanity, as alienating them. To catch the feeling of this effect, we might ask what would non-capitalist, unalienated production be like? Suppose we produced or provided whatever it is we make or do in a humane manner? Would we not be better able to affirm ourselves and our fellows? Would we not be better able to see something of ourselves in what we produce? Our product would do more than meet a human need. It would affirm what is humane in both others and ourselves. 24

Capitalism is a far cry from this. Work under capitalism has become a kind of commodity, to be bought and sold like any other. However severely constrained by state-making and the like, capitalists, in pursuing profit, seek out the cheapest source of it, and pay as little as possible for what they use. Much as they might struggle to find work satisfaction, workers tend to lose the sense of meaning and purpose their labour might otherwise bring. Everyone is supposed to be satisfied with material gain. What suffers is everyone's sense of relevance and community.

The social model of capitalism sketched above is highly simplified. Though historical materialists remain committed to the basic antimony between the bourgeoisie and the proletariat, class formation on a world scale is considerably more complex than this antimony suggests. Furthermore, contemporary patterns of global class formation belie the picture Marx and Engels drew one hundred and fifty years ago. Indeed, the contemporary pattern is the direct opposite of it. Rather than bourgeois nationalists confronting a global class of united wage-workers we find one international capitalist class confronting a splintered array of industrial and non-industrial labour.

The owners and managers of capital would now include the executives of global corporations and their counterparts at a local level. Among the working class, on the other hand, we would probably now include middle-managers, established workers, non-established workers (whose interests may differ considerably from established workers' ones), and those dispossessed by industrialisation. The last category would include marginal populations and, in particular, workers in informal sector employment. [25]

Marx did, of course, write before the great scramble for empire by the European states in the nineteenth century. His book on capital was only the first of six, and he died before writing the detailed study of the world market and the internationalisation of capital that he had planned. It fell to others to explain in detail, using his approach, why going global at least temporarily solved capitalism's key problems, and its class-making consequences.

Rosa Luxemburg, for example, saw imperialism as the result of over-production (or underconsumption, depending on how you look at it).

> Accumulation is impossible in an exclusively capitalist environment. Therefore, we find that capital has been driven since its very inception to expand into non-capitalist strata and nations ... The development of capitalism has been possible only through constant expansion into new domains of production and new countries. [26]

Lenin likewise concentrated on the importance of the export of capital, but he also emphasised the creation of monopolies and the merging of bank capital with industrial capital to create finance capital, which he saw as the paramount resource. Fundamentally imperialism was a 'special stage in the development of capitalism'. Free competition had given way to monopolies, and imperialism was capitalism in its monopolistic phase. Capitalism had to keep growing to keep going. Capitalists in general, and finance capitalists in particular, were bound to seek profits, and they did so regardless of state boundaries. They were state-makers themselves in many instances, and where they were not the relationship between the state-makers and the profit-takers was so close as to be irrelevant. The consequence was a territorial division of the world between the capitalist powers. [27]

In class terms, the consequence was also a growing transnational bourgeoisie, bearing state passports but trading, financing, buying labour and resources around the globe, and sharing more with each other than with fellow nationals not of their own class. By contrast the international proletariat, the wage-labourers — manual and mental — who directly made the world's wealth, remained unco-ordinated.

They have remained so to this day. On particular issues, like apartheid in South Africa or controlling nuclear weapons, they have had some impact, but on the whole the international division of labour has kept the 'head separate from the hand, and each hand separate from each other'. [28] While the bourgeoisie have busied themselves making one world out of capitalist enterprise, the proletariat have had to seek their common cause in civilising the system from behind their state borders. These borders are continually reinforced, however, by the more or less successful efforts of state-makers, even as they act, to service the needs of the bourgeoisie.

State-making and class-making

State-making and class-making (in the Marxist sense) work against each other in complex ways. While pluralist state-making purports to have the effect of consolidating people within local, territorial domains, the same process counterpoises people globally. People are pushed together in their state-defined environments, and at the same time are pulled apart by the rivalries this sets up regionally and world-wide.

The opposite happens with class-making. While capitalist class-making creates conflict between the bourgeoisie and the proletariat within states, the same process consolidates the respective classes (though the more mobile and self-consciously solidarist class in this regard is the bourgeois one). While people are pulled apart by their class conflicts locally, in other words, they are brought together by common class concerns world-wide.

This picture can be complicated even further by considering the countertrends within each component. The local cohesion state-making strives for can be frustrated by substate groups — nationalities, for example — determined to win greater autonomy for themselves. On the other hand the global dissonance state-making creates may be moderated by the work of global forums like the UN, or by associations and regimes set up to serve common interests (like regulating world trade).

By contrast, the local conflicts class formation sets up will be constrained by any practices, like imperialism, which provide the means to buy off dissent. The global cohesion of the bourgeoisie has to contend with a nascent but world-wide proletariat that is opposed to it.

Though the picture is complex it does appear to be patterned. Much of the crackle in world politics comes from the way state-making and class formation occur together. They move against each other in time to the grand fugues of sovereign centralism and of capitalist industrialism, with the occasional impromptu cadenza to remind us that whatever the patterns, there is always less order than there appears. It is the wildness of the world, as G.K. Chesterton once pointed out, that lies in wait.

Notes

1 J. Viner, 'Power Versus Plenty as Objectives of Foreign Policy in the Seventeenth and Eighteenth Centuries', *World Politics* vol. 1 no. 1, 1948, p. 4.
2 E.H. Carr, *The Twenty Years' Crisis 1919-1939*, Macmillan, London, 1946, 2nd edn, p. 114. For a contemporary defence of mercantilism, see H. Schmitt, 'Mercantilism: a modern argument', *The Manchester School of Economic and Social Studies* vol. 47, 1979, pp. 93-111.
3 R. Gilpin, *The Political Economy of International Relations*, Princeton University Press, Princeton, 1987, pp. 48-9.
4 ibid., p. 49. For a feminist critique of this see J. Tickner, 'On the fringes of the world economy: a feminist perspective' in C. Murphy & R. Tooze (eds), *The New International Political Economy*, Lynne Rienner, Boulder, 1991.
5 ibid., pp. 30-1.
6 E.H. Carr, op. cit., p. 121.
7 R. Ashley, 'Three Modes of Economism', *International Studies Quarterly* vol. 27, 1983, p. 481.
8 E.H. Carr, op. cit., p. 117.
9 K. Marx & F. Engels, *The German Ideology*, Lawrence & Wishart, London, 1977, p. 48.
10 ibid., pp. 42, 43. For excellent summaries of Marx's approach, its implications and ramifications, see V. Kubalkova & A. Cruikshank, *Marxism and International Relations*, Clarendon Press, Oxford, 1985; and T. Thorndike, 'The revolutionary approach: the Marxist perspective' in T. Taylor (ed.) *Approaches and Theory in International Relations*, Longman, London, 1978.
11 K. Marx & F. Engels, *Manifesto of the Communist Party*, Foreign Languages Press, Peking, 1975, p. 37.
12 ibid., p. 38.
13 ibid., p. 39.
14 ibid., p. 41.
15 ibid., p. 48.
16 ibid., pp. 56, 57.
17 R.W. Connell, 'Class Formation on a World Scale' in R. Connell (ed.), *Which way is up? Essays on sex, class and culture*, George Allen & Unwin, Sydney, 1983, p. 172.
18 R. Tawney, 'Foreword' in M. Weber, *The Protestant Ethic and the Spirit of Capitalism*, Unwin, London, 1930, p. 2.
19 K. Marx & F. Engels, *The German Ideology*, p. 47.
20 K. Marx & F. Engels, *The Manifesto*, p. 58.
21 H. Alker, 'Dialectical Foundations of Global Disparities', *International Studies Quarterly* vol. 25 no. 1, March 1981, p. 81.

22 J.M. Keynes, 'National Self-Sufficiency', *The New Statesman and Nation* 8 July 1933, p. 36.

23 R. Cox, *Production, Power, and World Order: social forces in the making of history*, Columbia University Press, New York, 1987, p. 355.

24 K. Marx, 'Estranged Labor' in *Economic and Philosophic Manuscripts of 1844*, International Publishers, New York, 1964.

25 R. Cox, op. cit., pp. 358, 368.

26 R. Luxemburg & N. Bukharin, *Imperialism and the Accumulation of Capital*, Allen Lane, London, 1972, p. 145.

27 V.I. Lenin, *Imperialism, The Highest Stage of Capitalism*, Foreign Languages Press, Peking, 1973, pp. 104-9.

28 S. Hymer, 'The Internationalization of Capital', *Journal of Economic Issues* vol. 6 no. 1, March 1972, pp. 103, 105.

The balance of productivity

What is the balance of productivity? What reading of world development does it prompt? What part do finance capital and multinational corporations play in this reading? What part do women as opposed to men play?

1. What is the balance of productivity? What reading of world development does it prompt?

Mapping state-making practices and class-making practices onto the one terrain, that of the human populace as a whole, allows a complex account of integrative and disintegrative trends that is considerably more sophisticated than either provides alone. State-making works to aggregate people on a national basis while setting them against each other internationally; class-making aggregates people (though more particularly the bourgeoisie) globally, while pitting bourgeois formations against proletariat ones locally.

Of course, class-making pits the bourgeoisie against the proletariat internationally too, but the confrontation is much less intense because the proletariat is more fragmented. The strife class-making creates locally can also be mitigated by the benefits of imperialism, for example, some of which can be used to blunt dissent.

State-making, on the other hand, with its policies of conscious integration, may involve bringing unwilling peoples together locally. It can entail a good deal of international co-operation as well as conflict.

What inspires this enormous amount of human behaviour? What

motivates so much synchronised yet dissonant activity? Perhaps a clue can be found by looking at the structure and the dynamics of the international political economy as a whole. Encouraged by seeing capitalists and state-makers working together on a global scale, some theorists take the world system itself as their focus and, in a rather grandiose fashion, look for causal forces in the whole way it has developed.

Those with traditional state-centric leanings see the world system as having been shaped for the last 500 years by a succession of world powers, first Portugal, then the Netherlands, then Britain (twice) and latterly the USA. George Modelski, for example, has drawn attention to the way 'world orders' are forged through wars out of periods of global disorder, and how this happens every 100 years or so. Hegemonic powers take a hold of the ring, and keep it until a serious challenge arises. The system then reverts to conflict and relative chaos.

Why every 100 years or so? Modelski suggests a 'systemic' explanation (whatever that means), and more recently a 'political learning cycle' (which is not much more precise). In more practical terms he also suggests that it may have something to do with life span and the fact that 100 years is about three generations - the first one builds, the second consolidates its inheritance, and the third fritters it away.[1]

From Modelski's perspective the global system is now well into its fifth long cycle. Political resolve remains the key theme in his narrative, though he is clearly aware of the significance of trade, industry and ultimately finance as motivating factors. The cycles are crafted by sovereign states and though their economic activity is of central concern, it is mostly neo-mercantilist activity from his point of view; the wealth-making taking place as part of state-making, rather than despite it.

A more economically minded analysis of the same historical sequence has been provided by Immanuel Wallerstein, who in a series of studies tells the story in terms of the capitalist world-economy as a whole. The globe-spanning practices he refers to make most sense, he says, in terms of a world that has a 'core', a 'semi-periphery', and a 'periphery'. State-makers and wealth-takers behave as they do depending on their place in this system. It is the overall structure of the world political–economy that matters most, since the doings of those in any part of it make sense only in the context of the making and maintaining of its three major zones or tiers.

Of course, some parts are more important than others since a superior ability to produce goods and render services, and to project military power, has made it possible over time for particular countries to be at the core. Again, we are looking at the Netherlands, the UK and the USA in turn. For Wallerstein, however, it is the story of the world system as a single, integrated entity that is the most interesting and revealing one.

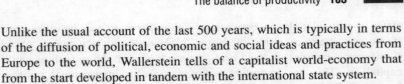

Unlike the usual account of the last 500 years, which is typically in terms of the diffusion of political, economic and social ideas and practices from Europe to the world, Wallerstein tells of a capitalist world-economy that from the start developed in tandem with the international state system.

For most of this period it has had a European core. The system once established grew as a whole, however, with the European and the non-European parts working together. For example, from the very beginning the capitalists who built the world-economy used labour as a commodity. The capitalists were European, but the labour was both European and non-European. (They didn't necessarily pay wages for it either. In the semi-periphery they used tenants, and in the periphery they used coerced labourers — slaves and serfs.)

Non-European labour was cheap. Those who owned or managed factories or plantations that could use cheap labour made money comparatively quickly. This led to different rates of economic development and different roles (who does what and where, or a 'division of labour') between core states and peripheral ones. It also led to a core class of capitalists separate from those working on the system's outer rim.

Like Modelski (and Toynbee and Spengler and Kondratieff before him) Wallerstein claims to see 'long waves' rising and falling through world society: long waves of geographic expansion and contraction; long waves of bust and boom in productive capacity; long waves of more or less interdependence and more or less intensive class formation. Unlike Modelski, however, Wallerstein emphasises the economic domain not the political state-making one (in the liberal sense, that is, of economics as distinct from politics.)

> In the late fifteenth and early sixteenth century there came into existence what we may call a European world-economy. It was not an empire [in the traditional, pre-capitalist version] [i]t was a kind of social system the world has not really known before ... [it was] an economic but not a political entity ...

It worked as an economic whole but it remained politically pluralistic.[2]

In liberal terms, such a system must be ideal, since it gives wealth-makers the freedom they need to make markets. Indeed, it allows much greater scope for individual economic initiative generally. In Marxist terms, however, it cannot disguise the class dominance of the bourgeoisie and the impoverishment and enslavement, waged and unwaged, of the (non-bourgeois) individual.

Whatever the perspective, the point of Wallerstein's analysis of the accumulation of capital on a world scale is to take as his unit of analysis the entire capitalist world-economy. The experience of individual nation states or particular classes between or within them can only be understood if we see them as parts of larger, globe-spanning structures whose significance emerges, as the world-system does, with the growth of world capitalism. This has important consequences for international politics, because if Wallerstein is correct international politics are only a footnote to world development; a side effect of how capitalist industrialisation has taken place and continues to take place in only some areas (core zones) and not others, which become peripheral, marginalised and poor.

International politics is only one dimension of a grander design. It is the outcome of many small decisions, none of which has necessarily been taken with this grand design in view. We must look beyond the nation state, in other words, to see what capitalism does in the world. The narrative of any state is the story of its place in the world system.

States are not static. They change in form and content and they move, in Wallerstein's parlance, from the core to the semi-periphery to the periphery, or back again, as circumstances dictate. The categories of core/semi-periphery/periphery have stayed constant, however, since 1640; since the beginning of the system itself. Furthermore, though state-makers strong enough to have appropriated a large and stable part of the world surplus and to be designated leaders of core states do conflict, one state typically emerges from this process as pre-eminent but not predominant. It has a hegemonic say but its pre-eminence is never great enough to parlay the system into an empire. The system, in this sense, remains pluralistic.

Wallerstein's conception is huge. It is a radically comprehensive way of viewing the world. Is it, however, very useful or true? Firstly, Wallerstein has to make some very general historical statements to get his schema to work, and historians have been very unhappy with the way he has forced particular stories to fit his grand design. The key problem is to convince area and issue specialists of the existence of a capitalist world-system with the three layers in it that overarch classes and states. Most historians think that global interactions haven't occurred in this patterned way over long enough periods of time for us to accept the autonomy and the logic of the system Wallerstein describes.

Secondly, Wallerstein makes very general statements about the world that do not seem to square with the way it works today. For example, he says it is not possible to see underdevelopment as a consequence, or even a partial consequence, of earlier ways of doing things. Since 1917, he argues, there has been only one social system in the world, with one mode of production and one division of labour, and that is the capitalist world-economy. Everything else was absorbed or eliminated during the geographic expansion of this capitalist world-economy from 1815–1917. Most liberals or even Marxists would not go this far, however, particularly given something as complex as contemporary world society.

Thirdly, he never explains why it was capitalism that became so success-ful a way of organising labour in the world, except to call it an accident. It may well have been, of course, but even accidents can be explained.

Fourthly, there is the whole problem of systems analyses like these that reify patterns of human behaviour and end up seeing them as separate from what human beings choose to do. Any particular human choice becomes, by definition, the outcome of abstract processes that seem to work regardless of human will. People cease to bring about change. It is the structure of the system that, in its autonomous and deterministic way, decides.

Fifthly, there is the radical liberal critique. This would see no reason why a core couldn't develop a periphery rather than underdevelop it, given economic growth and the benefits that radical liberals see for everyone in greater productivity, consumption and exchange.

Finally, there is the classical Marxist critique, that Wallerstein's understanding of capitalism concentrates too much on commerce and not enough on production. Consequently he downplays capitalism's class-forming significance. There is not enough class struggle in his schema. There is not enough sense, either, of superpowers manoeuvring for advantage, or of ecological limits to growth. There is too little sense altogether, one could say, of the complexities and contingencies of the real world.

Modelski and Wallerstein represent the extremes of world-system think-ing. Short of them we find the familiar neo-mercantilist, liberal and Marxist accounts of international political–economy already discussed.

Neo-mercantilism sees the national interest being pursued anywhere and everywhere by whatever means necessary—diplomatic, economic, ideological, or all three. If this means international capitalist enterprise, so be it. If it means autarky, independence, isolation even, so be it. (In Wallerstein's terms mercantilism has historically been a 'defensive mecha-nism of capitalists located in states which are one level below the high point of strength in the system'.[3])

Radical liberals applaud capitalism's productive capacities. The traditional sectors of any economy will be modernised, transformed, and made more efficient and rational by the untrammelling of the human propensity to haggle and trade. With uninhibited economic growth comes greater global interdependence. Though social and political factors do affect the process of modernisation in the long run it is the market which remakes the world as it expands and as capital accumulates, new technologies are developed, new ways of organising work and life are devised, cities grow, and money becomes the universal measure of worth and well-being.

A more system-conscious variant of the radical liberal approach argues that an open world economy can't be sustained without a hegemonic or leading power to establish and maintain liberal rules of the game. Hegemonic status is not seized by force. Other participants must acknowledge the pre-eminence of the leader, and lend their support to the leader's efforts to organise the system for the common good of all the main players. In the last century this role was played by Great Britain.

The Pax Britannica that ran from the end of the Napoleonic wars to the start of the penultimate European war (the First World War) was sustained by Britain's own example, plus the benefits supposedly obvious to all of having borders open to the world. These two factors were the ideological basis on which the tacit agreement by European and other states to respect the system and to play the game were said to rest.

At the end of the last European war (the Second World War) the USA established fixed exchange rates (the Bretton Woods system) and a general agreement on tariffs and trade (GATT) to promote the same sort of open order — one with a relatively free trading system and a stable currency. These devices were meant to solve the problem all radical liberals face, which is the way that, sooner or later, the harmony of an open economy is undermined by cheats and freeloaders who exploit the mutual benefits of the system for their own gain. Without a hegemonic leader, the argument runs, a radically liberal world order is most likely to revert to rampant economic nationalism, which to a radical liberal is a recipe for disaster.

Another problem radical liberals face is the way the opportunities offered by a radically liberal market result in the relocation of economic activity. Relocation can have profound effects on the global division of labour and the global distribution of industry. The very success of a well-led liberal world market undermines the pre-eminence of the market leader and creates a new distribution of material and military power. As Gilpin says, 'the inherent stability of the international market or capitalist system is highly problematic; it is the nature of the dynamics of this system that it erodes the political foundations upon which it must ultimately rest'.[4] With their relative decline, the system leaders may then change from being benevolent to being predatory (as the USA has often been charged with doing). The threat is even more general than this, according to Gilpin.

> In the final decades of the twentieth century the international economy confronts the dangers accompanying the relative decline of American hegemony. The international debt problem, the increase in trade protectionism, and other issues could trigger a crisis over which the United States and its economic partners could easily lose control. Such a failure of crisis management could once again bring down the liberal international economic order.[5]

Another Great Depression would follow, making life harder for many more.

To a Marxist, this would be entirely predictable, though for very different reasons. In the liberal view we face a failure of crisis management. In the Marxist view, however, the collapse of the world political–economy would not be a collapse but the inevitable outcome of the capitalist mode of production which is destined, because of the contradictions inherent in the organisation of its productive activities, to lead to class conflict and class war. Emiseration would be the immediate cause of such a war. Poverty, in this perspective, is produced by capitalist practices as efficiently as any of its other commodities. The underlying cause, however, as Ankie Hoogvelt argues, would be the 'triple alliance between international finance capital, international productive capital and the states [governments] of the ... Third World'.[6] Third world state-makers use military and policy power to foster capitalistic intervention while making land, natural resources and labour available in pre-capitalistic ways. [7]

The balance of productivity

How is this process most graphically conceptualised? What image best captures its main characteristics? One way to imagine wealth-making and profit-taking internationally is the way taken here, in terms of a balance of productivity. Like the balance of power (narrowly construed as the distribution of military power) the idea of a balance of productivity can be used to describe or explain or prescribe the practice of international politics in an extended sense, namely, that of international political–economy.

Using the schematic presentation of the balance of power made earlier, an analogous attempt can be made to map the balance of productivity. This entails describing it, explaining it, and finding out what it prescribes.

In descriptive terms, the balance of productivity refers to the distribution of productive capacity, or capital, in the world. It is the struggle for the world product, a struggle that potentially results in an even or uneven balance.

A radical liberal description of the process would draw attention to the geopolitical centres of the productive power in the world, such as Europe, the USA, and the countries of the Pacific rim, led by Japan. It would map the economic rivalry and the shifting economic alliances between them, and it would trace the diffusion of the world's wealth to the poor.

A classical Marxist description would highlight the accumulation of capital on a world scale by one wealth-making class. It would also note the impoverishment of the world's waged workers, particularly third world ones.

A feminist description, however (whether liberal or Marxist), would highlight the impoverishment of the world's women, again particularly third world ones. In doing so it would typically note the under-representation of female workers in formal statistics on labour markets, and the general (masculinist) tendency to underrepresent the full contribution women make to development as a whole.

In explaining such patterns the balance of productivity highlights the way the world polical–economy works to stop any part becoming preponderant.

In this regard the classical liberal version would emphasise the logic of comparative advantage. It would talk in terms of supply and demand within the global market.

The classical Marxist explanation would emphasise the logic of international capitalism. A number of mechanisms have been identified that have the effect of accumulating capital in the hands of the global bourgeoisie. All help to explain its dominance.

The feminist reading would fasten upon patriarchy or fraternity or any cognate concept that emphasises the way women are consigned to private as opposed to public domains. It would underline the reproductive as well as the productive role they play there, and the enormous significance of the unwaged work they do.

In making policy prescriptions, what the balance of productivity describes and explains determines what should be done to get a better balance. It says how to prevent one state or class or gender becoming preponderant, or how to redress preponderance where it exists already. The recommendations about the best mode of redress, and the best counterhegemonic strategies to employ, differ depending upon whether the description or the explanation is liberal, Marxist or feminist.

The balance of power and the balance of productivity are linked. If power is thought of in terms of its functional dimensions (political, material, military and ideological) and we take production (rather than just exchange) to be the core of the material realm, then productivity is a dimension of power, and the balance of productivity is a dimension of the balance of power.

Productivity, though by no means neglected by traditional analysts, is commonly treated as a secondary aspect of power. It is, however, a primary aspect. It is even, arguably, the primary aspect. To the extent that it is dealt with in a secondary way, balance of power theorists can be accused of failing to take their own core concept (power) seriously. They can be accused of not exploring far enough what makes for power and why the powerful can claim (in this traditional sense) to be so. They can be accused of restricting their analyses to the military or strategic dimension of power, and of not giving equal analytic weight to productivity. The result is a less than comprehensive reading of power, and of the balance of power itself.

What happens if we do try to take productivity seriously? Radical liberals, with their clear distinction between economics and politics, would look at the politico-strategic balance of power, and they would then wonder what an economic balance of power would involve. Theorists who have done so, however, have specifically discounted the worth of such a concept. For example, Charles Kindleberger has observed that:

> if we postpone ... the issue of imperialism ... [and note] where there is not exploitation or redistribution, it is hard to see that more income and wealth for the Soviet Union, for example, harms the United States and Europe in the same way that more military power does. Covetousness is a human weakness ... but it is hardly of sufficient importance ... to warrant us to contemplate a balance of economic power separate from the balance of political power.[8]

There are two telling flaws in Kindleberger's account. One is his failure to appreciate the importance of productive capacity as the basis for military capacity. Highly productive states are at least potentially militarily important states. Soviet state-makers could not bury the USA by increasing the Soviet standard of living, or vice versa. But economic power is not just measured in terms of the standard of living. It entails a country's capacity to mount and project armed might, and while this is not the same as the balance of power, it bears directly upon it. For this reason a map of the balance of productivity in the world looks very similar to a conventional balance of power map. Productivity is a primary component of any country's power. It is a necessary aspect of any consideration of comparative power in this respect, and therefore of any balance of power.

Productivity is important, then, despite what Kindleberger says, but is it also different enough to warrant its own concept? Kindleberger again thinks not. Here the dissimilarities between the two maps are very instructive. The qualifier used above to say that productive states can only be militarily important 'potentially' is necessary to account for countries like Japan and Germany. While both would be heavyweights in any balance of productivity map they do not feature quite so much in the balance of power map. There is also the reverse. The UK or France, for example, because of their nuclear arsenals, are more important in the balance of power than in the balance of productivity. Likewise, the makers of non-productive states may be receiving military aid as may non-productive insurgents or freedom-fighters. The two balances are not identical, therefore, which is why we can map the practices involved separately, and why it is useful to do so.

A state-centric map is only one possible reading of such balances. As indicated already, capitalists pursue profit wherever they can. This has led

to intense international activity and integrated practices that have transformed the context within which state-makers now work. The effect has
been a shift in the balance of productivity and the balance of power:

> away from nationally-organised labour movements (and nation states)
> towards internationally mobile capital. The state's dependence on
> internationally mobile capital means that state policy is mediated by the
> state's position as an economic unit in the world market, rather than
> formulated as previously in response to the balance of class forces within
> the nation.[9]

The second flaw in Kindleberger's argument is his attempt to hold to
one side the issues of imperialism, exploitation and redistribution. The
map of productive capacity in the world is very uneven. The patterns of
contemporary productivity are (among other things) exploitative and
maldistributive and even (neo)imperialistic. Can this be held to one side ?

Imperialism is a political phenomenon, but only the most doctrinaire of
liberals would also eschew its economic significance. The imbalance of
military power you get with an imperial hierarchy is typically mirrored by
an imbalance of productive capacity. The two are linked.

Marxists would see the balance of power and the balance of productivity as separate, since to be linked is to make the liberal assumption that
politics and economics are separate domains. They would see them as
fused. To quote Cox:

> Production creates the material basis for all forms of social existence, and
> the ways in which human efforts are combined in productive processes
> affect all other aspects of social life, including the polity. Production
> generates the capacity to exercise power, but power determines the manner
> in which productivity takes place.[10]

The balance of power between states and the strategic questions it raises
are only a part of the picture. They cannot be understood without
considering the balance of productivity and the questions about world
development (in the narrow sense of increased material output) that flow
from the various readings of how this has happened. As state-making tells
the story of the balance of power, so world development (in its limited
form of economic growth) tells the story of the balance of productivity.

Or should one say stories? More precisely, the story of world development (in this restricted sense) can be read many ways. Clearly, a narrative
so complex, with so many subplots and internal contradictions, cannot be
given more than the most summary treatment in a single, simple, sequen-
tial tale.

One approach, then, is to compare whether world development is actually
proceeding or not, with a 'moderate' or 'radical' reading of the process.[11]

This leads to four different analytic narratives: firstly that world development is actually taking place, albeit more slowly than might have been expected; secondly that it is stuck; thirdly that it is distorted; and fourthly that it is reversed. The first narrative is a classical liberal and Marxist reading. The other three are neo-Marxist alternatives.

More particularly, the first narrative involves a moderate telling of how world development is proceeding apace. As industry and agriculture become more mechanised and as gross national products grow, then there is evidence that development is occurring, albeit more slowly than many might have anticipated. This is the classical Marxist view.[12] It is also the liberal view, the difference between the two being the expectation as to outcome (wealth and harmony in the latter case, and class struggle and revolution in the former).

In the second narrative, a moderate account of how development is stalled, the process is seen to be blocked by capitalist penetration of pre-capitalist societies. This has made meaningful development impossible for the latter, who are condemned to their impoverished plight indefinitely.[13]

In the third narrative, development is proceeding, but in a dependent way. This more radical version of the process argues that those who got in on the ground floor distorted the development opportunities of all who followed. They used their historical advantage to skew subsequent events in their favour. The most significant defenders of this view have been the Latin American 'dependencia' theorists. The success of the newly industrialising countries of Asia, however, has made the cruder versions of the third and the second narratives more difficult to sustain.[14]

In the fourth narrative, development at the core is said to create underdevelopment at the periphery. This is also a more radical view of events. In this case development is seen as not proceeding at all; indeed, quite the reverse. Exploitation (resulting, for example, from the abuse of an underdeveloping domain's cheap labour) leads to a pattern of unequal exchange that further impoverishes the poor and enriches the already rich.[15]

In practice, examples exist of all four analytic narratives. This makes it difficult to find a logic to global capitalism and global industrialisation other than that of opportunism, which is not a logic, but the way of life of the entrepreneur. The plethora of possible approaches also makes it difficult to see world production processes becoming more homogeneous.

There is a great variety of ways in which production is carried out. That these ways also change is evident in the global restructuring of what capitalists require and how labour is used. It is also evident in the advent and the use of new technologies, like genetic engineering or robotics, which allow the most innovative firms to develop new commodities and new ways of manufacturing them. The advanced countries who host these firms are thus able to keep their productive edge.

Changes in the way production is carried out are also evident in the way manufacturers of light goods such as clothing, and heavy goods such as cars, use advances in communications, transport and organisational know-how to move their plants around to cost advantage. Less technologically developed countries also become (supposed) beneficiaries.

The complexity and diversity of such changes mean that whatever logic they have can only be construed in very general terms. The overall strategy seems to involve a move away from large, centralised, uniform productive units toward diversified and differentiated ones. This move is often international.

The complexity and diversity of the production systems involved is mirrored by that of the social relationships they entail. The fact of world development cannot be divorced, therefore, from its social causes and effects. These, like the balance of productivity itself, are very uneven, whether read in terms of state-based relationships in the world market, or in terms of capital versus labour, or of women versus men. The concept of the mode of production has consequently become much more problematic.[16]

2. What part do finance capital and multinational corporations play in this reading?

International finance

Capital is not one resource but many. Contemporary times have, however, been dominated by the kind of capital known as 'finance', detached from production but always in pursuit of profit and hence productive enterprise. Flows of finance capital are far larger than those of commodities, and are now counted in the tens of trillions of US dollars. In the words of one economist:

> A global financial and capital market may now be said to be in existence — with dramatic implications for the political independence of erstwhile 'sovereign' states. The discipline of external economic forces — a discipline operated through freely-flowing capital movements — has finally brought home to Finance Ministries of all countries the absolute importance of appropriate fiscal and monetary policies. They will 'buck the system' only at their peril — or, more importantly, at the peril of the inhabitants of those countries whose fortunes are in their hands.[17]

The general tone of this quotation is decidedly liberal, and it is not difficult to divine what 'appropriate fiscal and monetary policies' might mean to the author, or what the delights of 'discipline' entail. In radical liberal parlance, the free flow of capital allows capitalists to invest where they can make the most profit; where (in the jargon of economics) the 'marginal rate of return is highest and where it can therefore be employed most efficiently'.[18]

The outcome is meant to benefit everybody since it supposedly promotes the most productive use of the world's 'scarce supply of investable capital. This investment expands global demand and overcomes the inherent tendencies in a closed market economy toward under-consumption [over-production]'. It is also meant to overcome the situation where finance capital, though scarce, has no incentive to go anywhere, thereby becoming (despite a world shortage) unproductive.[19]

In Marxist parlance the predatory nature of capitalists in general and of financiers in particular is directly responsible for the neo-imperial exploitation of the world's poor. Lenin saw this aggressive greed as the driving force behind the imperialism of his day, and as the main cause of war, and all Marxists since have been more or less impressed by the capacity of capitalists to reproduce contemporary production methods and social relationships in the most remote and recalcitrant of the world's corners. They remain cynical, however, about the benefits involved, and pessimistic about the system's chances of survival given the maldistribution of those benefits.

Where in modern times has finance capital come from? There have been two principal sources. Firstly, the cost to the USA of running the Vietnam War was partly met by printing more US dollars. These became, mostly in the guise of Eurodollars (dollars held in Europe), an important part of the global pool of surplus funds.

Only a country of such dominant productive and political power as the USA could have used such a ploy, since it relied on the willingness of others to hold and deal in a national currency not their own. The persistent deficits the USA has ultimately incurred have not helped shore up the value of its dollar, which only drives dollar holders to try all the harder to make dollars work for them in world markets.

The other main source was the money earned by the oil-producing countries of the world when they took collective decisions to raise the price of their commodity (which was also set in US dollars). The first increases were made in 1973–74, and the second in 1979–80. The result was a large flow of funds into those countries, but these funds could be used only in pursuit of further profit.

The consequence has been what Susan Strange aptly called 'casino capitalism'.[20] The politically fragmented nature of the state system means there is no lender of last resort. Furthermore, the opportunistic behaviour of the world's wealth-makers tends to make financial investments speculative and fluid. The two phenomena together encourage international inflation, pressure on exchange rates, and put local monetary and fiscal policies at the mercy of punters who are way beyond the control of those who must make such policies.

With the proletarianisation of so much of the world's work, the wage cuts and the unemployment that follow unsuccessful gambles inevitably affect large numbers of people, which in turn has direct political effects. State-makers then compete to export their problems while colluding to attract the money they need to pay their debts. This makes them ideological allies of the very finance capitalists creating these problems, if they are not already self-conscious members of that class. Meanwhile the international financiers and the local profit-takers continue to work to maximise their short-term gains.

In Marxist terms:

> the victims once again [are] the working class throughout the capitalist world, trapped in a financial vortex beyond comprehension and control ... [U]nless visited by a fundamental socialist revolution — which, if only on a national scale, would probably entail a protective siege economy in the short term — it is a system that states and their populations cannot avoid.[21]

In radical liberal terms the stability of such a system depends on market forces retaining a dynamic equilibrium. The more faint-hearted (or the more realistic) tend to turn to the strongest economic power to protect the monetary basis of the world market by fixing, in de facto fashion at least, the main exchange rates. With United States state- and wealth-makers unable to get out of debt, and a continuing decline in the quality of what they export, they are no longer the obvious hegemon in this regard. The palm may have passed to the Japanese, who are the world's premier savers. It is falling more and more to them to foster the productivity of the system as a whole, to bail it out in times of crisis, and to back allied wealth-makers as well.

This is what British state- and wealth-makers did in the nineteenth century, albeit in their own interests. It is what their United States counterparts did in the twentieth, again in their own interests. It remains to be seen if the USA will retain its pre-eminence, how its once-undisputed hegemonic role may change, and whether United States/ Japanese 'bigemony' will ensue.

The stages whereby a hegemonic country goes from capital importing to capital exporting (and back again in the case of UK and the USA) have been mapped in some detail. Japan closely fits the contours of this map.[22] The long-term efforts of Japanese state-makers, since the Meiji restoration

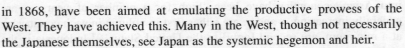

in 1868, have been aimed at emulating the productive prowess of the West. They have achieved this. Many in the West, though not necessarily the Japanese themselves, see Japan as the systemic hegemon and heir.

How desirable this would be is questioned by those who see a difference between an Asian and a Western concept of what constitutes fair trading practices. There is a sense — often condescending and sometimes racist — that Japan would not be a suitable hegemonic power. Evidence is cited of the way the Japanese wheel and deal at the highest political levels, the way a majority of commercial stocks are kept outside the market, and the way major stock beneficiaries can regulate their value.

The shift in the global balance of productivity towards Japan, however, as measured by shifts in capital flows or in the balance of trade, may mean it is the West that has to learn to adapt to the cultural and institutional traditions of the Japanese, not the other way around.[23] Though doubt persists as to the likely emergence of a Pax Nipponica, United States state- and wealth-makers face an unprecedented challenge. They are being outproduced though, as Huntington argues, if hegemony means producing '20 to 25 percent of the world product and twice as much as any other individual country', the USA still stands strong.[24] It is certainly in no position to claim the moral high ground. Its own lack of regard for business ethics, and the way it changes the rules of the game when it serves its own interests, would make the USA a hypocrite if it tried.[25]

Japan is also the world political–economy's main creditor. The decisions of Japanese wealth-makers as to which part of the world to favour with finance capital have important consequences. Japan continues to subsidise its erstwhile benefactor and ally the USA:

> partially for commercial reasons, to create a market for Japanese exports, and partly due to the attractiveness of high American interest rates [I]n the long run, [however], political concerns and interests will determine the willingness of Japan to continue financial support of American hegemony and prosperity. One political and psychological problem is that such a relationship converts the American military into a mercenary force defending Japan in return for Japanese capital.[26]

This problem can only last as long as Japanese state-makers continue to accept a military capacity that is notably inferior to their productive one. Meanwhile, as political allies of the USA on the one hand and as economic rivals on the other, their role is ambiguous at best.

Another obvious area of financial investment and aid is that of the Asia-Pacific region within which, in geopolitical terms, Japan is located. This domain includes the newly industrialising countries of South Korea, Taiwan, Singapore and Hong Kong, where Japanese wealth-makers have been investing heavily. As Derek Healey points out, Japanese capital flows into Asian economies have been 'high for a number of years ... are generally increasing ... and ... are either first in volume in each country or, at a minimum, are second [only] to the United States'.[27] Indonesia is the major regional recipient, though the fastest growing inflows are those to China. Investment in China is still relatively modest, however, and is of the 'wait and see' variety. Japan is also China's second biggest trading partner. Moreover, it provides over half of China's bilateral and nearly three-quarters of its multilateral aid.

Japanese investment in Asia is not just finance capital. It includes a host of private and public outflows, both direct and indirect, and the purpose and the mix have shown marked changes over time. Since the end of the first war of the Pacific investment has gone through three broad phases. In the initial period, until the end of the 1960s, Japanese state-makers and wealth-makers emphasised their need for resources, and set about securing raw materials for Japan's domestic industries. In the second phase, the 1970s, they shifted their investment towards labour-intensive manufacturing industries in countries where labour was cheap. The third phase, the 1980s, saw the focus swing toward increased investment in developed countries like the USA.

In line with the restructuring of the Japanese economy itself away from energy-intensive industries towards knowledge-intensive ones, investments have been made in technology-intensive manufacturing, particularly in the service sector. This presages a fourth phase during which Japanese capitalists may well choose to relocate their uncompetitive industrial production in lower-cost countries in the Western Pacific, a region that already accounts for one-fifth of total Japanese foreign direct investment.

It is the Japanese banks that will underwrite any loans involved. More important, however, will be the Japanese corporations. These corporations are the main transmission belts for Japanese capital flowing abroad. Indeed, corporations generally have become very visible since the last European war, and are now a dominant feature of the world political–economy.

Multinational corporations

Multinational or transnational corporations (TNCs), as the label implies, are firms with production facilities in more than one state. International economic activity of this sort, and the direct foreign investment involved, goes back to the great eighteenth century trading companies like the British East India Company and the Hudson's Bay Company. In the nineteenth century European and United States transnational firms diversified into agriculture, mining and manufacturing, and in the twentieth century, particularly since the last European war, they have come to provide the institutional framework for much of the world's business.

To a modern-day mercantilist the economic dependence or inter-dependence such companies promote is anathema. In radical liberal par-lance, however, they play an important part in diffusing technology, fostering economic growth and bringing the world economy together. In classical Marxist terms they are viewed likewise, pulling people out of their 'rural idiocy' towards capitalism and the light beyond. To neo-Marxists they are more likely to appear as 'imperialistic predators, exploiting all for the sake of the corporate few while creating a web of political dependence and economic underdevelopment'.[28]

The way multinational corporations have internationalised production affects the global political economy at all levels. They have carried capitalist enterprise far and wide, integrating and intensifying profit-taking practices wherever they have gone. Their world factories have played an important part in forging commodity chains and world production sequences that treat state boundaries as largely irrelevant.[29] Melvin Gurtov points out that:

> The prominence of global corporations in world politics can be gauged by noting their market dominance and size. About 500 TNCs (of over 10,000 worldwide) account for about 80 percent of total world production. A mere fifteen of them, and in most cases only three to six, control world trade in all basic commodities, from food to minerals. When their total output is matched against that of states, TNCs ... occupy forty-one of the top 100 places.[30]

There are nationally owned state trading multinationals, but these are not high on such a list. The large corporations are not state-makers' concerns. They are largely based in rich countries, and the profits they make contribute in no small part to what makes such countries rich. The 'high political' prerequisite for all this enterprise is world peace, though a number of TNCs make money from armaments and the preparations by state-makers for war.

The consequence at the lowest political level, that of society itself, is the part they play in transmitting the values and culture of the competitive, growth-oriented, materialistic, opportunistic and rationally managed centres of the world to its 'backward' and as yet unreconstructed peri-pheries. Little wonder analysts have proclaimed that:

> The global corporation is the most powerful human organization yet devised for colonizing the future. By scanning the entire planet for opportunities, by shifting its resources from industry to industry and country to country, and by keeping its overriding goal simple — worldwide profit maximization — it has become an institution of unique power.[31]

Everyone now feels this power. Nearly every country in the world actively pursues multinational corporations for investment in its people, its productivity and export capacity, and improvement of its know-how, employment prospects and earning capacity.

What this all portends generates an intense and continuing debate. To elaborate: on the one hand the protagonists of TNCs would say they foster freer trade and comparative advantage, provide finance for development and research, encourage the manufacture and distribution of goods on a global basis, and contribute to the peaceful environment in which this can take place. On the other hand TNCs ostensibly promote oligopoly and the evils of restricted enterprise, undermine state sovereignty, foster dependence, and generally contribute to the underdevelopment of the poor by propping up repressive regimes, manipulating markets and the movement of know-how, retarding indigenous enterprise, underpaying workers, and undermining local values and ways of life.[32]

The intensely opportunistic nature of these globe-spanning enterprises is well caught by Anthony Sampson in his study of International Telephone and Telegraph (ITT). He recounts his impressions of the annual ITT barbecue. As a guest at this exclusive event he recalls feeling as if he had entered a 'nomad's encampment'. From the barbeque marquee (as he subsequently described it) ITT's managers, like a group of bourgeois Bedouin, looked out onto a world 'benighted with prejudice and unreason; where governments were merely obstructing the long march of production and profit; where nations were like backward native tribes, to be placated, converted, and overcome'. The duality implicit in the company's stance Sampson found 'baffling'. On the one hand ITT was a 'highly responsible world organisation, constantly mindful of its 200,000 shareholders, its 400,000 employees, its seventy host nations and held together with an accounting system of the strictest control'. On the other hand Sampson sensed a company 'accountable to no nation, anywhere ... How can governments ever control such an organism which is, like a jellyfish, both everywhere and nowhere? And how does the multinational corporation, of which ITT is a convenient caricature, fit in with modern notions of politics and diplomacy? How does it, or should it, relate to the nation-state ?'[33]

At the time Sampson was writing, multinational corporations were seen as a direct threat to the sovereign state. They were wanted for their economic promise, but state-makers feared their capacity to erode the autonomy of state-making practices wherever they went or were asked to go. One effect of the oil price rises of the early 1970s, however, was to prompt state-makers to nationalise a number of oil company subsidiaries within their borders. Sovereign dominion did still make a difference, though the result was more often a renegotiation of contracts than meaningful economic autonomy. The results were nonetheless dramatic.

'World history', in Gilpin's words, 'records few equivalent redistributions of wealth and power in such a short period'.[34]

The list of multinational corporations is still dominated by companies based in the USA. The number of non-United States corporations has been growing, however, as European and Japanese multinationals, and now those from newly-industrialising countries like Brazil, India and South Korea, join in the hunt for markets and resources and new deals. State-makers collude with wealth-makers to augment the developmental opportunities 'their' multinationals enjoy in global, not just regional or local, markets. When we find British capitalists, however, using Euro-dollars to buy Australian iron ore for Japanese steel-mills it does become difficult to tell just what 'their' might mean.[35]

Japanese corporations are the most conspicuous of the new wave of economic internationalists. Initially, as indicated above, Japanese corporations invested abroad to get raw materials or low-cost components for home processing and for re-export in the form of finished goods. Tariff barriers to Japanese goods entering the USA, Europe and elsewhere, however, prompted Japanese corporations to invest and produce more abroad. Neo-mercantilism only spurred Japanese producers on to greater efforts. The growing multinationalisation of the firms involved has come to represent a major shift in the balance of productivity.

Equally remarkable has been the way United States multinationals have responded to the eclipse of United States industrial hegemony, to large national trade deficits and to a burgeoning national debt. United States based corporations could not be accused of acting as patriots, except in the most extended and liberal sense (what is good for the world and good for us is good for the USA). They show scant regard for the material and social malaise of their home country. Indeed, neo-mercantilist critics argue that United States corporations should put their capital, including their technological know-how, to work in the domestic market rather than putting it where other states benefit and become competitors. They fear their country's loss of industrial capacity, and see the strategies of vertical integration pursued by such corporations, that is, the consolidation of the productive chain from raw material to the table, as undermining United States self-reliance.

It is the state-makers and the wealth-makers in poor states and new states, however, who have been most concerned with the impact of TNCs. Foreign investment by corporations in the less organised areas of the world has had a long history. Plundered and colonised, the peoples who lived in these areas were subsequently decolonised and mostly given formal independence. Neo-colonial means had then to be found to keep access to the raw materials, the crops and the cheap labour the big firms had previously taken for granted. There were many locals willing to keep borders porous in this respect. Where they were less willing, and erected tariff barriers to encourage local production and to provide local substitutes for foreign imports, corporations found new ways to jump the barriers to establish branch plants and manufacturing subsidiaries. The picture has become progressively more complex with: 'cross-licensing of technology ... joint ventures ... marketing agreements, secondary sourcing, off-shore production of components ... [and] cross-cutting equity ownership'.[36] The result has all too often been enclave development; distorted and inappropriate and inefficient development; and further exploitation.

At this point it is a common ploy to argue that poor countries are irrelevant in the larger scheme of things, and to question what the fuss is all about. Thus we find J.D.B. Miller pointing out that 'the rich countries' trade and investment is primarily with one another, and their major profits appear to derive from this'. Their relationships with the third world, he concludes, are 'largely incidental'.[37]

To talk of countries, however, as Miller does, is to betray an obdurantly liberal view of the global political–economy, and demonstrates a singular lack of awareness of the extra-statal nature of corporate practices. Furthermore, to talk of profit-making and the economic hierarchies it creates as not deliberate and as nothing but the involuntary outcome of making money is to surrender quite uncritically to a marketeer's conception of how the world works.

The marketeer's conception is a radical liberal one, in which economic dominance (or domination) is as it should be. It is the price of progress, and can be minimised only by state-makers choosing to facilitate rather than frustrate corporate practices. Close relationships between transnational capitalists and host and home government state-makers are both the consequence and cause of a growing politicisation of these practices, foreign investment among them. The dynamo is economic, however, and politics is best kept at one remove (except when socialising losses. Gains, of course, are capitalised).

In Marxist terms, corporate managers and their state-making allies are classmates. Their relationship has always been political, as it has always been economic. State-makers are the creatures of those who make the material means whereby their rule is sustained. They are collaborators. Corporate capitalists rarely become state-makers. They don't need to. This is not to deny political resistance in the USA, for example, to Japanese corporations building vertically integrated industrial conglomerates there. Marxists would ask who is resisting and why, and would be less interested in nationalistic or jingoistic reactions than in the way collusion between

United States and Japanese firms exploits United States and Japanese wage-workers.

3. What part do women as opposed to men play?

In reading the story of world development (in its limited and partial sense as material capacity, or capital accumulation), two main themes emerge: the sheer progress since the last European war; and the highly uneven way it has happened. Earth's people are now said to be so productive that the question of ecological limits to such growth is becoming acute. The geopolitical spread of uneven outcomes is also most notable. Much of black Africa, and of Latin America, is mired in debt, with many of their growing populations having to survive outside the productive schemes of the major wealth-makers and the state. Growing prosperity is evident among only some sectors of the newly industrialising countries, and in parts of a few of those still largely underdeveloped (or in the process of being so).

The uneven quality of world development, and the uneven balance of productivity this indicates, can be read either in terms of state-based relationships in the world market, or in terms of capital versus labour; as changing class relationships in a world political–economy. As indicated already, however, there is a third reading that can be made, and that is in terms of gender. The global political economy is not only capitalist. It is also sexist, patriarchal, fraternalist, and man-dominated. The state-makers, as noted above, are overwhelmingly men. So are the conspicuous wealth-makers — the overt capital accumulators — whether we talk of them as a simple category, or as a social formation; a class.

Even the second and more dynamic formulation, that of class, has been accused of being 'gender-blind and therefore gender-biased'. Thus Hartsock argues that it is a category based on 'men's experience, a category that mistakes men's experience for the general human experience ... Our society ... is structured not simply by a ruling class ... but also by a ruling gender, defined by and dependent on the sexual division of labor'.[38]

Hartsock is not alone in this view. 'It must now be accepted', Connell concludes, 'that gender divisions are not an ideological addendum to a class-structured mode of production. They are a deep-seated feature of production itself ... Gender divisions are a fundamental and essential feature of the capitalist system; arguably as fundamental as class divisions ... Capitalism is run by, and mainly to the advantage of, men'.[39]

If this is so, then we must look at the balance of productivity in terms not only of state-making and class formation but in terms of the distribution of productive practices by gender. We must look at men and women as productive beings, and as reproductive ones, and if as suggested above there are patterns, we must try to account for them.

The global pattern is compelling. Note the much cited summary by the International Labor Organisation that females, who comprise half the world's population and one-third of its official workforce, do two-thirds of the world's work. For this they get one-tenth of the world's income. They also own less than one-hundredth of the world's property.[40] A more recent summary by Caporaso likewise concludes that:

> all societies have a gender division of labor ... this division of labor excludes women from certain jobs, it segregates them from status and income categories within broad job classifications, it gives unequal pay for similar jobs, and it has the effect of under-valuing or not valuing (meaning nonpriced rather than unappreciated) women's work in the home .[41]

A capitalist world political–economy needs capital. It also, of course, needs labour, and the cheaper the better for making the profits that capitalists prize. Capitalists conduct business in poor countries and use young women for less skilled factory work since they are highly unlikely to have unions, they can be paid a pittance, and local state-makers often offer support services, all of which maintains or increases employers' profits. Another effect has been to take such work away from those women who do it in the richer, more industrialised regions of the world. In those regions, however, women have more of a chance to improve their skills and to get other jobs in higher wage brackets. They must contend, nonetheless, with 'housewifisation', as indicated below.

The female workforce is not uniform. Industrial capitalist wealth-making has, however, favoured the creation of a domestic domain that is almost exclusively female. Nuclear families, with women at home in a private capacity, are used to gestate and raise more potential workers and home-makers. This is meant to free men to labour for wages and to attend without distraction to their jobs.

There is rarely a physiological reason for such a division of labour along sex lines. It must be explained, therefore, in terms of patriarchy or fraternity; patriarchy or fraternity which, furthermore, is reinforced by capital gain. Women can be used, in such a system, as a reserve army of labour that can be drawn into the formal workforce as demand dictates, and returned to the home when no longer needed. They constitute a large pool of relatively inexpensive, unorganised, willing and flexible workers, rather than labour in their own right. Thus they are pulled into the waged sector of the economy in time of war, or whenever else there is a labour shortage, and put back on domestic duties when paying jobs become scarce again.

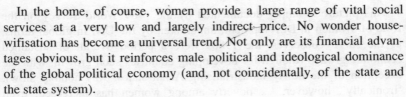

In the home, of course, women provide a large range of vital social services at a very low and largely indirect price. No wonder house-wifisation has become a universal trend. Not only are its financial advantages obvious, but it reinforces male political and ideological dominance of the global political economy (and, not coincidentally, of the state and the state system).

Note the argument by Maria Mies:

> Contrary to what is commonly accepted women, not men, are the optimal labour force for the capitalist (and the socialist) accumulation process on a world scale. Though this has always been the case, in this phase of development of the world economy this fact is openly incorporated into the economic strategies of national and international planners. Women are the optimal labour force because they are now being universally defined as 'housewives', not as workers; this means their work, whether in use value or commodity production, is obscured, does not appear as 'free wage-labour', is defined as an 'income-generating activity' and can hence be bought at a much cheaper price than male labour.[42]

Despite the use in less developed, undeveloped or underdeveloping countries of young, relatively unskilled women as cheap labour for capital-intensive manufacturing or assembly lines, the trend seems to be toward a global division of labour between men and women where the men are free wage-workers and the women are non-free housewives. The more developed the economy, the more apparent this becomes. This trend is reinforced by the way women in developing countries lose control of the land. The use of male-centred development models, and the sort of agricultural modernisation that follows, has dispossessed many women in the poor and newly industrialising countries of the one capital resource they controlled.

It is radical liberal theology that this is part of the diffusion process and ultimately beneficial. It is distinctly illiberal, but no less plausible, to suggest that rather than being left out, women are used as an integral part of the process, all too often in exploitative ways.

The United Nations Decade for the Advancement of Women (1975–85) defined as key goals the need to win greater recognition for women's unwaged labour and, more particularly, the right to be paid for it. It also argued the need for state-makers and wealth-makers to overcome a discernible trend towards the feminisation of poverty. At the end of that decade, however, it was apparent 'with few exceptions ... [that] women's relative access to economic resources, income, and employment ha[d] worsened, their burdens of work ha[d] increased, and their relative and even absolute health, nutritional, and educational status ha[d] declined'.[43] Poor women had got poorer, in other words, more women were poor, and women were getting poorer compared to men.

This picture is amply documented by the 1989 World Survey on the Role of Women in Development, undertaken by the UN. In global terms, as the survey observes, the 1980s were a period overall of sustained economic growth (though for developing countries such growth, with the exception of the newly industrialising Asian states, was notably slow). 'Ironically', however, '... poverty among women has increased, even within the richest countries ... The bottom line shows that ... at least for the majority of developing countries, economic progress for women has virtually stopped .'[44]

This amounts in practice to a massive assault on (or in less provocative language, the erosion of) the life-choices and life-chances of half the human race. In Mies's memorable phrase, women are the 'last colony'.[45]

Is the solution to women's poverty and oppression a basic needs strategy that provides improved welfare services and more paid work? This would be the liberal response. What if, however, the marginalisation of women's work and ways is the direct result of their incorporation into the contemporary world market; a consequence of the international division of labour under the capitalist mode of production? Non-liberal analysts would say it is. The feminisation of poverty is due, they argue, to exploitation, not maldistribution. If this is the case then liberal measures to ameliorate women's plight would probably make matters worse.[46]

It clearly makes a difference, in other words, what ideological position is adopted, as it not only influences description given or the explanation made of women's plight in world affairs, but affects prescriptions for change. For this reason I shall now turn to the balance of ideologies in the world.

Notes

1 G. Modelski (ed.), *Exploring Long Cycles*, Lynne Rienner Publishers, Boulder, 1987.

2 I. Wallerstein, *The Modern World-system: capitalist agriculture and the origins of the European world-economy in the sixteenth century*, Academic Press, New York, 1974, p. 15. See also A. Toynbee, *A Study of History*, Somervell abridgement, Oxford University Press, Oxford, 1946 and 1957, and O. Spengler, *The Decline of the West*, Knopf, New York, 1961, vols 1 and 2. On N. Kondratieff see J. van Duijn, *The Long Wave in Economic Life*, George Allen & Unwin, London, 1983.

3 I. Wallerstein, *The Capitalist World-economy*, Cambridge University Press, Cambridge, 1979, p. 19.

4 R. Gilpin, *The Political Economy of International Relations*, Princeton University Press, Princeton, 1987, p. 64.

5 ibid., p. 80.

6 A. Hoogvelt, *The Third World in Global Development*, Macmillan, London,

1982, p. 210.

7 See J. Caporaso, 'The International Division of Labor: a theoretical overview' in J. Caporaso (ed.), *A Changing International Division of Labor*, Lynne Rienner Publishers, Boulder, 1987.

8 C. Kindleberger, *Power and Money: the economics of international politics and the politics of international economics*, Basic Books, New York, 1970, p. 69.

9 C. Vogler, *The Nation State: the neglected dimension of class*, Gower, Aldershot, 1985, pp. 161-2.

10 R. Cox, *Production, Power and World Order: social forces in the making of history*, Columbia University Press, New York, 1987, pp. 1, 4.

11 The idea of this 2 x 2 matrix was first suggested, as far as I'm aware, by Rex Mortimer.

12 B. Warren, 'Imperialism and Capitalist Development', *New Left Review* no. 81, 1973, pp. 3-44.

13 G. Kay, *Development and Underdevelopment: a Marxist analysis*, Macmillan, London, 1975.

14 F. Cardoso, *Dependency and Development in Latin America*, University of California Press, Berkeley, 1979.

15 A. Frank, 'The Development of Underdevelopment', *Monthly Review* vol. 18 no. 4, September 1966, pp. 17-31.

16 R. Cox, op. cit., p. 397.

17 D. Healey, 'Japanese Private and Public Capital Outflows and Asian Economic Development in the 1980's', OECD Development Centre, Paris, Doc. No. CD/R(88)34, p. 149.

18 R. Gilpin, op. cit., p. 306.

19 T. Thorndike, 'The revolutionary approach: the Marxist perspective' in T. Taylor (ed.), *Approaches and Theory in International Relations*, Longman, London, 1978, p. 83.

20 S. Strange, *Casino Capitalism*, Basil Blackwell, Oxford, 1986.

21 T. Thorndike, op. cit., p. 84.

22 D. Healey, op. cit., pp. 27-8. The liberal reading of these stages does obscure the extent to which the 'economistic orientation of [Japanese] labor ... [has been] the consequence of the overt repression of workers interested in self-management, and the planned substitution of right-wing unions for ones striving for worker empowerment'. See J. Rytting, 'Class Struggles in Japan', *Restructuring and Labor* no. 19, March/April 1989, p. 26. This is a review of M. Ichiyo, *Class Struggle and Technological Innovation in Japan Since 1945*, International Institute for Research and Education, Amsterdam, 1987.

23 Adapting to these traditions involves in part learning about the Japanese as a people. This is not as simple as it might seem, since Japanese national characteristics, while fairly readily identifiable, can be depicted more than one way depending upon whether or not one is well-disposed towards the Japanese. See R.P. Dore, 'The Japanese Personality' in G. Wint (ed.), *Asia Handbook* (rev. edn), Penguin, Harmondsworth, 1969.

24 S. Huntington, 'The U.S. — Decline or Renewal?', *Foreign Affairs* vol. 67 no. 2, Winter 1988/89, p. 84. Huntington believes Japan has 'neither the size, natural resources, military strength, diplomatic affiliates nor, most important, the ideological appeal to be a twentieth-century superpower' (p. 92). The prospect of a Pax Nipponica is discussed further, though not endorsed, by R.

Leaver in 'Restructuring in the Global Economy: from Pax Americana to Pax Nipponica', *Working Paper no. 61*, Peace Research Centre, The Australian National University, Canberra, 1989. See also R. Sinha, 'U.S. Hegemony and the Japanese Challenge', *Coexistence* 25, 1988, pp. 264-8.

25 R. Sinha, op. cit., pp. 247-8.

26 R. Gilpin, op. cit., p. 238.

27 D. Healey, op. cit., p. 74.

28 R. Gilpin, op. cit., p. 231.

29 C. Chase-Dunn, 'Interstate System and Capitalist World-Economy' in W. Hollist & J. Rosenau (eds), *World System Structure*, Sage, Beverly Hills, 1981, p. 34.

30 M. Gurtov, *Global Politics in the Human Interest*, Lynne Rienner Publishers, Boulder, 1988, pp. 23, 25.

31 R. Barnett & R. Muller, *Global Reach: the power of the multinational corporations*, Simon & Schuster, New York, 1974, p. 363.

32 C. Kegley et al., 'The Multinational Corporation: Curse or Cure?' in C. Kegley & E. Wittkopf, *The Global Agenda* (2nd edn), Random House, New York, 1988, p. 274.

33 A. Sampson, *Sovereign State: the secret history of ITT*, Hodder & Stoughton, London, 1973, pp. 15-21.

34 R. Gilpin, op. cit., p. 232.

35 R. Connell, 'Class Formation on a World Scale' in R. Connell, *Which way is up? Essays on sex, class and culture*, George Allen & Unwin, Sydney, 1983, p. 177.

36 R. Gilpin, op. cit., p. 256.

37 J.D.B. Miller, *The World of States*, St Martin's Press, New York, 1981, p. 102.

38 N. Hartsock, *Money, Sex and Power*, Longman, New York, 1983, pp. 5, 9, 149.

39 R. Connell, *Gender and Power: society, the person and sexual politics*, Polity, Cambridge, 1987, pp. 103-4.

40 Cited, for example, in J. Langmore & D. Peertz (eds), *Wealth, Poverty and Survival*, George Allen & Unwin, Sydney, 1983, p. 67.

41 J. Caporaso, 'Labor in the Global Economy' in J. Caporaso (ed.) op. cit., p. 206.

42 M. Mies, *Patriarchy and Accumulation on a World Scale: women in the international division of labour*, Zed Books, London, 1986, p. 116.

43 G. Sen & C. Grown, *Development, Crises and Alternative Visions: Third World Women's Perspectives*, Monthly Review Press, New York, 1987, p. 16.

44 *1989 World Survey on the Role of Women in Development*, United Nations, New York, 1989, pp. 5-6.

45 M. Mies et al. *Women: the last colony*, Zed Books, London, 1988.

46 A. Bandarage, 'Women in Development: Liberalism, Marxism and Marxism-Feminism', *Development and Change* vol. 15, 1984, pp. 495-515.

3 Society

PART

6

Society, culture and social movements

What does society mean in the context of international politics? What sort of society is defined by the cosmopolitan culture of modernity? Who is critical of this culture and why? When do such critics constitute social movements? In what respect are social movements the keepers of the moral flame?

1 What does society mean in the context of international politics? What sort of society is defined by the cosmopolitan culture of modernity?

World society

The conventional approach to international politics discusses state-making, the international system of state-makers, and the balances of power (defined in strategic and military terms) that state-makers strike within this system. State-making and all it entails is not, however, the only, or even the most important, part of world affairs. A more comprehensive analysis will include an account of the international political–economy and, more particularly, an account of the mercantilist version of it that sees state-making as meaningless without material self-sufficiency, as well as an account of the radical liberal version of it that sees state-making as obstructing the workings of the world market (a market destined, if allowed open and free performance, to provide prosperity and peace for all).

It will also include an account of the classical Marxist version. This version of how the international political–economy works believes that state-makers are members of a global ruling class. As owners or controllers of the means of production the interests of the members of this class conflict with those of the workers who make them wealthy. Broadening our perspective in this way we add to the usual reading of the balance of power an appreciation of it as a balance of productivity.

The conventional reading of world affairs can be carried even further, however, to consider the social domain in which state-making, marketeering and class-making take place; to consider, that is, the nature of the social domain these practices define and defend; and, more importantly perhaps, what lies beyond them that might be of relevance to international politics. Here we encounter world society. We undertake world studies in its most comprehensive sense.

International politics is a complex, shifting array of social practices which are shaped or determined by the feelings, the values and the ideas that people have about the international political–economy and the international polity. Whether we think the right verb should be shaped or determined will depend on whether we think feelings, values and ideas cause world affairs or merely condition them.

Social practices assume some sort of society. The concept of society assumes in turn some sort of culture, or rather, an ongoing process of culture-making. In global terms these are difficult concepts to pin down.

In feminist terms, for example, world society is most meaningful as a description of how men and women collude in defining and marginalising women's work and women's ways. Since male domination seems to be universal, the practices involved could well be seen as defining a global society. This society (to use Walker's terminology) is a two-worlds one, however, with men as the state-makers and wealth-makers, and women mostly relegated to the domestic domain, which is inferior in terms of its political importance, material rewards and social status. The culture-making that defines global socialising practices is that of the ruling gender. It is the masculinist culture of patriarchy or fraternity. It is (from this perspective) exploitative, assertive, competitive and afraid.

In Marxist terms world society is defined by industrial capitalism. It is those social relations that capitalists create wherever they invest or establish their productive facilities. This approach is also a two-worlds one, though the difference between the worlds is marked by differences in class not gender. The ruling class defines the ruling culture, which is therefore bourgeois. Its culture-making practices serve the wealth-making ones. They are interventionist, innovative and ultimately self-defeating.

In the conventional reading, however, world society is the story of European state-makers scrambling for empire in the late nineteeth century and taking with them not only their armies and their administrative practices, but their traditions of interstate alliance, their codes of international law, their commercial traditions and their diplomatic culture. As state-making became universal and as the leaders of the colonised became the leaders of sovereign states whose task it was to define and defend their territorially tangible independence, such leaders became the representatives of states. They set up embassies in other state capitals, commissioned flags, and coached themselves in the protocols of diplomatic practice. They applied to join interstate organisations. They studied international law. In short, they set about joining a society of peers, a society with its own cultural practices. It was a society that generations of European state-makers had developed to define state status, to exclude those not eligible to join, and to facilitate regular dealings with each other.

The modern world society, in the sense of a diplomatically mediated system of sovereign state-makers, did not fall fully clothed from history's closet. The concept of ambassadors, in the sense of envoys and resident representatives, was familiar long before the advent of the modern state system. The suzerain lords of the ancient world, for example, would send delegations to imperial courts to petition the emperor, pay taxes, or demonstrate formal and ceremonial subservience. Emperors would exchange representatives, as would local regimes.

The point here is the way sovereign authorities took over the notion and made it a two-way one, an exchange. The practice of exchanging representatives has been dated from 1603 when a Huguenot diplomat first drew the distinction between emissaries sent between states (ambassadors) and emissaries sent either from states to private individuals (agents, commissioners) or from private individuals to states (deputies).[1] This distinction made clear the policy of the time. It also gave belated recognition to the success European statesmen had had in monopolising diplomatic traffic and making their own way of behaving into the most authoritative one.

The diplomatic traditions state-makers inherit today were devised to cope with conflict; they were ways of managing the international relations of an interstate system. They were highly particular ways, however, that clearly betrayed their origins. With the reduction of the papacy by state-making aristocrats from its status as the international European government of Christendom to that of an Italian principality, it was the kingly courts that came to provide the models and manners of civilised self-restraint. The sanctimonious procedures of the Church were superseded by or incorporated into the rites and rituals of secularising monarchs. The mores of these monarchs defined European diplomatic practices and, in due course, those of the whole world.

Anthropologists and historians have provided many descriptions of peoples, geographically removed from each other, finding ways of relating. A shared culture is not necessary to provide the rules required, although it clearly facilitates such a process. It is no accident that the cultural practices of European state-makers, having taken control of much of the globe and then relinquished it, were carried over into the way the new world was arranged.

In many cases indigenous elites were also familiar with local practices of a similar sort from pre-colonial times. However, as Bull and Watson argue:

> the most striking feature of the global international society of today is the extent to which the states of Asia and Africa have embraced such basic elements of European international society as the sovereign state, the rules of international law, the procedures and conventions of diplomacy and international organisation.[2]

Modernity

Bull and Watson make the further point, that: 'International legal, diplomatic and administrative institutions ... rest upon a cosmopolitan culture of modernity, to which the leading elements of all contemporary societies belong even if the masses of the people do not.'[3] This is a key point because if we are to locate the social dimension of international politics or, from another perspective, the social domain of which international politics (narrowly defined) is one dimension, we have to be able to describe its main cultural characteristics.

The members of a cosmopolitan interstate society will act in the light of meanings established by the culture-creating practices of that society. They will enact those meanings in how they behave, and what they enact, as Bull says, is something called modernity.

What is modernity?[4] What does it mean to be a modern human being, a practitioner of this cosmopolitan milieu, and a member of the cosmopolitan society this sort of culture-making defines and defends?

These are very large questions. In brief, however, it seems that the key characteristic of the non-modern (pre-modern or post-modern) individual is his or her close and unexamined sense of continuity with the cosmos. To think and feel in a non-modern way is to have an intimate subjective relationship with the world that reason may elaborate and confirm but does not deny. By contrast, the mind of a modern person has no intuitive sense of this link. Reality is thought of as outside the self.

With a mind-set of the modern sort we can look back on the world, on the universe, even on the self and the sense of self. This one leap of the

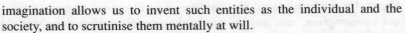

imagination allows us to invent such entities as the individual and the society, and to scrutinise them mentally at will.

We also invent the opposite of being modern, namely, being traditional. Traditional practices are not, in this sense, those hangovers from the past that we learn from our ancestors without having to think about them. They are not, that is, our customs. They are those practices we choose or make for ourselves, or that are chosen and made for us by state-makers, wealth-takers, or mind-shapers, that provide us with a past appropriate to our modernity. In a modernising age, in other words, the past is no longer taken for granted. It is no longer an endless realm of myth and legend. It becomes concrete, finite and a place in itself.

In choosing or making a past in this way we typically attempt to provide ourselves with a sense of continuity and authenticity or, if we are state-makers, with a sense of our legitimacy. The past having become, like everything else, some thing, out there, it can be rationalised, it can be used as an ideology, and it can be quarried to affirm particular notions of the present.

Radical objectivism

The Greeks were the first systematically to explore the objectivising mind-set — the 'Archimedean point' — in any detail. Their mental break with the cosmos having been made, the Greeks found they could create a new sense of continuity which was, however, different from the close and unexamined one that had gone before it. In this new view humankind appeared as a part of the natural world, but as a separate part, while the world itself appeared more material and objectivised. It began to seem less mystical and less all-of-a-piece with the self.

The effects of radical objectivising were profound and enlightening. They presaged science and the use of reason in more extensive ways. They allowed the use of the intellect to theorise with rather than as something to be used to work out the means necessary to achieve particular ends. They also had a number of important corollaries. [5]

The act of naming, for example, tended to become one of labelling only. Naming no longer had the power to make magic. Non-modern people, in the sense used here, tend to have a feeling for language and the cosmos as close to each other, or interconnected. A change of mind, for example, to a non-modern mind can mean a change in reality. To the modern mind, however, the enchanted use of words is unthinkable and intolerable. Such a use implies that a change of mind can change the world.

To a radical objectivist, like the contemporary scientist, words are no more than arbitrary sounds that by mutual and learned consent denote things. He or she tends to say that there is no objective evidence for any other assumption, and that we are well advised not to believe that the cosmos shuffles about in response to our human fancies — not, that is, if we want reliable, cumulative knowledge. Appeals to the unseen for agents of change in the world — animal spirits, for example, or ghosts, or gods — no longer suffice. They are not convincing enough. They don't explain. They tend to explain away. They tend to leave the objectivised mind dissatisfied, disbelieving and disapproving.

Modernists sometimes seem nostalgic for their lost innocence in this regard, that is, nostalgic for a time when people didn't objectivise so much. Most of them do accept, however, that having detached their view of reality from reality itself, the words we use in talking about what we think and feel are also detached from reality. Most modernists would accept that working magic is the domain now only of illusionists.

Hoisting oneself up by one's mental bootstraps in an objectivising fashion has a second effect. Having learned the leap of the imagination that radical objectivising requires, those with mental detachment of this sort seem to have an enhanced capacity to think about a secular cosmos in abstract ways.

Holding their mental constructs apart from reality as models of that reality and as analytic realms in their own right, radical objectivists seem to be able to manipulate their models and reflect upon reality relatively free of their own emotional and aesthetic interests in the matter. They can create, for this very useful and exploratory purpose, a without and a within. They can construe reality as a depersonalised realm outside themselves, oblivious to whatever human qualities they feel they have inside. They can interrogate the natural order they see outside in a sceptical and relatively impersonal way, without feeling that their own sense of themselves has been put in doubt. They can experiment, hypothesise and share what they learn with sceptical individuals like themselves around the world. They become, in a word, rationalists.

Because rationalists tend to stand aloof mentally from everything around them, they develop a powerful sense of their personal interests, which will then compete with whatever else they value — honour for example, or faith — for primary status.

A third effect of radical objectivising is what it seems to do to our sense of space and time. Space becomes geometric, time becomes linear, and both get quantified. Time can be saved, for example. It can be expended; it can drag; it can pass quickly; it can be measured and budgeted; it can also seem less human somehow, and less a part of the undifferentiated flow of life. It can erode the non-modern feeling (again in the sense used here) of time as something we experience like we do the air we breathe or the water we drink.

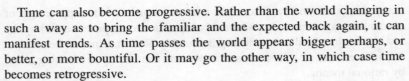

Time can also become progressive. Rather than the world changing in such a way as to bring the familiar and the expected back again, it can manifest trends. As time passes the world appears bigger perhaps, or better, or more bountiful. Or it may go the other way, in which case time becomes retrogressive.

The importance of changed perceptions of time led Lewis Mumford to identify temporal regularity as modernity's main characteristic. 'The clock, not the steam engine', he argued, 'is the key machine of the modern industrial age ... no other ... is so ubiquitous. Furthermore, ... by its essential nature the clock dissociates time from human events and helps create the belief in an independent world of mathematically measurable sequences'.[6] It helps create the sense of a neutral world that can be explored rationally. It helps foster the technical application of the results of these explorations and this, in turn, means more mechanisation, more machine manufacture, and an ongoing industrial revolution.

Radical objectivising has led even further in this regard, to the concept of space-time. It was Einstein who first linked these two abstractions in a scientific way. His findings, though a mental tour de force, can only be comprehended in the universal symbolic language of mathematics. Despite their authority as science this makes them less accessible; less so, perhaps, than a number of analogous conclusions drawn over the years by religious mystics. (Men and women have had intimations like Einstein's for millenia, though couched of course in the subjectivised language of pre-modernist discourse.)

Returning to the industrial revolution, it is commonplace to observe how much the material achievements of this radical turn of events have improved the living conditions of large numbers of people. As new knowledge has magnified human productive power, so has the capacity to enhance human welfare grown. It is also commonplace to note the environmental costs that have been involved. Less common is an account of the psychological and social costs that have been incurred as well.

Mumford points to a 'modulation of emphasis, a matter-of-factness ... a quiet assurance of a neutral realm in which the most obdurate differences can be understood'.[7] What has been the effect of feelings like these? We know that the search for rules in nature of the sort that radical objectivism has inspired has been turned back on society itself in an attempt to regularise human behaviour. This has also led, however, to a very high value being placed upon rationalistic decision-making. The problem here has been where societies have begun to assume that by observing particular rationalistic means, the substance of efficiency will surely follow. The bureaucratic practices this can prompt (while serving additional functions like holding at bay an importunate public who ask too many things of too few resources) tend to emphasise the appearance of rational management only. Where this happens the purposes served by the institutions involved can be lost quite quickly. Rationalism can become an end in itself, not just the means to it. Reason can end up celebrating itself, by rational means.

The fourth effect of radical objectivising, already hinted at, is what it does to the sense of self. One consequence is alienation. Radical objectivists tend to become strangers in their own universe, since it can be rather hard to feel at home in a cosmos that is an object, that is material, and that seems devoid of divinity.

One obvious outcome in this regard can be the cost to feelings of social immediacy and human mutuality, a cost often increased by the emotional effects on people of industrial production systems and the bureaucratic polities they build to promote their pursuit of material gain. Does knowledge won this way have to have no meaning for human existence? Is it truly the case that if we know with our selves and our feelings we live in a personal timeless universe, but that if we know with the 'objectified, operational "I", there can only be sub-atomic waves and particles; and the void?'[8]

A cogent case has been argued both ways. Regardless of the conclusions drawn, however, radical objectivism does seem to have the effect of loosening the ties that bind the individual to society, and to inspire a change in self-identity. People modernised in this respect do seem to think less in terms of 'who I am' — based largely on hereditary status — and more in terms of 'what I do'. This can be seen, for example, in the way the modern primary and secondary school will teach individuals to internalise notions of personal ability in the meritocratic way required by the labour market. [9]

Capitalist industrialism

Growing numbers of individuals, we are told, want the products that contemporary science, technology and industry can provide, however contrived those wants might be. To satisfy their desires they are ostensibly willing to accept the spiritual costs involved. The question then becomes one of social effects. Will industrialisng peoples change their cultural environments into places as standardised and as predictable as the products of their machines? To what extent and in what ways will Tokyo become the same as Rio de Janeiro or Dar es Salaam? Can we expect the relegation of organised religions to ephemeral status and their replacement by secular equivalents such as nationalism or shopping? Was the resurgence of fervour in Shi'ite Iran, for example, no more than a futile attempt to stem this tide?

Contemporary industrialism has certainly undermined and overwhelmed every social order it has encountered, a process prosecuted by force of arms, economic opportunism and force of example. Barrington Moore argues, however, that there is no evidence that the mass of the population anywhere has wanted an industrial society, and plenty of evidence that it has not. At bottom all forms of industrialisation have so far been revolutions from above, the work of a ruthless minority.[10]

This is an extreme position, and doesn't do justice to the demonstration effect (people seeing products they want). Neither does it do justice to the ingenuity with which materialism has been combined with local beliefs. It does, however, heighten our sense of how unnatural this phenomenon has been. It also provides a useful reminder that what we live with today has not always been the case, nor has it always been welcome.

Modern industrialism proletarianises. In its capitalist form people sell their labour for wages. As the system has grown so has the size of the waged workforce. Any collective awareness on the wage-workers' part that this is a system that may exploit them has been checked, however, by the tendency for technological advances to replace labour with machines. Labour-shedding pits wage-workers against each other for whatever jobs there may be. At the same time capitalists continue to seek labour where it is cheapest, either among marginalised groups nearby (recent immigrants, the racially stigmatised, women) or among diverse populations further afield.

Labour for a wage need not necessarily, although it does, tend to reduce the meaning of work to the material rewards it brings. Work as the affirmation of a sense of society and, through that sense, of the self, is very difficult to sustain when effort is rewarded with money, that is, with a medium of exchange rather than some more integral good. Effort sold like this becomes a commodity too, as Marxists have long been aware. Work then reinforces people's feelings of alienation. Indeed, it becomes a primary source of what seems meaningless about life and the day.

This is not all. To fix upon changes in human labouring is to miss the much more pervasive effects of the industrial milieu and, more particularly, the capitalist version of it. According to Marx:

> The bourgeoisie cannot exist without constantly revolutionising the instruments of production and thereby the relations of production, and with them the whole relations of society ... [U]ninterrupted disturbance of all social conditions, everlasting uncertainty and agitation distinguish the bourgeois epoch from all earlier [or other] ones. All fixed, fast-frozen relations, with their train of ancient and venerable prejudices and opinions, are swept away, all new-formed ones become antiquated before they can ossify. All that is solid [or privileged and established] melts into air. [11]

Marx was very impressed with the dynamism of capitalist industrialisation. To maximise profits capitalists push to the perimeter every other value. Heritage becomes irrelevant. Recreating the present becomes a physical and mental imperative without any apparent conclusion. Buildings are torn down to be rebuilt to be torn down again to be rebuilt. Whole cultures are remade in like fashion. Whatever equilibrium is achieved can only be precarious and dynamic at best, and growth is the only authentic measure of progress, which leads one to wonder what sort of human beings capitalist industrialism produces.

A lust for renewal would seem to be the main trait of such a way of being. Anything else would inhibit the workings of the market and therefore the making of more goods and services. In practice such an extraordinary conception generates a compelling set of human practices and a terrifying outcome:

> from the clothes on our backs to the looms and mills that weave them, to the men and women who work the machines, to the houses and neighborhoods the workers live in, to the firms and corporations that exploit the workers, to the towns and cities and whole regions and even nations that embrace them all — all these are made to be broken tomorrow, smashed or shredded or pulverized or dissolved, so they can be recycled or replaced ... and the whole process can go on again and again, hopefully forever, in ever more profitable forms.[12]

Marx likened the plight of the bourgeois to that of the sorcerer who, having summoned the demons of hell, discovers they are too powerful to keep under his or her spell.[13] No wonder, it is argued, the bourgeoisie tend to shrink from the logic they ostensibly espouse. No wonder they qualify the free market by introducing a host of self-protective measures, using their own power and that of the state to provide self-serving safeguards, and confounding open consideration of the process by choosing a consensus of mutually enforced mediocrity.[14]

Industrialism not only proletarianises, but it is profoundly individualistic. Modernisation of this sort, carried to its logical extreme, would render any community incoherent. The notion of sustaining collective activity under such circumstances would seem absurd, yet despite the deconstruction of their societies and of their sense of themselves people continue to practise culture-building and socially-binding practices of equal — some would say, pre-eminent — significance. Chaos has not ensued.

Bureaucratisation is one such set of practices. Where the resources permit, the provision by the state of a wide range of goods and services requires administrators in large numbers. The more efficient the administrator the more effectively he or she will have learned the disciplines of discretion, precision, speed, deference to his or her superiors, and the discharge of his or her specialised duties in a self-effacing way. Individualism of any

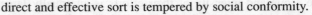

direct and effective sort is tempered by social conformity.

The same qualities are required in more commercial contexts. The result is invariably a kind of social machine, reliable and predictable and devoid of human idiosyncrasy, despite the quirks of its human components. Habitual, methodical and obedient behaviour is what the rigours of modernisation seem to be about. Despite the maelstrom of change within which we live a good deal of mechanistic human activity goes on as well, replete with compliance and depersonalisation rather than openness and self-development.

Consider also the rigours of city living and of urbanisation more generally, which is the most obvious adjunct to capitalist industrialism. Urban life is not yet the norm in the world, nor, indeed, is it new. A conspicuous feature of modern times, however, is the rapid increase in the number and size of large urban centres. The movement of people towards them constitutes the greatest mass migration in written history.

The impersonality of city life can be a welcome relief from the relationships of the village or town. It is exacerbated by the job specialisation a large human enterprise like a city requires to make it run. It is also exacerbated by the welter of human events city living provides. Events are consumed as objects by participant subjects, and remain outside the life-world of their audience who can feel, if not excluded, then largely irrelevant as a result.

Cities are, however, social machines. They work in regular and predictable ways, and would not be the desired social milieu for many of earth's people if they did not. As they alienate so they order, and for many the order is preferred, if only because it is so obviously made by humankind by and for themselves.

2. Who is critical of this culture and why?

Bull and Watson argue that international society rests upon a cosmopolitan culture of modernity. There has been nothing restful, however, about the dynamic way scientific, technological, commercial and diplomatic values have been globalised. The way in which cultural practices conducive to the modern state system in general and to industrial capitalism in particular have been promoted internationally, and the extent to which they have received popular acceptance, are key features of contemporary times.

Pre-eminent as a proselytiser for modernist values, since the last European war at least, has been the USA. Whether defending democracy, or making money, or both, United States culture-makers are ubiquitous.

Documenting the scope and intensity of their efforts is an equally large task. It is sufficient to take one small, eccentric and revealing example that instructs us 'How To Read Donald Duck'.

Ariel Dorfman and Armand Mattelart, the authors of this polemic, point out how much Walt Disney, as a contemporary culture-maker, has done to disseminate the sort of myths that sustain modernist culture of the American sort. Disney has been an important producer of cultural commodities. His work is not, however, value-neutral. It actively fosters a sense of 'innocence' supposedly universal, beyond place, beyond time — and beyond criticism.[15] It is argued that this sense has helped to legitimate commercial and political practices that in reality have been anything but innocent.

The USA is the liberal, hegemonic, grand capitalist power in the world. The myth of its innocence has long been dispelled by the policies of its state-makers and profit-takers. Their strategic and economic interventions have too often been too callous and too self-serving for anyone to consider them benevolent, yet the Great American Dream of cultural naiveté still pervades the global imagination. It still feeds the feeling that somehow any abuse can be justified or undone because it is ultimately all good, clean, wholesome, democratic, harmless, parent-approved Duckburg fun.

It is far from that, of course. Inside Mickey Mouse's little white glove, as Dorfman and Mattelart intimate, lie the greedy, supple fingers of the practised cultural entrepreneur. The values of purity, leisure and wealth that Disney comics promote, for example, are so much at odds with the lives of most of the reading audience that their promotion, as a profit-making mind-shaping venture, can only seem cynical, even grotesque.[16]

Dorfman and Mattelart wrote their text in 1971, in the midst of an attempt by a short-lived Chilean regime to rescue Chile from its neo-colonial dependence on the USA. The Chilean political–economy was dominated, then as now, by United States multinational corporations. The country, then as now, was heavily indebted, and though the state-makers of that short-lived regime did regain control of Chile's main assets, it proved much harder to counter the cultural influences of their capitalist antagonists. The Dorfman and Mattelart text was a specific part of that counteroffensive.

All such initiatives came to an end on 11 September 1973, with a violent counterrevolution mounted by the Chilean armed forces. Mickey and Donald were brought back to help obliterate any residual trace of socialism and to restore virtue and innocence to an ideologically corrupted country. Virtue and innocence? Mickey and Minnie Mouse, and Donald and Daisy Duck, are eternal fiances. There is no worldly love or sexuality in Disney's world. Furthermore, there are no parents since everyone is an uncle, a cousin or a nephew. The world of Disney has no primary family relationships; no paternal or maternal care.

It is also a world, as Dorfman and Mattelart demonstrate, where foreigners are primitive, being either barbarians or members of cultures in decline. They live in picturesque huts or tumbling-down towns. They are usually childlike and harmless, and where they are violent they are stupid or crass. They readily accept gifts, and in turn provide riches and treasures which they do not use themselves. They tend to confront mechanical objects as toys, their language is babyish, and their economy is most commonly a subsistence one. They are ruled by kings, and whenever a king is overthrown the monarchy is immediately restored. There is no religion. Their cultures radiate simple goodness. They have no industrial processes, no workers, and no-one ever dies.

This is, of course, a Marxist reading of Disney and not the only one possible. But it is a compelling account, drawing attention to how the relationships in Disney's world are:

> compulsively consumerist; commodities in the market-place of objects and ideas ... Under-developed peoples take the comics, at second hand, as instruction in the way they are supposed to live and relate to the foreign power center ... The misery of the Third World is packaged and canned to liberate the masters who produce it and consume it. Then, it is thrown-up to the poor as the only food they know. Reading Disney is like having one's own exploited condition rammed with honey down one's throat.[17]

Mattelart developed this analysis in a more general way in a work on multinational corporations and the control of culture.[18] In dissecting what he called the 'ideological apparatus of imperialism' he highlighted the sense of the struggle for survival and the urge to prevail that animates global image-makers. For United States state-makers and wealth-makers, for example, it is not just a matter of universalising United States political and business practices but of fostering the global acceptance of its legal practices, educational methods, administrative and managerial regimes, and popular mores and culture. At the same time as they seek to make universal the parochial value preferences of the USA, however, they also adapt them to local cultures. Which culture wins depends not only on what takes place but on one's view of what is taking place; whether, that is, one subscribes to the Trojan Horse theory (the values of the imperialist culture-makers being disguised and smuggled in as comics, TV soap operas and the like), or whether one believes that in the present phase of accumulation of capital, the internationalisation of business makes a wave of 'cultural nationalism.[19]

There is also a composite theory that posits the spread of Western culture as both adaptive and as a Trojan Horse; as cultural imperialism but in a decentralised form; as a kind of contextual practice which privileges the most camouflaged. The mediators in this theory are the national or (where nationalism is rudimentary or non-existent) the creole bourgeoisie. As mediators they service the world system at the same time as they seek to conserve their domestic hegemony. It is they who are the porous elements who must adapt the global to the local, while still working within the terms set by international industrial capitalism. It is they who must craft policies sufficiently parochial to sustain at least a modicum of legitimacy at home, while collaborating in the culture of the world political–economy.

These polemics are only two among the many of those that challenge the tenets of modernity. The whole concept has been called into question, and every aspect of the modern milieu has now been rendered problematic.

It is argued, for example, that modernity is merely propaganda for the liberal political–economy. It is no accident, perhaps, that the main protagonists of modernity have been industrial capitalists, who see themselves as the end products of all desirable change, as inherently progressive, and as quintessentially modern.

One way they have argued the case for modernism has been to draw a straight line with traditionals at one end and moderns (themselves) at the other. The modernising community is one that is proceeding along this line in the desirable direction.

Drawing such a line, and acting as if it had common credence, is highly questionable. For those who receive the results of modernisation, becoming modern is not necessarily all that marvellous, given that modernism has made possible the subordination of atomised individuals to high surveillance states and the capacity for species suicide, and that it has made many feel unhappy. Furthermore, those who have experienced the traditional for themselves have often found, or knew already, that in practice traditional means complex and highly sophisticated, particularly so when the criteria of complexity and sophistication being applied are not technological.

Non-technological criteria have, of course, been overshadowed at the moment by the singular success of scientists in providing reliable and cumulative knowledge, and in augmenting military power. Many of the victims of industrial capitalism have begun to feel, however, or have never forgotten, that non-technological criteria are no less important a measure of progress than those espoused by state-makers and wealth-makers.

The simple scale that links the traditional to the modern obscures the extent, for example, to which the failure to modernise in some parts of the world may be necessary for modernity to happen in others. Underdevelopment may be just as modern as development. Poverty and wealth may be the systematic outcome of one world process that has both effects.

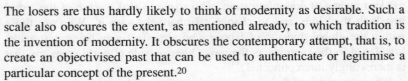

The losers are thus hardly likely to think of modernity as desirable. Such a scale also obscures the extent, as mentioned already, to which tradition is the invention of modernity. It obscures the contemporary attempt, that is, to create an objectivised past that can be used to authenticate or legitimise a particular concept of the present.[20]

The idea of modernity has also been questioned by a growing number of so-called critical theorists, who question the 'intellectual imperialism of the modern ..."scientific" approach to knowledge and society'.[21] Critical theory finds problematic the whole attempt to talk of human behaviour in terms of a detached and objectivised individualism. It stresses social, historical and cultural themes in ways that put them at odds with the rationality and materialism of science and technology. It highlights the way language is used to construct our sense of reality, and the seeming impossibility of ever getting objective knowledge. It leads to a comprehensive reassessment of the familiar ways in which we look at the world, and it casts doubt upon the way the story of the modern is told by all the major Western theoretical traditions.

The purpose of such critical theory, whatever its stripe, has not been to question modernity just for the sake thereof. Its main goal has been to open up and sanction a larger intellectual space within which such questions can be asked in the first place. It has been to extend our concerns so that 'voices otherwise marginalised can be heard ... questions otherwise suppressed can be asked ... points of analytical closure can be opened for debate ... [and] issues and arguments effectively dismissed from the mainstream can be seriously reconsidered and re-evaluated'.[22]

Jim George, whose words are cited above, gives as an example of good critical theory Walker's interrogation of the idea of one objectivised world, an idea that informs much thinking about international politics. He endorses Walker's notion of other worlds; of many worlds; of alternative realities derived from alternative readings of post-Renaissance European history. This notion is an important antidote to more conventional views, not least because it heightens our awareness of social movements and their contemporary significance.

3. When do such critics constitute social movements?

Whose voices come through the cracks to which critical theory draws attention? Who are the marginalised, now being heard in international politics despite their formal irrelevance? Who are the national groups who resist state status? Who are the religious groups who do likewise? Who are the feminists, the indigenes, the ordinary people confronting each other via modern means of communication, who strive to make sense of the world in which they live, and to change affirmatively with it? Who are those within the global division of labour who are effectively being cast aside, 'displaced to the margins as the new Other outside a world economy that is increasingly interconnected?'[23]

We make sense of these processes by acknowledging the contemporary significance of social movements. It is those who belong to such movements who are bringing a new dimension to the discourse of world affairs. What are social movements? In Walker's words they are 'part of a broad process of social invention that carries the possibility of reconstructing the conditions for a decent life from the bottom up'.[24] They are the more or less spontaneous efforts by underdogs to bring about social change, despite their marginalised status and lack of power in the conventional sense. Though formally powerless such groups are not helpless, given the Carrollian competences they possess and which many are now exercising in ways that directly impinge on world politics and world political–economy (see appendix 3).

Social movements, as inferred above, represent many different human concerns. They articulate a more or less coherent defence of peace, human rights, global ecology, women's rights, urban renewal, community identity, greater autonomy for indigenous peoples, a host of unconventional ideas about a preferred political economy, and survival itself, whether the threat be starvation or nuclear obliteration. Specific examples of social movements would include movements as diverse as the Polish Solidarity party before it came to power, the Chinese students who demonstrated in Tiananmen Square, the Greenpeace supporters of the *Rainbow Warrior*, and the women at Greenham Common. It would also include neo-fascist groups and religious fundamentalist groups.

Social movements are the result of immediate and particular experiences and they arise, it seems, when societies are stressed or distressed.[25] They are people's response to a future perceived as threatening. The response is not, however conventional. If it were, the social movement concerned would be vulnerable to police, military, material, or ideological repression or co-option, and would soon cease to be a social movement.

Why are we seeing social movements in such numbers? With the exception of environmental movements, they are not new. If they grow out of particular experiences, and under conditions of social stress and distress, what are those experiences? What are the contemporary sources of stress and distress?

In line with the discussion of modernity above, one key source would seem to lie in the fact that society 'no longer has a nature, it is no longer based on any value or invariant; it is only what it makes itself, for better or for worse'.[26] To reiterate the Marxian vision of bourgeois capitalism, perhaps the sense that (modern) society is nothing but the changing, unstable, loosely coherent product of social relations, cultural innovations, and political processes has something to do with it. This picture certainly applies to world society where change, 'necessary, unceasing, and enforced' is the 'order' of the day.[27]

Change prompts people to respond, and their response is not always progressive. The age of the European enlightenment, for example, that of the eighteenth century, saw those who exalted rationality prevail over tradition-minded aristocrats. One consequence of the triumph of intellectual reason, however, was rationality carried to extremes. Reforms effected in the name of this sort of enlightenment led to un-reason of the most reactionary sort. The ideals of the French revolution, for example, became in part the ideology of a victorious bourgeoisie, and workers were shot in the name of the republic. The seeds were also sown for a compound European imperialism that was to cost earth's people dearly.

The nineteenth century saw science and scientific thinking exalted as the way to liberate all humankind. Science was billed as reason's most productive child. Progress was universal, providing more for more people than had ever been dreamed possible. The negative aspect of such progress, however, was the proletarianisation of millions of men and women at home, and imperialism abroad, as already mentioned.

The twentieth century saw science and scientific thinking carried to new heights and depths. Progress, now called technological advancement and global development, eliminated smallpox. It also made genocide possible. Ruthless regimes were not slow to use the tools that rational thought made possible. Nazis systematically used 'high-tech' means to murder millions of Jews, Slavs, political dissidents, gypsies and homosexuals. Stalin, with his policy of forced industrialisation, killed more than twice as many people in constructing the modern Soviet state.

Mass assassination was also perpetrated by more covert and indirect means. The deaths of uncounted millions around the world can fairly be attributed to the construction of a capitalist world economy that has always prized profit before the meeting of human needs. The marketeers of Europe and the USA have much to answer for in this regard. Meanwhile, like Damocles' sword, there has hung over the whole world for more than a generation now the daily threat of thermonuclear holocaust.

Change, in other words, affects different people differently. In Touraine's terms we can segregate local societies, and world society in general, into three key categories: players, who develop the strategies of change; operatives, who execute them; and a large mass of the marginalised. In this last category Touraine places the unemployed, the inhabitants of underdeveloped or underdeveloping regions, members of dominated ethnic groups, temporary workers, workers in subcontracting firms (mostly women), peace activists, feminists and environmentalists.

These three categories, Touraine says, are not classes. They are not defined by relations of production as master to slave or industrial capitalist to industrial labourer. They are defined rather by their relationship to change: the players leading change; the operatives protected from change; and the marginals suffering it. [28]

Marginals may well constitute the majority of earth's inhabitants. They are certainly mostly poor. They also mostly live in poor countries. The rest dwell elsewhere in the third world, as well as the second and first worlds. The liberal diffusion of the world's wealth does not reach them, nor does economic imperialism since neither they nor their resources are worth exploiting.

This has led to a huge hiatus in global vision. In Hoogvelt's words:

> [u]nable to free ourselves from the chains of the capitalist world economy, we cannot or will not concern ourselves with the plight of those who are increasingly expelled from that same world economy. We may try to understand, and improve, the conditions of life of those who live within our world system, we cannot even think about those outside it. [29]

4. In what respect are social movements the keepers of the moral flame?

Social movements provide an opportunity to voice dissent from, even to mitigate the effects of, reactionary change. To say that social movements are the keepers of the moral flame is to say that the state and the market are not; that state-makers and wealth-makers are indifferent to what is right and wrong.

The ideology of state-makers is not amoral, but it certainly marginalises moral behaviour. It has led us, for one thing, to the brink of species suicide. There have been few notable displays of moral distress along the way.

Even when state-makers have adopted a righteous policy in the form, for example, of sanctions against South Africa, such practices have resulted as much from the pressure on state-makers of domestic social movements as from any innate sensibilities on the part of state-makers themselves. The ideology of non-interference in the affairs of others remains the basic norm. The order imposed by state-makers through the state system as a whole is what they value most.

The market is no better. In liberal terms free enterprise benefits all, however, the manifest disparities in wealth between rich and poor both within and between states suggest that the market is not as morally neutral a concept as liberals suppose. Marxists never believed it was. Those who think that no-one deserves to live in poverty, that many living in wealth do not deserve to do so, and that it is no use waiting for the logic of capitalism and the laws of history to emancipate the repressed and the destitute, have to look beyond wealth-makers for the radical changes required.

For those who must fight what is all too often a losing battle to meet their basic needs, living a dignified, creative life is well-nigh impossible. Looking to state-makers for help is unrealistic since they either are the marginalisers themselves or collaborate with them. An attempt to assume state-making power itself would likely mean co-option, and the subsequent negation of radical grievance. Waiting for the class war that results in socialism is tantamount to waiting for Godot.

The alternative need not be inaction. It might be the exercise of one of the Carrollian competences identified earlier. Social movements have no military power. They have no economic power. They have only their sense of outrage and the moral purpose such outrage springs from and serves. Their appeal is directly to values denied or neglected by technocratic, modernist modes of government and production. Such a sense and such an appeal can be important political forces, however, as recent events in Eastern Europe proved.

Some social movements are reactionary. In this sense they are hardly custodians of the human conscience, and of what is fair or just. Though motivated by a sense of what is right or wrong, they would be better designated forces of darkness than of light. One would be hard pressed to call a racist riot an example of a social movement that keeps the moral flame alight, unless one were racist oneself.

Some social movements promise the security of a golden age, for example a return to seventh century Islam, or bucolic communalism. Though not always or necessarily evil, neither are such groups particularly progressive.

Whether a social movement advocates going to these extremes or not, it is usually a sense of injustice, of repression, of lack of opportunity or ill-being, that motivates most of its members. That sense will be a personal one. The experience of oppression or exploitation can be both close and strong. It can be readily apparent in daily life, and need not be imagined. To quote Andre Gunder Frank and Marta Fuentes: 'the more powerful and uncontrollable the forces of the world economy [and, one might add, the state system] ... the more do they generate social movements ... which claim both autonomy and immunity from these world economic [and strategic] forces and which promise to overcome them or to isolate their members from them'. [30] The autonomy claimed above is a moral one. The immunity also mentioned denotes ethical antibodies, not military or economic ones.

The values social movements espouse are the key to their appeal, in other words, which comes from the 'moral force of their promise to free their participants from the deeply felt unjust (threat of) deprivation of material necessities, social status, and cultural identity ... [O]bjectively irrational hopes of salvation appear as subjectively rational appeals to confront reality'. [31]

The moral purpose of social movements has led many explicitly to espouse the doctrine of human rights, or one or more of its specific strictures. Human rights are moral claims. They are strong claims; rights talk is strong talk; and the doctrine attempts to define the basic standards any culture must meet in the treatment of its members if it is to warrant civilised status. The United Nations Universal Declaration of Human Rights provides a specific and quite comprehensive list of such entitlements.

The articles in the Declaration have only the force of common agreement behind them. There is nothing graven in granite on the subject, which means that these rights rest only on the arguments given for them. Since rights are strong claims, the reasons have to be good ones to sustain them. What is considered good differs from one moral tradition to another, which made initial agreement on a single list difficult and, because of differing interpretations of specific articles, hard to sustain. The interesting thing is that global agreement was ever reached. Enforcement has remained superficial and uneven, but the Declaration remains the first and only broad statement of minimum moral standards to have received universal recognition.

The point here is that agreement of this sort does empower people. It is strong knowledge in itself. Knowing what has been universally affirmed does strengthen people's sense of purpose and inspires them to express their feelings of frustration or outrage. It is this sense that has inspired many contemporary social movements. In this sense such movements are the latest chapter in a long saga of social struggles for civil freedom, equality of opportunity, and global relationships that are harmonious and free.

Their victories are rarely obvious or direct. Where social movements are actively repressed they can use only covert means to make their point. If we return to Carroll's analysis of power as competence, however, we find that the disintegrative, inertial, explosive or innovative potential of social movements may be manifest only in the longer term. They may do their most effective work in an indirect way, over extended periods of time, subverting the myths that make the status quo seem invulnerable, and providing deeply valued alternatives to its moral ideals and political and economic practices.

Being partial, fragmented, and dispersed, social movements tend to stay that way, never mounting more than sporadic and marginal raids on the powers that be. Confined to their own immediate concerns, social movements are usually of limited political relevance in the short term. In many a peace body, for example, the difficulties of defining what peace means in a positive sense, that is, as other than the absence of war, can lead to endless debate about purpose and how to proceed. Whether mounting spontaneous demonstrations of their peace awareness (demonstrations, camps, marches, occasional acts of violence and the like) or making more structured attempts to pressure state-makers to abjure the war option and, in particular, eschew the use of nuclear weapons, such groups can remain largely peripheral.

Ecological movements likewise find it difficult to agree on their general goals. The members of such movements who hold utopian and anarchistic ideas about what is to be done and how to do it find themselves at loggerheads with the more pragmatic activists, who are more prepared to accept compromise. The same applies to feminist movements where arguments for reforming patriarchal and fraternal systems by winning more opportunities for women within them are counterposed by those who would see these arguments as reinforcing such systems rather than reforming them. For the latter, much more radical efforts are required to effect true equality of opportunity.

None of this is to decry the moral fervour which animates the sense the members of such movements may have of their particular cause. It is only to point out the difficulties moral fervour itself can present.

The big issues persist nonetheless. If high productivity and the ethic of non-stop economic growth, whether liberal capitalist or command socialist, should fail to deal adequately with the ecological consequences of endless wealth-making; if the plight of the unemployed and the poor should continue to worsen; if material progress should lead not to people's affirmation but their growing despair, then we can expect to see them turning, as they have in the past, to common interest groups and a wide range of social surrogates — an enhanced sense of nationalism among them — to survive.

The issue of survival is spiritual as well as physical. The turn to common interest groups denotes the social decision not to feel so alienated and the aim, however unformed, of making public policy, economic planning, and the environment — both material and moral — something more habitable for human beings. An important tool, given current constraints on populist resolve, might well be social movements. Should that be the case it would mean a new lease of life for an old paradigm of oppositional discourse. [32]

Notes

1 J. Holzgrefe, 'The Origins of Modern International Relations Theory', *Review of International Studies* vol. 15, 1989, p. 17. See also J. Der Derian, *On Diplomacy: a genealogy of Western estrangement*, Basil Blackwell, Oxford, 1987.

2 H. Bull & A. Watson (eds), *The Expansion of International Society*, Clarendon Press, Oxford, 1984, p. 433.

3 M. Berman, *All That Is Solid Melts Into Air: The Experience of Modernity*, Simon & Schuster, New York, 1982, pp. 87-129.

4 ibid., p. 435.

5 See the use of this (common) distinction by H. Marcuse, *One-Dimensional Man: the Ideology of Industrial Society*, Sphere, London, 1968, p. 130. Also R. Williams, *Keywords* (rev. edn), Fontana, London, 1983, pp. 252-6. There are, if Foucault is to be believed, three modes of objectification, not one. Each transforms human beings into subjects. The first is the scientific perspective described here. The second includes what he calls the dividing practices, that turn people into the sick and the healthy, for example, or the criminal and the good. The third involves the way human beings turn themselves into subjects, for example, by learning to recognise themselves as subjects of sexuality. The second two are clearly derived from the first. See M. Foucault 'The Subject and Power', *Critical Inquiry* vol. 8, Summer 1982, pp. 777-8. The anthropologically particular character of the concept of person implicit here, and its oddness as an example of possibilities within the world's cultures, is well caught by C. Geertz, '"From the Natives Point of View": On the Nature of Anthropological Understanding' in M. Gibbons (ed.), *Interpreting Politics*, Basil Blackwell, Oxford, 1987.

6 L. Mumford, *Technics and Civilization*, George Routledge & Sons, London, 1934, pp. 14-15.

7 ibid., p. 362.

8 A. Shultz, *A Theory of Consciousness*, Philosophical Library, New York, 1973, p. 425.

9 J. Caporaso, 'Labor in the Global Economy' in J. Caporaso (ed.), *A Changing International Division of Labor*, Lynne Rienner Publishers, Boulder, 1987, p. 221.

10 B. Moore, *Social Origins of Dictatorship and Democracy*, Penguin, Harmondsworth, 1966, p. 506.

11 K. Marx & F. Engels, *Manifesto of the Communist Party*, Foreign Languages Press, Peking, 1975, pp. 36-7. The further predisposition of industrial culture to violence and instability is explored, among many others, by A. Jones, 'The violence of materialism in advanced industrial society: an eco-sociological approach', *Sociological Review* vol. 35 no. 1, 1987, pp. 19-47.

12 M. Berman, op. cit., p. 99.

13 K. Marx & F. Engels, op. cit., p. 99.

14 M. Berman, op. cit., p. 113.
15 D. Kunzle, 'Introduction to the English Edition' of A. Dorfman & A. Mattelart, *How to Read Donald Duck: imperialist ideology in the Disney comic*, International General, New York, 1984, p. 11.
16 loc. cit.
17 ibid., pp. 96, 98.
18 A. Mattelart, *Multinational Corporations and the Control of Culture: the ideological apparatuses of imperialism*, Harvester Press, Sussex, 1979.
19 ibid., p. 231.
20 See L. Rudolph & S. Rudolph, *The Modernity of Tradition: political development in India*, University of Chicago Press, Chicago, 1967, particularly the introduction; also E. Hobsbawm & T. Ranger (eds), *The Invention of Tradition*, Cambridge University Press, Cambridge, 1983, ch. 1.
21 J. George, 'International Relations and the Search for Thinking Space: another view of the third debate', *International Studies Quarterly* vol. 33 no. 3, September 1989, p. 270.
22 ibid., p. 273. See also A. Heller, 'Marx and Modernity', *Thesis Eleven* no. 8, 1984, pp. 44-58 and P. Rosenau, 'Once Again Into the Fray: International Relations Confronts the Humanities', *Millenium* vol. 19 no. 1, Spring 1990, pp. 83-110.
23 R. Walker, 'The Concept of Culture in the Theory of International Relations' in J. Chay (ed.), *Culture and International Relations*, Praeger, New York, 1989. See also his 'World Politics and Western Reason: Universalism, Pluralism, Hegemony' in R. Walker (ed.), *Culture, Ideology and World Order*, Westview Press, Boulder, 1984, particularly section III, 'The Concept of Culture and Its Contradictions'. Categorising social movements has become a sociological industry in its own right. See, for example, the whole issue of *Social Research*, vol. 52 no. 4, Winter 1985, as well as J. Pakulski, *Social Movements: the politics of moral protest*, Longman Cheshire, Melbourne, 1990. For a social psychological perspective, see B. McLaughlin (ed.), *Studies in Social Movements*, The Free Press, New York, 1969.
24 R. Walker, *One World, Many Worlds: struggles for a just world peace*, Lynne Rienner Publishers, Boulder, 1988, p. 8. See also K.-W. Brandt, 'New Social Movements as a Metapolitical Challenge: the social and political impact of a new historical type of protest', *Thesis Eleven* no. 15, 1986, pp. 60-8.
25 ibid., pp. 29, 26.
26 A. Touraine, 'Triumph or downfall of civil society', *Humanities Review* vol. 1, 1982, p. 220.
27 ibid., p. 219.
28 ibid., p. 223.
29 A. Hoogvelt, *The Third World in Global Development*, Macmillan, London, 1982, p. 214.
30 A. Frank & M. Fuentes, 'Nine Theses on Social Movements', *Thesis Eleven* nos 18/19, 1987/88, p. 159.
31 loc. cit.
32 C. Boggs, *Social Movements and Political Power: emerging forms of radicalism in the West*, Temple University Press, Philadelphia, 1986, p. 4.

7

The balance of ideologies

What is ideology in the context of international politics? What is the balance of ideologies? How should we read world thought in this regard? What does such a reading tell us about the invisible dimension of gender?

1. What is ideology in the context of international politics? What is the balance of ideologies?

An industrialising world of competing and colluding state-makers and of competing and colluding wealth- and class-makers is highly complex. It is one in which ideas, though never to be divorced from those who have them and from the material contexts in which they live, can and do take on a life of their own. As Lewis Mumford once argued: 'Every culture lives within its dream'.[1]

The dreams, the visions that people share, are perhaps their most powerful possession. International politics, in the most comprehensive sense, is no less a place of dreams and visions and, some would argue, is becoming increasingly so. Thus Stanley Hoffmann has described international politics as:

> in considerable part the product of a conflict of wills, of a contest of active perceptions competing for the privilege of defining reality ... When force loses some of its prominence, power — my exercise of control over you — becomes the art of making you see the world the way I see it, and of making you behave in accordance with that vision. International politics in the past was often an arena of coercion without persuasion; it is tending to become an arena of persuasion, more or less coercive.[2]

How does one assess a conclusion like this? Is the world becoming an arena of persuasion, more or less coercive? Certainly coercion without persuasion is still commonplace. However, so is the attempt to win hearts and minds. And what about that grey area where coercion and persuasion merge into one another, where coercion occurs in more subtle forms, shaping convictions by non-violent means, or where by coercion we establish some discrete domain within which only one kind of argument is allowed, thus pre-empting debate and making persuasion unnecessary?

Whatever we make of questions like these in global terms, implicit and often explicit in what is happening today is not just a struggle for some kind of productive advantage, not just a race for local or global strategic parity or superiority, but a battle for the 'world mind'. (The concept of the world mind denotes what people are thinking, wherever on earth they live.)

The balance of ideologies

This battle has three dimensions. It can be construed, most obviously, as the psychological (ideological) component of any conflict between the makers of states. The world, in terms of the disposition of military forces, has been dominated by the central balance between the USA and the Soviet Union. The most important ideological confrontation (lately mitigated) is likewise, and not coincidentally, that between these same two states. ('States' in this regard should be read not as sovereign territories, with lines of inclusion and exclusion drawn on the ground, but as states of mind, with the lines drawn in citizens' heads.)

This confrontation was most acute during the Cold War. The two sets of state-makers concerned were each convinced of the thoroughly malevolent intent of the other. The Cold War was not only about military might. Although each side maintained large standing armies, there were violent clashes by proxy over respective spheres of influence, and both sets of state-makers were wont to retreat to the trees, from the tops of which they would posture obscenely with their nuclear bananas.

The Cold War was also about the comparative potency of the competing ideologies of the respective state-makers, and of their more or less patriotic citizens. It was a sustained attempt to establish the superiority of liberal capitalism as opposed to command socialism, with the rest of the world either looking on or taking sides.

State-making is idea-mongering itself, of course, since the state, however determined in the last instance by material life, is an ideological construct. 'States ... define, in great detail, acceptable forms and images of social activity and individual and collective identity; they regulate, in empirically specifiable ways, much — very much, by the twentieth century — of social life'.[3] Thus we find state-makers fostering nationhood (the 'illusory community' as Marx called it); fostering, that is, a solidarist 'us' and an alien 'them', the latter to be found both within and without. Thus the state, while a descriptive label and seemingly 'neutral, natural, universal, [and] obvious' is an 'impositional claim ... The idea of the state', as Weber stressed, 'is a "claim" to legitimacy'.[4]

The second dimension of the battle for the world mind is the ideological component of the story of world development. This story can be told either in terms of the market and the material and social gains to be made from free enterprise, or in terms of modes of production, exploited labour, and unequal economic exchange. In the latter case, for example, attention is drawn to the way the bourgeoisie at the world's productive centres exploit and fragment the wage-workers at the periphery, relying on hegemonic influence rather than co-ordinated oppression to do so.

Both the liberal and Marxist stories have variants. Each offers different explanations for world poverty, and together they have inspired a number of different prescriptions for how state-makers and wealth-makers and people in general should act to achieve greater material well-being.

The third dimension of the battle for the world mind is between the scientific mode of cognition and the sorts of understandings that preceded it, or that persist still in many minds, or that seek to displace or transcend it today. It talks about the extent to which modern ways of thinking and feeling have supplanted non-modern ones, only to be challenged in turn by those who find the ideology of rationalism that lies at the heart of the modernist enterprise in some way inhumane.

These three sites of mental struggle are brought together by the concept of the balance of ideologies. This concept can now take its place in the analytic narrative beside the concept of the balance of power (narrowly construed as the distribution of military power) and the balance of productivity (read in either neo-mercantilist, liberal or Marxist terms).

If proponents of the balance of power took their own concept seriously enough, of course, they would use its portmanteau character to account for general and local balances of productive and ideological as well as military significance. They would develop the concept of the balance of power in a comprehensive way, describing and explaining its material and mental dimensions as well as its political and strategic ones. However, they don't. They typically fail to do justice to political–economy, hence the need for a separate concept, the balance of productivity. They also fail to do justice to the ideological domain, hence the need for the notion of a balance of ideologies. By providing specific labels for these neglected dimensions, we can see more clearly their full significance.

What is ideology?

Ideology denotes ideas in action; ideas in practice; ideas used as levers for change. The emphasis is on practice, since it is actions that make for change, not ideas as such. The privacy of introspection becomes socially relevant only when it engages the world in public ways; when it becomes an ideology. Ideas have power, in other words, only in concrete contexts where they articulate capacities of another sort — military, political, political-economic, or spiritual.

As Michael Howard once put it, 'the word is commonly used to describe a particularly rigorous, comprehensive and dogmatic set of interrelated values, based on a systematic philosophy which claims to provide coherent and unchallengeable answers to all the problems of mankind ... When we speak of an ideologue ... we mean: a priest of a secular religion'. In addition to this definition Howard cites a 'broader, looser, and less codifiable' use of the term that is used to refer to a 'value-system, a "mind-set".'[5]

The word was coined in the eighteenth century by the rationalists of the European enlightenment to describe what they believed was a new science; a science of ideas.[6] They saw what they were doing as very different from traditional metaphysics, though their inspiration came from the ancient Greek metaphysicians (literally, 'those who enquire into non-physical affairs using principles appropriate to physical ones').

The revolutionary nature of the step these thinkers took was appreciated at once by conservative critics, who saw and disliked its inherent democratic possibilities. If people were encouraged to think in systematic and objective ways they were quite likely to use their thoughts as reasons for changing the world. This was quite likely to put established privilege at risk, as indeed it did. Science, after all, fosters technology. From scientific theories about how the world works flow prescriptive ideologies about how it might work better, and this applies to the social as well as the physical realm.

The conservative response, then, was to decry the whole notion of a science of ideas as 'abstract, impractical or fanatical'.[7] It was to render the term pejorative, as in the use of the double standard: 'I have a doctrine; you have an ideology'. This was not the only attack on the concept. Since the idea of a science of ideas implied a realm of thought detached from any material and historical context, it was also criticised by the decidedly unconservative Karl Marx.

Marx sought to establish the practical ground of all such mental figuring, including his own.

> We set out from real, active men and on the basis of their real life-process we demonstrate the development of the ideological reflexes and echoes of this life-process. The phantoms formed in the human brain are ...

necessarily, sublimates of their material life-process, [however], which is empirically verifiable and bound to material premises. Morality, religion, metaphysics, all the rest of ideology and their corresponding forms of consciousness, thus no longer retain the semblance of independence. They have no history; no development; but men, developing their material production and their material intercourse, alter, along with this their real existence, their thinking and the products of their thinking. Life is not determined by consciousness, but consciousness by life.[8]

Calling ideas phantoms suggests they are illusions. Calling them forms of consciousness suggests something more tangible and less false, though always expressive of how people live, and the conditions under which they do so. Given that different people live in different ways, however, might there not be many ideologies, rather than one universalist, rationalist and scientific ideology? The prospect that there might be contravenes the claim of the term's originators to have found an Archimedean point somewhere outside the real world from which they might unambiguously know it and move it. It questions, in other words, the whole project of the European enlightenment.

Such a critique renders knowing highly problematic in every respect. We all, in this sense, become ideologists. Short of death, we can't escape the material conditions of our existence and hence, by the logic above, we can't have ideas that are unconditioned and free. Nor can we know a priori that the science of ideas is superior to any other mode of cognition. There is no place to know from. To know in this sense is not, as rationalists would have it, to 'construct a coherent representation that excludes contesting interpretations and controls meaning from the standpoint of a pure presence, a sovereign identity already in place'; one that is 'beyond history and independent of politics'. To know is also (or rather) a process of representation. As such, in Ashley's words, knowing 'cannot re-present a pure presence already given. None simply and self-evidently exists. A work of representation can only be a work of writing meaning: a work that imposes a territorial ground, a domicile of being, a mode of subjectivity capable of deciding meaning'; a site of struggle, no less, where ideas are actions and 'power is conspicuously at work'.[9]

From such a perspective there can be no perspective. Despite Ashley's own lapse at this point into radical rationalism there can be no overview, no point up high, other than the point we make for ourselves. There can only be 'motion, discontinuities, clashes, and the ceaseless play of plural forces and plural interpretations on the surface of human experience'. There can, in other words, be 'no constants, no fixed meanings, no secure grounds, no profound secrets, no final structures'. There can only be a 'historically fabricated network of multiple themes, concepts, narratives, and practices that can be ordered, recombined, dispersed, and relatively stressed'.[10]

The outcome, as the last sentence suggests, is a virulent relativism. It becomes seemingly impossible to establish a hierarchy of values, or to say that one ideology is not only different from another, but better or worse than it. On reflection, however, relativism is not as problematic as this. It is only impossible in the light of the above to establish a lasting hierarchy of values, not a hierarchy as such. A lasting hierarchy would hardly remain relevant to human affairs for long anyway, since human affairs change. A lasting hierarchy of values would denote static, stereotyped practices that would eventually become irrelevant, repressive, or both.

This suggests a way to proceed. If we are not unduly arrogant or ambitious and if we don't presume to make value judgements that will hold for all time and in all places then there is nothing to stop us making such judgements. We have to be prepared, however, to reformulate the value hierarchies we build in the light of the arguments and circumstances of the day. The judgements we make using this relative kind of relativism consequently may never be conclusive. The arguments never end, and there is always a danger in their not doing so. We do know, however, that if they did end, likely so would we.

2. How should we read world thought in this regard?

The most potent of the contemporary ideas in action are the Westernising ones. (Potency does not mean superiority. The judgement in this regard is about spheres of influence, not about intrinsic merit.) Not only is the ideology of the West self-consciously universalistic, it has been aggressively universalised. Ever since the thinkers of the European enlightenment first provided a coherent formulation of it, state-makers and wealth-makers have used it to rationalise their ambitions. Indeed, the ideology was formulated in no small part to articulate those ambitions in the first place. The key aspect of it, namely rationalism (objectifying reason), can now be seen enacted in every aspect of human living, world-wide. Earth's people continue, of course, even when they use the same words, to mean many different things by them. However, the degree of global uniformity in material and mental life that has been achieved in modern times is unique.

Modernity again, and non-modernity

A phase like this in the patterning of world thought (without which it would not be meaningful to talk of world thought at all) is, however, only a phase. We have been living with modernity long enough now to realise how dependent and parochial it is, and that it is regressive as well as progressive. However appealing rationalism may be to the state-makers, wealth-makers and mind-shapers of the world, and however successful they may be in getting people's acceptance of the concepts and values involved, many people (and whole peoples) continue to or have come to resist the modernist presumption that the 'different must always be resolved into the same'. They continue to be, or they have become, 'increasingly wary of the extent to which the analysis of structural transformation remains caught within what are essentially seventeenth and eighteenth century [European] conceptions ... which do not seem to be very useful in understanding the implications of either contemporary military technologies or the global rearticulations and velocities of capital'.[11]

The resistance of custom to modernist mores is fairly easy to explain. Cultures are never static, but are always changing. There are always innovations from within, or new influences to be accommodated from without. Even where people want to change, however, and to incorporate new ideas and practices into their lives, they find large or rapid change difficult to adjust to. Most people show a marked preference for the familiar, and have a profound psychological capacity to rescue and retain it in the face of contradictory ideologies. They seek to conserve a specific and safe understanding of how the world works. Indeed, the modernist ideology of traditionalism itself, as indicated in the previous chapter, has been one such response.

One particularly striking example of custom at work in a non-modernist way is that of the cargo cults of Melanesia. These cults represented an ingenious attempt to deal with the novelty of white men and women in terms of Melanesian ideas of the cosmos, while at the same time laying claim to the new commodities the whites brought with them. In traditional Melanesian parlance, for example, every commodity, from pigs to sweet potatoes, had its own god. Rituals ensured that each god provided each commodity as required. When white missionaries came they talked of a special God called Jehovah. For specific groups of Melanesians this became the deity to contact when they wanted to secure modern goods, or 'cargo'. The rituals were improvised, and included the building of life-size replicas of aeroplanes out of bush materials. These were placed on landing strips as lures to entice real planes down from the sky, where their cargo could be unloaded by those below.

Using this wrongly-conceived but sophisticated ideology, Melanesians were able to assimilate into their own belief systems the highly disruptive influence of the newcomers, as well as their material possessions, and even their spiritual ideas. They were able to maintain essentially intact their own familiar cosmic concepts, and their own ideological frameworks as these pertained to production and consumption. It must be emphasised that neither were they fools. They were no less perceptive and adaptive than any other people in the world. Indeed, there are clear parallels between this sort of behaviour and contemporary accounts of how scientific revolutions proceed.[12]

Eventually, as anomalies proliferate within, it becomes harder and harder to preserve a belief system intact. If an old paradigm is no longer able to solve problems simply, in a way that unifies the apparent diversity of events, and if it no longer makes accurate predictions, then ideological turmoil ensues. A new paradigm is devised, usually by younger minds, which is better able to explain the anomalies in what is happening. Even then the adherents of the old paradigm usually prefer to grow old and die with their preconceptions intact rather than have to revise them.

In this respect scientists in general, and social scientists in particular, are little different from the cargo cultists of Melanesia. Modern-day rationalists would see themselves as ultimately more open-minded than this. They would defend the rational use of reason — its capacity to objectify — as less likely to produce ideological closure, and as more likely to question custom. They would see their pottering dialogue with the unknown as much more productive of cumulative knowledge, and as more creative. Is it a dialogue or is it, as critical theorists would now argue, more a monologue? Does it really open the mind, or does it lead to more subtle forms of closure, manifest in more subtle forms of social and political repression?

The post-modernist resistance to modernist mores doesn't only take the form of the intellectual critique touched upon here. The social movements (of which cargo cults wouuld be one, albeit traditionalising, example), also discussed in the previous chapter, are often clear expressions of such resistance, and their opposition takes many different forms. As anti-modernists, the members of social movements espouse alternatives to the universalising progress of modernity and its relativistic nihilism. They give voice to a wide range of particular and affirmative ideologies, and make it possible to reconceptualise universality in non-modernist ways. They are symptomatic of a growing inability on the part of state- and wealth-makers to appear authoritative and hence legitimate. And they have opened up post-modernist possibilities that objectifying reason, in the name of bureaucratic rationality for example, or technological progress, has tended to close. [13]

Meanwhile, however, the Westernisation of the world proceeds apace. Its scientific-industrial values are familiar to, if not actively shared by, the world's state-makers and wealth-makers. The same goes, to a varying and lesser extent, for those who inhabit the states that these people make; for those who work for their productive enterprises or buy their goods and

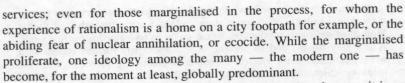

services; even for those marginalised in the process, for whom the experience of rationalism is a home on a city footpath for example, or the abiding fear of nuclear annihilation, or ecocide. While the marginalised proliferate, one ideology among the many — the modern one — has become, for the moment at least, globally predominant.

This is the big battle. It is, in a sense, the hardest to see because it is so pervasive and so profound. This gives problems of perspective, since it is difficult to know what is happening, and more particularly what is going to happen, from where we stand, which is, despite our much-vaunted objectivity, in the middle of it all. There is also a problem of coherence. Given the wide range of ideas that Europeans have entertained in the last few hundred years it can seem more than a little crude to lump them all together under the label of rationalism, or see them all as ultimately derivative of one such concept. There is a third problem, however, in that the minds of those involved do not live in one mass. Part of the Westernising of the world has involved the making of nations and states. The story of world thought cannot be told without describing how the ideologies of statism and nationalism have been used to weld people into territorial aggregates.

Statism and nationalism

This story has been told in part in earlier chapters. Here it will suffice only to emphasise the importance of state-making and nation-making as ideological enterprises. State-making, for example, involves not only establishing a particular form of government (policy-making), particular ways of implementing governmental decisions (administrating), particular coercive practices (military and police enforcement), and particular forms of adjudication and incarceration (court-rulings and imprisonment). It also involves less overtly dominant and less potentially violent institutions, which Louis Althusser calls 'ideological state apparatuses'. Under this heading he specifically identifies religion, public and private schools, the family, political groups and parties, the legal profession, trade unions, the press, radio and television, as well as literature, the arts and sport.[14]

In pre-capitalist Europe, Althusser argues, the predominant ideological apparatus was that of the church, which performed 'not only religious functions, but also educational ones, and a large proportion of the functions of communications and "culture" as well'.[15] In contemporary Europe, however, and in its derivatives around the world, he sees the school as the dominant ideological state apparatus. It is in school that the young are systematically coached in what they need to know to keep the world going.

In Althusser's view, the school takes children from an early age and inculcates a:

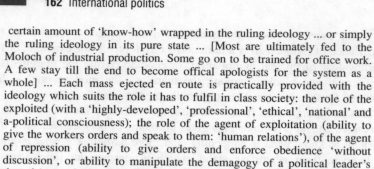

certain amount of 'know-how' wrapped in the ruling ideology ... or simply the ruling ideology in its pure state ... [Most are ultimately fed to the Moloch of industrial production. Some go on to be trained for office work. A few stay till the end to become offical apologists for the system as a whole] ... Each mass ejected en route is practically provided with the ideology which suits the role it has to fulfil in class society: the role of the exploited (with a 'highly-developed', 'professional', 'ethical', 'national' and a-political consciousness); the role of the agent of exploitation (ability to give the workers orders and speak to them: 'human relations'), of the agent of repression (ability to give orders and enforce obedience 'without discussion', or ability to manipulate the demagogy of a political leader's rhetoric), or of the professional ideologist (ability to treat consciousnesses with the respect, i.e. with the contempt, blackmail, and demagogy they deserve), adapted to the accents of Morality, of Virtue, of 'Transcendence', of the Nation, [or] of ... World Role.[16]

Althusser is a Marxist and his critique of schools and schooling is part of a larger, highly deterministic argument about the reproduction of the social relationships that make capitalist exploitation possible. His analysis is general enough to apply to state-making, wherever there are the resources to see it through. Even in an ostensibly Marxist state like the Soviet Union schooling could be described in similarly cynical terms. Of course, the Soviets would say that they have what amounts to a doctrine rather than an ideology in the pejorative sense. They would argue that, far from indoctrinating their young, they provide them with the skills with which to understand the world and to make their own contribution to it. They are, however, not immune from Althusser's argument.

For many of the world's state-makers, particularly the newer ones, inculcating a sense of a singular nation that coincides with the borders of the state is their most urgent task. Their own legitimacy is derived in no small part from fostering the feeling of one land–one people, and an obvious place to push for such a sentiment is the schools.

That 'imagined community floating in homogeneous, empty time' that is the idea of the nation is an integral part of the ideology of the Western state.[17] Its significance did not escape the notice of those who led movements for colonial self-determination, particularly the literate and bilingual ones. Indeed, they turned it back on their imperial overlords as part of the claim for independence. They were themselves typically products of colonial school systems that had nation-making consequences, even where these systems did not have nation-making intentions.

These schools drew from far and wide, though not typically from outside the colonial domain. Thus:

the tender pilgrims made their inward, upward way, meeting fellow-pilgrims from different, perhaps once hostile, villages in primary school; from different ethnolinguistic groups in middle-school; and from every part of the realm in the tertiary institutions of the capital [or of the metropole, where the capital had none]. And they knew that from wherever they had come they still had read the same books and done the same sums. They also knew, even if they never got so far ... that all these journeyings derived their 'sense' from the capital, in effect explaining why 'we' are 'here' 'together'.[18]

The consequence, as in the West, was to make 'nation-ness ... virtually inseparable from political consciousness'. [19]

The general picture sketched above would apply to most of the colonies of the nineteenth century European powers. I have given earlier my reading of the story of industrial capitalism and the extraordinary way capitalists propelled themselves around the world. The empires that they, their allies and their lackeys created were vast. Even with the contemporary technologies of transport and communications, the need to recruit and train local clerks and administrators was acute. The schools built for this purpose taught more than technical skills. They included lessons on what Europeans had learned about the power of collective action and of nationalism, and became the seed-beds for local hybrid forms of the same ideologies, which were later to flower into movements for independence.

Once independence had been won, more widespread schooling of the Western sort became a key plank in all developmental platforms. Schools and their curricula became part of the struggle by the new state- and nation-makers to order their domains and to develop. Classrooms became sites, as they have long been everywhere else, of an intense struggle between traditionalist and modernist ideologies. The battle for the world mind was joined, and it was and remains intensely political.

Schools were not the only sites of such struggles, of course. To return to where this study began, that is, with the press, newly independent state-makers quickly found that global news reporting lay in the hands of a few temperate-zone agencies, which systematically discriminated against the socioeconomic tropics. This monopoly inevitably meant a bias toward temperate-world views and temperate-world concerns, thus underrepresenting those of peoples living where temperate-world interests were not immediately affected. State-makers in the tropics were quick to realise how dependent they were upon the world press for the sort of image they and their countries had elsewhere, and for the information about foreign affairs they received themselves.

Awareness grew among the more radical of the newly independent state-makers of the need to free communications systems from temperate-world control. This, it was felt, was an important part of the more general attempt to win greater autonomy for tropical communities. It was part of the attempt to be informed more objectively, instead of having to receive the biased reporting of the global North. Talk of objectivity had a modernist ring. It did not answer the question of what objectivity in this context might mean. Nor did it settle the issue as to whether development was better served by national thought control, or by relatively open debate, or indeed, whether there was any middle way or other way to proceed that could avoid the stifling character of the first course or the potentially chaotic consequences of the second.

Whose news? is a critical question for more than development debates. It raises other and equally important issues. On the battle for information, for example, hangs the power to determine the language in which political discourse is conducted.[20] Since political language is always loaded, this power is important. In it, for instance, are inscribed the poetics of power; the rituals that make authoritative what state-makers do.[21] Rituals consolidate a sense of order and continuity, and make any particular order seem natural. Since order is the highest value to which state-makers typically subscribe, control of language ensures that it is their rituals (like the diplomatic courtesies that help sustain the state-system, or the routines of international negotiation) that are considered correct. This, in turn, helps order world affairs. It clearly matters to state-makers, then, who writes the words in which their discourse is conducted, and for whom.

Those who would disorder the state or the state system in the name of another value, will seek a language appropriate to their task. They will use this language to question the meaning of state-making rituals, to contest the authority of state-makers' commands, and the legitimacy of wealthmakers' motives. They will meet, at very least, 'withering indifference'[22] and casual dismissal. They will meet, at most, overt oppression, their writings banned, their broadcasts jammed, their minds and their bodies broken or put behind bars.

So pervasive has Westernisation been that the values they articulate are usually couched in terms of freedom, justice, equity or fraternal wellbeing, which were the ideological slogans of the French and American revolutions. The values have inspired many to support the radical changes that material self-interest has made desirable, but leave much unresolved. Freedom for whom, for example? Freedom for the individual as such, or for the whole group to which the individual belongs? Equity for the particular citizen, for classes or categories of citizen, for peoples, or for states?

Individualism and collectivism

Running through ideological claims like these is an unresolved tension between individualist and collectivist conceptions of the good life and how

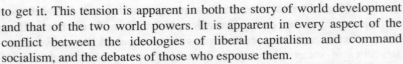

to get it. This tension is apparent in both the story of world development and that of the two world powers. It is apparent in every aspect of the conflict between the ideologies of liberal capitalism and command socialism, and the debates of those who espouse them.

The ideology of liberal capitalism is an individualistic one. The invention of the individual, as argued already, in no small part made objectivity and objective reasoning possible. A belief in human autonomy was the foundation stone on which the edifice of enlightened Europeanism was built, and it was upon this edifice that modern capitalism was made.

The concept of society denoted by the belief in human autonomy is fragmented. People are held together, it suggests, by reciprocal needs of a pragmatic sort as much as by a sense of fraternity. They are an aggregate of selves. We belong to a society because that way we get things we otherwise couldn't, and we as individuals rather than the group as such are the more fundamental, original and real phenomena.

A command socialist consciousness, on the other hand, is a collectivist one. People's sense of the group is supposed to be synergistic. Individuals look to the group for sustenance and support. Thus while those in the USA, as liberal capitalists, tend to place precedence upon personal integrity, freedom of speech or thought or movement, and equality before laws that are fairly and impartially applied (the civil and political rights as they are called), the Soviets give priority to full employment, the right to work, to be housed, and to be healed and taught, in line with their general notion that for civil and political rights to be meaningful, one must first secure social, economic and cultural rights.

Both sets of state-makers buttress their respective approach with an appropriate image of human nature. At the heart of the ideology of individualism and the competitiveness it creates lies a belief that primarily we are egoists, and hence ought to be so. It is no accident that this should make more efficient the sale of labour in the marketplace for a wage (people compete to have their labour-power bought, which bids down their price and pushes up their need to acquire more skills).

At the heart of the ethic of collectivism, on the other hand, and the ideal of mutual aid that it supposedly fosters, lies the assumption that primarily we are and hence ought to be altruistic. It is likewise no accident that this made seemingly natural, and not just necessary, the self-sacrifices on the part of the people that sustained Communist Party control for so long.

Liberal capitalists see human consciousness, then, as something detached; as a realm of its own. While they happily admit the influence of society on how we think, they emphasise self-realisation and the freedoms they see as safeguarding the individual domain.

Command socialists, however, see consciousness as crafted by how we produce things; by patterns of material production that then define the sort of awareness possible at any particular point in time. In the last instance the productive substructure determines the political and cognitive super-structures of society. Ideology is dependent upon who controls a community's material resources. Given how contingent and dependent our consciousness can be, and despite the best of our analytical intentions, a mentally free people can only be one that holds its resources in common; that owns and controls how it makes what it needs to live and to prosper.

Marx, from whom command socialists derive their ideology, believed himself that historical progress would ultimately undo all constraints. With communism every individual would be finally free. Liberated from the malevolent influence of bourgeois competitiveness, each would be able to do whatever he or she could, receiving in turn his or her necessities. With the collapse of capitalism a collective utopia would finally be possible, where unfettered human beings could fulfil their diverse capacities under socioeconomic conditions of plenty and peace.

For Adam Smith, from whom liberal capitalists derive much of the classical economics of their ideology, or for John Locke, from whom they take much of their political rationale, the key revolution has already occurred. With a free market, and a citizenry exercising its natural rights, the tools for human liberation are already to hand. Productive systems obedient to the laws of supply and demand tap the entrepreneurial desire for self-gain in socially acceptable ways. Governments that protect the individual's entitlements in terms of basic goods and services, and in terms of his or her personal autonomy and self-realisation, thereby ensure that any inequalities that do arise don't matter. The good world is already here.

In practice, liberal capitalists have proved to be a mixed blessing. The impressive productivity of those whose initiative it allows to flower has come at a high human cost. Likewise command socialism, which on the one hand has provided — in the Soviet Union and China alone — basic necessities for a quarter of humankind (though not yet in the democratic and decentralised way the first socialist reformers envisaged) has centralised and bureaucratised political rule in highly repressive ways that stultify the will to produce.

Despite the compromised quality of both regimes, and the widespread capitulation of the command socialist model in the late 1980s, the battle of the ideologies goes on. When ideologues compete they are trying to convert each other. The greatest power of all is the capacity to define consciousness; to define, that is, what is thinkable by another human being. No coercion, no overt controls are necessary, if someone is convinced. Persuade another of your superior purpose, and he or she will motivate and monitor him or herself. He or she will do what you want, unbidden. If devout enough, he or she will endure extraordinary privations and even death to do so. It is hardly surprising, therefore, that this sort of competition can be intense.

The intensity of the competition can obscure, however, the common ground on which people stand. In the case of the competition between liberal capitalism and command socialism, this common ground is scientific rationalism and industrial technology. Both lots of state- and wealth-makers would have us modernise. Both would exalt growth. Both would prefer to defer indefinitely the costs involved to the physical environment, for example, or to the human spirit. Both would prefer to gloss over the likely consequences of a collapse of the nuclear balance of terror.

Nuclearism

The balance of terror refers to the distribution of nuclear weapons in the world and the fact that no one set of state-makers has a commanding amount of them. It is the balance of power in its crudest form, as it works with regard to nuclear armaments, which are weapons of very great explosive and pollutant power.

Though the stocks they hold differ in composition, the two state-makers with the largest arsenals, those of the Soviet Union and the USA, stand in a generally balanced relationship with each other, as the distribution of the nuclear forces at their disposal is roughly even.

The balance of terror between these two peoples does not consist only in the relative numbers and kinds of weapons involved. It consists also in the relationships that result. A balance is maintained because to have nuclear arms is to deter erstwhile enemies, more particularly the nuclear- armed ones, from employing them. The ideology of the balance of terror is in practice that of mutual deterrence, which involves not just estimates of other state-makers' stockpiles, but of their willingness to use such weapons in war.

This leads at once to a paradox: how can such weapons present a credible threat when their use would trigger retaliation so destructive as to make such an act seem suicidal? Getting in first becomes a huge gamble, given the number of targets that need to be hit, and the extent to which nuclear weapons are protected from just this eventuality. Not getting in first means running the risk of losing, if losing can have much meaning under these circumstances. Indeed, it has recently become evident that nuclear war may not be an option under any circumstances because of ecological factors heretofore largely unseen.

It seems that nuclear weapons may have given the species the capacity to commit suicide as a whole. A big nuclear war, it has been argued, would not only blow up or poison huge numbers of people, but could conceivably create ecological conditions that would kill all the rest. This secondary effect is far from certain, and scientific opinion is currently backing away from such a conclusion. Who is to know, however, when scientific opinion might again change, to advance that premise as readily as it now retreats from it?[23]

Any behaviour that risks death on such a large scale is probably pathological. Psychopathology is specifically concerned with the study of behaviour that is maladaptive or inappropriate and that can be seen as a source of 'undue distress, threat or detriment' to the society or self.[24] Defining what is maladaptive, inappropriate or undue distress, threat or detriment means making judgements about what we value most. In the light of the risk of species suicide, however, the most relevant judgement would seem to be in terms of the preservation of all life itself. This is a basic value, and a necessary condition for the persistence of international politics of any sort.

There are circumstances where it might be reasonable to prefer death to life. Faced by a lethal dictatorship, for example, we might choose to risk death rather than become its willing victims. We have seen enough lethal regimes in our times to know what they can do. Neither the United States nor the Soviet is such a regime. Neither great nuclear power advocates exterminating some part or all of its erstwhile opponent, or anyone else for that matter, except in self-defence. This being so, and given the risk of decimation and even of species suicide, we might ask whether it is any longer sane to plan for a major nuclear war, rather than a policy of 'live and let live' that includes the possible surrender of either power to the other.

How do United States and Soviet state-makers, and their strategists, behave in this regard? Does their general behaviour defend life on earth? Most would say that it does. They would say that the nuclear gamble is a calculated one meant to secure other values too. Given the risks, and the fact that neither power is inherently evil, can the gamble be justified? Why are these people not appalled at our common plight?

They might, I suppose, be ignorant of it or simply unimaginative. They might be divinely detached from the whole issue. If they are none of the above, however, then in the light of the definition of psychopathology given already, they can only be insane. A sane response to the prospect of species decimation would be quite different. An aware, thoughtful and engaged individual would, by this reasoning, feel only high panic or utter dismay. In the story of world thought, in other words, we seem to have opened a new, decidedly irrational and perhaps conclusive chapter.

What of those who directly advise the state-makers on this issue? Firstly, none are divinely detached; none are saints. Secondly, one might expect them not only to be highly informed (that is, they are not ignorant) but also to have a vivid awareness of the implications of a big nuclear war

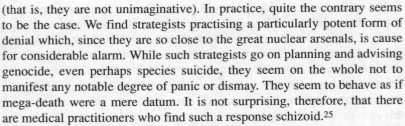

(that is, they are not unimaginative). In practice, quite the contrary seems to be the case. We find strategists practising a particularly potent form of denial which, since they are so close to the great nuclear arsenals, is cause for considerable alarm. While such strategists go on planning and advising genocide, even perhaps species suicide, they seem on the whole not to manifest any notable degree of panic or dismay. They seem to behave as if mega-death were a mere datum. It is not surprising, therefore, that there are medical practitioners who find such a response schizoid.[25]

Some authors have documented this ideologically curious outcome in considerable detail. Carol Cohn, for example, in listening to civilian strategists explain their subject in detail, found herself 'aghast, but morbidly fascinated' by their 'extraordinary abstraction and removal' from what she thought of and felt to be reality.[26] Their professional discourse was consistently dispassionate and couched in a specialised language that was concise, closely argued and utterly devoid of any sense of 'horror, urgency, or moral outrage'.[27] She was most disconcerted to encounter such lack of awareness among a group of men (they were all men) otherwise charming, funny, clever, decent and concerned.

The most conspicuous feature of their discourse was the abundance of euphemisms.[28] Bland words do, of course, seem more objective. They help defuse emotionally fraught subjects. However, their habitual use can and does mislead.[29] It makes it possible, for example, to detach talk about nuclear war from talk for it. This might be admissible if detachment had no policy implications, but talk about nuclear strategy is used to craft policy for the use of nuclear weapons on a mass scale, and if the talk is emotionally detached so will the policy be. Again, this would not matter so much if the policy was on a subject like beef quotas in international trade, for example, but it applies to potential death and destruction on a very large scale. The argument for keeping the planning language as close to the policy consequences as possible is therefore very strong.

Some of the euphemisms and the language are far from bland, however, which is revealing in itself. Cohn became acutely aware of the sexual and patriarchal connotations of some of the key images used by the 'white men in ties discussing missile size' who gave the lectures she attended.[30] What she found most intriguing, however, was how this imagery was used to construct a work world that was felt to be habitable, comfortable and tenable. Therefore, along with some memorable examples of stereo-typically masculinist dominance-language, instances of sexual trivialisation and male creation fantasies, Cohn also noted that by domesticating nuclear weapons and finding comfortable analogues for them in their minds, the strategists involved were able to minimise the lethal meaning that rockets and bombs really have.

The self-deception was and is obvious, of course. However cosy it is made, the realm of nuclear strategy is not friendly and familiar. It is a place of inhumane calculations which denote potential mass murder and ecological mayhem. Strategists make their discourse technically precise and ideologically compelling. Since their work involves planning species decimation, however, it is legitimate to ask whether what in a less appalling context would be natural, normal, even endearing behaviour, is not in this case psychopathological.

The language and imagery of strategists is not neutral, then. It may sound that way, but it is ideologically loaded. Much of it is self-referential too, policy being recommended with regard to calculations of strategic ends and means, rather than political or even military ones. Given the degree of acceptance such recommendations have found, particularly among the state-makers in the USA, it is conceivable that nuclear war and thus the decimation of the species could now occur not because it serves any human value or purpose, but because it fits the logic of strategic discourse alone. The incentive for such a war would be the affirmation of the weapons themselves, 'not human lives, not even states and state power'.[31]

Most disturbing is the extent to which strategists may exacerbate the very security dilemmas they are supposed to resolve. Not only do these security dilemmas justify an international armaments culture that is highly profitable and cynically oblivious to basic human needs but, more subtly, strategists talk of world politics as anarchic, then proclaim themselves uniquely qualified to manage the consequences. They are little interested in anything but the state. Strategic ideology, in other words, is part of the larger ideology of nation statism.

As discussed above, this larger ideology takes a single, albeit highly successful, socioeconomic and political structure (the state), assumes its pre-eminence, posits individual state-makers, defines threats as originating outside the separate state domains, and then tells these state-makers how to cope with them. Debate is limited to one highly-technocratic discourse to the detriment of questions like where did states come from in the first place? Where might they be going to? How do they fit into the international political economy? How does nuclearism reinforce statism? What is the ideology of nuclearism and what might it mean?

State-makers seek to secure their respective territories. In the USA it has been fear of communism and its diverse iniquities, and confidence in the United States' democratic superiority, that have long been used to rationalise the defence of the realm in nuclear terms. Militant democratism and capitalist enterprise have always been formally preferred. In the Soviet Union it has been fear of capitalism and its undesirable features, and confidence in socialist superiority, that have conventionally served this purpose. Communist Party orthodoxy and centralised socialism have been the values and institutions that Soviet state-makers have more or less diligently defended. Both sets of state-makers have found ideological neutrality anathema. As state-makers they have been highly competitive.

As major participants in the larger human project of modernisation, however, they collude. They have shared an unacknowledged commitment to what E.P. Thompson has called 'exterminism', by which he means 'those characteristics of a society — expressed, in differing degrees, within its economy, its polity and its ideology — which thrust it in a direction whose outcome must be ... extermination'.[32]

Something of the power of this ideology, in the USA at least, is shown in the response to a suggestion Roger Fisher made 'that the code required for the President to authorise the firing of nuclear weapons, instead of being carried near the President in an attache case, should be implanted in a man's chest, so that the President, when he wanted to get at it to fire the weapons, would first have to hack him open personally with a butcher's knife'. Fisher says that friends in the Pentagon were horrified at the suggestion."'That's terrible", they said, "having to kill someone might alter the President's judgement. He might never press the button"'.[33]

It is the ideologists of peace and a sustainable environment who typically provide the wider perspectives in which to view the balance of nuclear terror and what it portends. Facing the prospect of species decimation is not easy, and is one of those things best done out of the corner of one's mental eye.[34] By averting the gaze from what is an emotionally blinding prospect we allow a modicum of humility, which prevents us losing sight of what the ideology of nuclearism could achieve. It is an antidote for human pride and humanity's preoccupation with its practical achievements, of which nuclear weapons are one.

3. What does such a reading tell us about the invisible dimension of gender?

While all the above is clearly of concern to analysts of international politics, there remains one aspect of the battle for the world mind that is only just beginning to find its way into the conceptual arena, namely, that of human gendering. International politics, in gender terms, is one of the last great bastions of male privilege and power.[35]

What has gender to do with world affairs? Firstly, as indicated earlier, women have been made invisible there. It is as if the issues raised by discussions of human gender are not relevant to global socialising practices, and need not be part of the study of international politics. Is this because women are in fact irrelevant?

That is a truly preposterous notion. However, not only is there almost total silence on the issue of gender in international politics, but the conventional definition of the subject — as state-making and as issues of state policy — actively excludes the discussion of gender. It renders the issue irrelevant, a rendering made easier by the male-dominated nature of 'high politics' itself, of its foreign ministries, of its ministries of defence, and of its related policy bodies. Women are seen by the men already there as unsuitable (compared with themselves) for the responsibilities involved. (The female exceptions to the rule are revealing in the different ways in which they are exceptional.)

What is most extraordinary is that this radical value assumption is successfully sold as value-neutrality. Male domination of international politics is explained in terms of international politics as a gender-neutral realm. This is analogous to saying that owning a slave is not a problem because the system of slave-owning is not a problem. And, of course, both male dominance and its pervasive nature are problems.

The second reason for highlighting gender as an issue in world affairs, therefore, is the way more than half the human race are denied the opportunity to contribute to international politics and to help solve the problems it presents. Gender means, in this context, that women are confined to subordinate roles, with direct and very specific consequences for women and men.

We can see this clearly in the definition of power most commonly used in world affairs, namely, power as dominance/subordinance rather than power as competence (as mutual enabling; as co-operation rather than conflict). We can also see this in the feminisation of world poverty. Simply put, therefore, international politics oppresses women. It does so systematically and it does so world-wide.[36]

The full significance of such an awareness is well caught by the summary statement that while women make up the majority of earth's people, they are built into its institutions as if they are were a minority. The implications of this statement are far-reaching. As Lerner points out:

> While women have been victimized by this and many other aspects of their long subordination to men, it is a fundamental error to try to conceptualize women primarily as victims. To do so at once obscures what must be assumed as a given of women's historical situation: Women are essential and central to creating society ... Women have 'made history', yet they have been kept from knowing their History ... Women have been systematically excluded from the enterprise of creating symbol systems, philosophies, science, and law.[37]

Women have always created symbols and knowledge and laws of their own, of course, but mostly as women, not as those who think and speak for all.

International politics, I repeat, deals in the main with the macro-issues of state-making and wealth-making. A gender-critique of such issues quickly reveals the notable absence of female state- and wealth-makers (and of course, a concomitant plethora of male ones). It also highlights the gender-based disparities in wealth and the capacity to generate wealth, that are such a feature of world affairs. When we consider mind-shaping, we find the macro-concerns of international politics directly related to the micro-concerns of world feminism.[38]

What is this relationship? It has been a key part of the feminist project to explore the ways in which the personal is the political. Much attention has been given to the sexual politics of the home and to the construction of the family (variously defined) as not a natural institution but as a socially, economically and ideologically determined one, where male interests predominate. Though this might seem remote from the concerns of international politics, it is not. The family is central to the maintenance of all political order. As the family goes, so goes the world.

The relationship between women and world politics is also clearly apparent in the role women play in war, where they are widely used as support labour and prostitutes, and as a rationalisation for fighting in the first place. The rationale for war, for example, is typically cast in terms of the need to defend wives/mothers/sisters from the depredations of the enemy. The relationship between women and the world political–economy is also close, with women playing an essential part in world development, though largely to their detriment.

The seeds of the feminist critiques of this relationship were sown in the late eighteenth century. As the liberal doctrine of natural rights was extended to women and it was recognised that, in rights' terms at least, they were the same order of being as men, a sustained attack was made on marriage as a form of female bondage. The attempt to realise full citizenship, enhanced educational opportunities and legal equality became the features of an emancipatory programme that was meant to transform women's lives.[39] What liberals did not achieve, however, was any change in the basic division of labour that as a matter of course put men outside the home and women in it. Neither did they question the hierarchy of power within the family whereby men dominated women nor question the global consequences of having such a hierarchy.

A parallel critique by Marxists, and those influenced by Marx and by Engels, emphasised the political–economy of women's plight. They emphasised the proto-class nature of women's possession in marriage, both as property and as the bearers of legitimate heirs to whom property might pass.[40] 'Capitalism', it was argued, 'was partly constituted out of the opportunities for power and profit created by gender relations. It continues to be'.[41]

The demonstrable failure of socialist societies to provide parity of opportunity for working women has rendered rather false the claim that female emancipation would come about with socialist reform and women's material independence. Clearly material autonomy makes a difference, but by any measure — material, political or sexual — women are still subordinate in socialist societies, as in the world at large. A greater commitment to equity has not yet appreciably changed the hierarchical nature of male/female relationships that such societies display.

This suggests that the cause of women's oppression is complex and profound. Since the relationship between women and world affairs is a subject that has only recently made its way onto the research agenda, the reasons for this are not as clear as they might be. No single factor seems sufficient to explain female oppression, and no superficial reform seems able to lead to a sustained and comprehensive women's liberation.

How then does one describe and explain such intransigence? Contemporary attempts to do so turn on two key concerns: one with the ideology of patriarchy; the other with the question of the nature and extent of sexual difference.

Patriarchism

Patriarchy denotes the rule of the father and, by extension, by men as a whole. It is a problematic concept, since the power of the father has varied in individual societies over time. It is also different in different societies for the same point in time. Furthermore, in the modern society patriarchy is no longer paternal at all, which is not to say that male dominance has come to an end there. Quite the contrary. It has merely taken a different and more modern form, namely, that of fraternal patriarchy.[42]

'The basis of paternalism', Lerner argues, 'is an unwritten contract for exchange: economic support and protection given by the male for subordination in all matters, sexual service, and unpaid domestic service given by the female'.[43] We can emphasise the contractual nature of this exchange, in which case we then need to add to accounts of the social contract and its story of freedom another account, heretofore repressed, of the sexual contract and the story it tells of subjection to gender.[44] Beside the law of the state and the law of capitalist production, in other words, is the law of male sex-right, which is women's subordination to men as a fraternity.[45]

Equally significant is the way such subjection has excluded women from the human enterprise of constructing abstract thought.[46] From this perspective the female enlightenment has only just begun — a chapter in the story of world thought that promises to be as revolutionary as the male-run one that gave the world modernity.[47]

In terms of international politics, one immediate consequence has been the revelation of the ways in which male-centric readings of the subject have obscured the extent of global inequality. Gender is a socially relevant difference used to sustain inequality between the sexes. It is the result of social processes of subordination. It is a key aspect of international politics, and of the patterns of systematic dominance practised there.[48]

This being so there is no need to genderise the subject, as it is already genderised. International politics involves, that is, a particular set of (male-centric) ideas and practices that are universalised and made to seem objective and natural when they are not. Their ostensible objectivity and seeming naturalness have been predicated historically upon female suppression. They describe as reality one point of view, which is turned into Reality, which is made in turn into the object to be described. The ideology of patriarchy is reproduced under such conditions in a reified and magnified form. Scholarship then becomes a kind of narcissism, enacting and perfecting itself, with the obvious casualty being the pursuit of truth.

Genderism

Gender denotes what people are taught to be as masculine or feminine beings, themselves culturally specific notions. It is a socially constructed concept, and as such is amenable to change. How much change, however, remains in dispute.

Gender is usually differentiated from the concept of sex, which is a biologically acquired characteristic, the significance of which is also in dispute. Opinions stretch along a continuum. In the middle lie politically liberal feminists who would see such a difference as insignificant, and exaggerated by sociocultural conditioning. They assert the primacy of our common humanity, and see any person's sex as of secondary concern.

To the left of this position is that of the radical feminists, who would see sex as fundamental, though they would then go on to argue that any essential difference between men and women does not denote female inferiority. On the contrary, they would endorse in a very positive way what women's bodies and minds might mean. Women are not only different from men; they are distinctive.[49]

The continuum bends back on itself like a keyring, as all political spectrums do, so that the extreme to the right, the conservative position, is a parallel but fundamentally opposed one. In the words of a particularly committed nineteenth century patriarchist, 'men are stronger than women in every shape. They have greater muscular and nervous force, greater intellectual force, [and] greater vigour of character', a 'fact' he uses to justify a sex-based division of labour and to assert the futility of reform; to argue, that is, against equality of opportunity for women.[50]

In terms of international politics sexual difference is expressed in many important ways. State-making, for example, has had much to do with war-making, which is very much a male domain. Male domination of the state as a political form is closely related, therefore, to militarism.

Militarism, Reardon argues, requires an excess of the 'strength, bravery, and responsibility necessary to fulfill male social functions'.[51] If this denotes an essential difference between men and women, then women stand to be condemned indefinitely to a subordinate role because they do not have those qualities in male amounts. Alternatively they could promote other, non-male qualities as preferred and as previously largely denied. If the essential difference is not significant, they can either join the fray or resolve, having been largely excluded from it for so long, to make a virtue out of their heretofore subordinate status and to assert the superiority of non-militarism.

To talk about women in the way done so above, and on a global scale, is to suggest that they share a common plight. This is a much debated assumption, raising issues of race, class, religion and nation, as well as those (already complex) of sex and gender. Clearly the subordination of women as women cuts across other political, economic, social and spiritual concerns and has to compete with them for ideological attention. It is, however, the most ubiquitous of them:

> embedded [as it is] in the social division of labour in the most funda-
> mentally integral fashion ... This is why women's oppression is difficult to
> see, why women can so easily be divided. It means ... that women have no
> pre-existing social institution on which to base their struggle and on the
> other hand that eliminating sexual inequality would require the most far-
> reaching social upheaval of them all.[52]

In terms of the balance of ideology it informs every aspect of the battle for the world mind.

Notes

1 L. Mumford, *Technics and Civilization*, George Routledge & Sons, London, 1934, p. 28.

2 S. Hoffman, 'Perceptions, Reality and the Franco-American Conflict' in J. Farrell & A. Smith (eds), *Image and Reality*, Columbia University Press, New York, 1967, pp. 57-9.

3 P. Corrigan & D. Sayer, *The Great Arch: English State Formation as Cultural Revolution,* Basil Blackwell, Oxford, 1985, pp. 3-5.

4 ibid., p. 7.
5 M. Howard, 'Ideology and international relations', *Review of International Studies* vol. 15 no. 1, January 1989, p. 1.
6 R. Williams, *Keywords: a vocabulary of culture and society* (rev. edn), Fontana, London, 1983, pp. 153-7.
7 ibid., p. 154.
8 K. Marx & F. Engels, *The German Ideology*, Lawrence & Wishart, London, 1977, p. 47.
9 R. Ashley, 'The State of the Discipline: realism under challenge?', unpub. paper, pp. 52, 47, 53. Also R. Bernstein, *Beyond Objectivism and Relativism: science, hermeneutics and praxis*, Basil Blackwell, Oxford, 1983, pp. 47-8: 'It has become a well-entrenched dogma of modern thought that only after we resolve the "hard" issues of epistemology and come to grips with scientific knowledge can we turn to the "softer" and "fuzzier" concerns of moral, social, and political philosophy. This is a prejudice that is being questioned in the new conversation about human rationality'.
10 R. Ashley, 'The Geopolitics of Geopolitical Space: Toward a Critical Social Theory of International Politics', *Alternatives* vol. 12, 1987, pp. 408, 410.
11 R. Walker, 'Ethics, Modernity and the Theory of International Relations', unpub. paper, p. 19. See also A. Bozeman, *Politics and Culture in International History*, Princeton University Press, 1960.
12 T. Kuhn, *The Structure of Scientific Revolutions* (2nd edn), University of Chicago Press, Chicago, 1970.
13 R. Walker, op. cit., p. 9. Also C. Boggs, *Social Movements and Political Power: emerging forms of radicalism in the West*, Temple University Press, Philadelphia, 1986, p. 29.
14 L. Althusser, 'Ideology and Ideological State Apparatuses (notes towards an investigation)' in his *Lenin and Philosophy and Other Essays*, Monthly Review Press, New York, 1971, pp. 142-3.
15 ibid., p. 151.
16 ibid., pp. 155-6.
17 B. Anderson, *Imagined Communities: reflections on the origin and spread of nationalism*, Verso, London, 1983, p. 107.
18 ibid., p. 111.
19 ibid., p. 123.
20 R. Righter, *Whose News?: politics, the press and the third world*, Burnett Books, London, 1978. See also H. Mowlana, *Global Information and World Communication*, Longman, New York, 1986; G. Wood, 'The Politics of Development Policy Labelling', *Development and Change* vol. 16, 1985, pp. 347-73.
21 C. Geertz, *Negara: the theatre state in nineteenth-century Bali*, Princeton University Press, Princeton, 1980, p. 123.
22 Derived from Ashley's concept of withering nonchalance. See 'The poverty of neo-realism', *International Organization* vol. 38 no. 2, 1984, p. 285.
23 See for a recent overview S. Thompson & H. Schneider, 'Nuclear Winter Reappraised', *Foreign Affairs*, Summer 1986, pp. 981-1005; also the subsequent comments and correspondence in *Foreign Affairs* Fall 1986, pp. 163-78. Parts of the following section have appeared already in R. Pettman, 'The Psychopathology of Nuclear Deterrence' in G. Rodley (ed.), *Beyond Deterrence*, Centre for Peace and Conflict Studies, University of Sydney,

1989).

24 J. Page, *Psychopathology*, Aldine, Chicago, 1975, p. 3.

25 H. Caldicott, *Nuclear Madness*, Jacaranda, Brisbane, 1978, p. 71. See also J. Dyer, 'The Psychopathology of Nuclear War', *Bulletin of the Royal College of Psychiatrists* vol. 10, January 1986, p. 3. For the voice of reason see The Harvard University Nuclear Study Group, *Living with Nuclear Weapons*, Harvard University Press, Cambridge, 1983.

26 C. Cohn, 'Sex and Death in the Rational World of Defense Intellectuals', *Signs* vol. 12 no. 4, Summer 1987, p. 688.

27 ibid., p. 690.

28 See also P. Chilton (ed.), *Language and the Nuclear Arms Debate*, Frances Pinter, London, 1985.

29 Phrases like 'collateral damage' or 'countervalue attack' do not have the same connotations as 'guts', 'blood' or 'burnt mothers'.

30 C. Cohn, op. cit., p. 692.

31 ibid., p. 711. The logic is not unlike that of the parent who says to the child: 'eat up your peas or I'll blow up the house'. The end and the means are not commensurate. The logic betrays a parent more interested in explosives than child nutrition.

32 E.P. Thompson, *Zero Option*, Merlin Press, London, 1982, p. 64. See also A. Rapoport, 'Preparation for Nuclear War: the final madness', *Journal of Orthopsychiatry*, vol. 54 no. 4, October 1984, pp. 524-9.

33 Cited by J. Dyer, op. cit., p. 3.

34 L. Thomas, *Late Night Thoughts on Listening to Mahler's Ninth Symphony*, Bantam, New York, 1983, p. 12.

35 L. Alexandre, 'Genderizing International Studies: Revisioning Concepts and Curriculum', *International Studies Notes* vol. 14 no. 1, Winter 1989, pp. 5-8. See also the issue on women and international relations, *Millenium* vol. 17 no. 3, Winter 1988.

36 J. Seager & A. Olson, *Women in the world: an international atlas*, Simon & Schuster, New York, 1986; R. Sivard, *Women: a world survey*, World Priorities, Washington, 1985.

37 G. Lerner, *The Creation of Patriarchy*, Oxford University Press, Oxford, 1986, p. 5.

38 The distinction between gender-critique and feminism I have taken from Barbara Caine, though she would not agree with my linking of the two. My discussion more generally, however, is an attempt to follow her current thinking on the subject.

39 J.S. Mill, *Subjection of Women*, Massachusetts Institute of Technology Press, Cambridge, 1970; M. Wollstonecraft, *Vindication of the Rights of Women*, Penguin, Harmondsworth, 1975.

40 F. Engels, *Origin of the family, private property and the state in the light of the researches of Lewis H. Morgan*, Foreign Languages Publishing House, Moscow, 1952.

41 R. Connell, *Gender and Power: society, the person and sexual politics*, Polity Press, Cambridge, 1987, p. 104.

42 C. Pateman, *The Sexual Contract*, Polity Press, Cambridge, 1988, p. 3.

43 G. Lerner, op. cit., p. 218.

44 C. Pateman, op. cit., p. 2.

45 ibid., pp. 219, 3.

46 G. Lerner, op. cit., p. 225.
47 J. Bernard, *The Female World from a Global Perspective*, Indiana University Press, Bloomington, 1987.
48 S. Brown, 'Feminism, International Theory, and International Relations of Gender Inequality', *Millenium* vol. 17 no. 3, Winter 1988, pp. 467, 473.
49 V. Randall, *Women and Politics: an international perspective* (2nd edn), Macmillan, London, 1987. The concept of a distinctive difference has been developed at length by French feminists.
50 J. Stephen, *Liberty, Equality, Fraternity*, Cambridge University Press, Cambridge, 1967, pp. 193-4.
51 B. Reardon, *Sexism and the War System*, Teachers College Columbia University, New York, 1983, p. 15. Also C. Enloe, 'Feminists Thinking About War, Militarism, and Peace' in B. Hess & M. Ferree (eds), *Analysing Gender: a handbook of social science research*, Sage, Newbury Park, 1987.
52 V. Randall, op. cit., p. 48.

Conclusion

An account of world affairs in terms of the balance of power is something we largely take for granted. It has become part of the every-day language of international politics; part of an analytic vocabulary we tend to use without thinking. Using words without thinking can be a trap, however. Remaining mindful of what words mean is an important part of being aware of their ideological implications. As George Orwell once said:

> the worst thing one can do with words is to surrender to them. When you think of a concrete object, you think wordlessly, and then, if you want to describe the thing you have been visualizing you probably hunt about till you find the exact words that seem to fit. When you think of something abstract you are more inclined to use words from the start, and unless you make a conscious effort to prevent it, the existing dialect will come rushing in and do the job for you.[1]

In conventional parlance the existing dialect is a discourse on the state and the interstate system. The power implied is military force. The value most esteemed is the order of the system. The balance of power is primarily understood to be the balance of military power. In these terms we are told a familiar tale of sovereignty, territorial integrity, and the legitimacy of state-making itself.

The existing dialect is, however, only one way of accounting for world affairs. Power is a portmanteau concept that denotes not only military, but material and mental practices. If we are serious about exploring power in all its aspects — if we are serious, in other words, about understanding all the aspects of the balance of power — we need to look at more than its strategic dimension. We need to tell the story in other terms, like those of political–economy.

Here we find three different accounts of how the world works. In their most extreme form they represent the neo-mercantilist, liberal and Marxist approaches.

Each account is complex, diverse and riven by internal debates. For summary purposes, however, we can say that neo-mercantilists consider wealth-making to be part of state-making, and that it is politically motivated. The main motive is nationalism. The main policy is protectionism.

Radical liberals, in contrast, consider polity and economy to be separate realms, more or less closely linked. The activities of entrepreneurs in the local and global marketplace are seen as the key to both individual and collective prosperity. It is their self-aggrandising behaviour that generates prosperity and peace. The motive is ever-increasing wealth. The preferred political environment is a non-interventionist one, and state policy is condoned only where it seems necessary to protect the freedom of the market itself and to provide those public goods the market does not.

Marxists, on the other hand, consider polity and economy to be fused, and the political–economy to be determined by the predominant mode of production (in our own time, that of industrial capitalism). The relationship between capitalists and wage-workers is one of symbiotic antagonism. The emiserating effects of capitalist profit-taking lead, in classical Marxist parlance, to revolution. The proletariat whom capitalists exploit (wage-workers) are supposed eventually to overthrow the system and achieve emancipation. (Neo-Marxists are not so sure that capitalism need come to this apocalyptic conclusion, though like all Marxists their main desire is to achieve worker self-determination.)

To accommodate these different narratives, it is necessary to extend the discourse on the balance of power to include the balance of productivity. This concept draws attention to the world as a productive whole. It highlights those who make the world's goods and perform the world's services, and it asks: who is this all for?

In general terms the balance of productivity tells the story of world development. Neo-mercantilists extol the virtues of self-sufficiency, especially, it seems, in the light of the effect of marketeering on the weak. Radical liberals talk about the growth of the world market, and the distorting effects politics and state-making have had on the honest efforts of entrepreneurs to build a more bountiful economy. Marxists highlight the exploitative nature of this process, the part state-making has played in it, and the cost to the world's workers of the pursuit of private profit. A more recent reading, by radical feminists, speaks for the world's women, who are mostly unwaged.

Besides the balance of productivity, however, there is another dimension to the balance of power that the existing dialect and its military/strategic concerns do not explore. This is the social/ideological dimension. Again, there are different accounts of what is important. State-centric analysts and practitioners highlight world society's shared rules and arrangements.[2] Those of a more radical bent see state-making and wealth-making in terms of an international milieu that is being industrialised and modernised by global entrepreneurs. Others find 'modernity' itself problematic, and their voices are heard in the words and practices of a wide range of contemporary social movements. They articulate such values as freedom, equity, community, well-being (and other less liberal values too). They aim to resist or reform international society in part or whole.

To accommodate social movements I have extended my reading of the balance of power even further to include a balance of ideologies. This concept draws attention to the battle for the world mind, that is, the struggle to define what people think. The most obvious dimension of this struggle is the propaganda war between the great powers. This has ramifications for the story of world development, and for current prescriptions as to how this should happen. More subtle is the ongoing effort to legitimise the idea of the state itself. More subtle again is the masculinist bias built into both ideas.

The balance of power (narrowly defined in military terms) is a balance of productivity and a balance of ideology as well. Likewise, the balance of productivity impinges upon the balance of power (narrowly defined) and the balance of ideology. The balance of ideology also impinges upon the balance of power (narrowly defined) and the balance of productivity. Neither can be adequately discussed without involving the others.

This is not yet the common view. In the continuing struggle to define the parameters of the discipline and to police its content, international politics is still understood largely in terms of the state and the balance of power and 'high politics'. As argued above, however, this is only part of what goes on in world affairs. The significance of 'low politics' and 'even lower politics' has been discussed in detail, and they demonstrate very clearly the richness of the concept of power. They demonstrate at the same time the need to interpret as broadly as possible the meaning of international politics.

How are the three domains — high, low and even lower — to be synthesised? Eclecticism would hardly be adequate, since the attempt to construe the three as merely co-present, while a necessary antidote to a one-dimensional approach, does not do justice to the way they inter-relate. There is no simple answer to this question. One way to begin, however, would be to consider first the balance of productivity rather than the balance of power.

The balance of productivity is of growing significance, and linked directly with the balance of ideologies. We live in the middle (if middle it proves to be) of the most materially productive period in written human history. The industrial revolution, which is what we call this era, continues to have profound material and mental consequences for all humankind, and for international politics.

However we define international politics, the study of it has to take the far-reaching consequences of such a radical increase in human productivity into account, or risk irrelevance. Perhaps by starting here we might fall less often into the trap of reifying and privileging the state and the state system, and we could recover more readily the lost domains that conventional studies of the subject still neglect.

This is both a materialistic and an idealistic conclusion. Emphasising human productivity sounds like materialism and indeed it is, though I would emphasise the new and humanistic materialism rather than the old and the contemplative kind. (This distinction is drawn from Marx's 'Theses on Feuerbach'. There he specifically criticises what he calls old materialism, which he sees as symptomatic of those preoccupied with single individuals and civil society. Materialists like this fail, in his view, to understand 'sensuousness as practical activity'. The new materialism, in contrast, he sees as one that is interested in human society. He see it as an attempt to understand how we perpetuate our social humanity. [3])

Materialism of the second kind is a conscious affirmation of human community. To perpetuate a human community means using productivity in humane ways. Where productivity is inhumane social movements emerge that articulate people's concerns about the environment, about poverty, about human rights, and about the affairs of women. Their concerns are idealistic ones, but they are not irrelevant. Quite the contrary. They seek to civilise materialism, and to have it serve social humanity. They seek to change the world. It is here that the sense of human community is most active and immediate and meaningful. It is here, perhaps, that international politics must turn for its ultimate inspiration and its ultimate rationale.

Notes

1 G. Orwell, 'Politics and the English Language' in M. Stein et al., *Identity and Anxiety,* The Free Press, Glencoe, 1960, p.18.

2 Such 'arrangements' are currently called 'regimes'. See, for example, S. Krasner (ed.), *International Regimes,* Cornell University Press, Ithaca, 1983.

3 K. Marx & F. Engels, *The German Ideology,* Lawrence & Wishart, London, 1977, p. 123.

APPENDIX

Glasnost and perestroika

What was the policy, initiated by Soviet state-makers in the late 1980s, of restructuring? Why did they make the changes they did? What light did their doing so throw on state-making in the modern world?

Though many examples of modern state-making could have been chosen, the Soviet Union is a particularly dramatic one, and well placed to illustrate the dynamics of the process. Few other countries this century have had such an extraordinary history. Moreover, the general story that is told of events in this part of the world radically changed in the late 1980s when leading local state-makers began to instigate far-reaching politico-economic reforms. Not only did their actions reveal much about how states are made, but about how they are unmade too.

Why 'perestroika'? Why 'glasnost'?

Like any aspect of international politics, interpreting Soviet affairs is a hazardous business at best. With regard, for example, to the Soviet policies of perestroika (restructuring the economy) and glasnost (greater political freedom), Robert Kaiser found them:

> enthralling — nothing so interesting or exciting as Mikhail Gorbachev's reforms has happened in Russia in modern times. The world is rightly transfixed by the spectacle of Russians telling the truth about their past and their present, encouraging private enterprise, urging a diminished role for the Communist Party and generally committing mayhem against Marxism–Leninism ... We are ... witnessing the beginning of the end of the Soviet empire. The fear of Soviet conquest and hegemony that dominated

world politics for more than a generation should now dissipate. We have passed the high-water mark of Soviet power and influence in the world.[1]

On the other hand Graham Allison — conservative, sceptical, opportunistic, American — thought that '[t]o the extent that Gorbachev's analysis is leading him to take steps that serve our interests, good. To the extent that the Soviet Union turns inward for a decade or two, and concentrates on rebuilding Soviet economic strength, we should cheer'. However, to him the appropriate response for outsiders was to test and probe: 'As the U.S.S.R. passes such tests, some in the West will proclaim prematurely that peace has broken out. Others may be lulled. We could be tricked. The web of interdependence we spin could entangle the West more deeply than the Soviet Union'.[2]

A different view again was taken by Cornelius Castoriadis. He was scathing, pessimistic, radically dismissive. He contended that:

> there are only very narrow margins within which the Gorbachev attempts to 'reform' Russian society can make some substantial difference without unleashing a grand social, ethnic and political crisis and/or inducing (in response to or in anticipation of such a crisis) a backlash from the military and Party establishment leading either to an emasculation of the 'reforms', or to the appointment of Mr. Gorbachev to some hydro-electric plant of the Lena region ... The Gorbachev illusion is the idea (predominant today in the West, possibly shared by Gorbachev himself) that substantive reforms, in a country like today's Russia can be introduced strictly from above, that you can retain the absolutist power of bureaucracy whilst dismantling the social and economic bases of this power — in brief, that ... you can change the system without changing it.[3]

Then there was the ostensible instigator of these reforms himself, Mikhail Gorbachev, General Secretary of the Communist Party of the Soviet Union, seemingly concerned, sensible, frank, even ingenuous. 'There are different interpretations of perestroika in the West', he wrote.

> 'There is the view that it has been necessitated by the disastrous state of the Soviet economy and that it signifies disenchantment with socialism and a crisis for its ideals and ultimate goals. Nothing could be further from the truth ... Of course, perestroika has been largely stimulated by our dissatisfaction with the way things have been going ... But it has to a far greater extent been prompted by an awareness that the potential of socialism has been underutilized.[4]

Underutilised seems something of an understatement. As Evgeny Chazov, then Soviet Minister for Health, pointed out, the Soviet Union was fiftieth in the world for infant mortality (after Mauritius and Barbados), and thirty-second in the world for life expectancy (the only industrially developed country where this rate was decreasing). Half its schools did not have central heating, running water or a sewerage system, and half its schoolchildren, on the admission of the Chairman of the State Committee on Public Education at that time, were 'not in good health'.[5]

Given the range of opinion about what was going on, and the rather unreliable nature of any statistics that attempted to tell the story in numbers,[6] a clear picture was hard to draw. Even an unclear picture was not a happy one.

At its centre was the command structure of the Soviet political economy. Soviet productive systems were highly administered ones. There was no market in the capitalistic sense. Economic performance criteria were laid down by planners. Supervision of the productive process was centralised, and bureaucrats determined what resources went where. Investment patterns, the costs of production, and prices, were the result of party-political and administrative decisions rather than those dictated by supply and demand.

Not surprisingly, there was chronic bureaucratic hypertrophy. 'Economic planning', one analyst observed, 'absorbs the energies of 700 administrative organs (including 100 central ministries) employing more than 15 million people. According to *Izvestiya*, every year 850 billion different documents are issued by the bureaucracy in the Soviet Union'. [7] Another result of centralised planning was the absence of anyone outside the system, except perhaps black-marketeers, whose behaviour might be monitored to determine how it performed.

In capitalist economies, where politics and economics are treated as separate realms, feedback is available in abundance. There are several key indicators which are scrutinised annually, weekly, daily, hourly, even moment to moment, that summarise the economic behaviour of the participants and suggest states of play. Interpreting these indicators is an industry in itself.

A Western capitalist economy in crisis will manifest clear symptoms of ill-being. The stock exchange will reflect quite quickly any large lack of confidence in the viability of current patterns of production. Brokers' businesses will start to crash, dole queues will lengthen, growing numbers of commercial concerns will declare themselves bankrupt, highly involved groups like chambers of commerce or trade unions will give public voice to the lack of confidence in prevailing governmental policies, and the media will report upon the crisis and offer comment on its causes and the possible cures.

Compare this with the Soviet Union where objective evidence of crisis must be read from the shortage of mass-produced consumer goods, the notable absence of entrepreneurial activity, the productive surges that go into meeting monthly, quarterly or annual plan targets, the extent of the black market, and tangential signs of low worker morale such as alcoholism. Gorbachev talked of slow economic growth, idle capital, the spiralling expense of resources and other measures of economic stagnation, but any statistical demonstration of these phenomena had to be read in the context of a command economy. Production was not related to consumption via buyers' opinions as summarised by their market choices (the black market remained the exception, and a most revealing one). Buyers were only relevant in a formal fashion, via the political process.

In a country like the Soviet Union, the political symptoms of lack of confidence in what state-makers provide have historically been censored and suppressed. Indeed Ferenc Feher has argued that since economics and administration have been so interlinked in Soviet affairs, 'there is only a single criterion of Soviet economic crisis: a statement by the leadership to that effect'.[8] This radically overstates the case, but it does highlight the importance of party-political recognition of a problem before there can be reform. [9]

The pervasiveness of Communist Party rule was apparent not just in the productive realm, but elsewhere. Soviet citizens did not inherit their state. It was consciously constructed in modern times along modern lines for the new Soviet human being. The main state-maker was the Communist Party, which had its committees in every factory, farm, office, school and block of flats, persuading, supervising and getting things done. Using the nomenklatura network the Central Committee controlled appointments to all responsible posts in society. It was the Party that sorted out the 'muddles and bottlenecks which inevitably ... [arose] when the planning system [got] tangled in its own tentacles'. It was the Party's right to sole rule that Marxism was said to endorse, a right 'bestowed upon it by history, of which its guardians profess[ed] a superior understanding'.[10] The ideology of the Party was comprehensive and pervasive, founded in a faith in ideas, and particularly 'all-embracing, systematic ones'.[11] Little wonder that the popular response to glasnost was often highly cynical. [12]

The totalising nature of Soviet state-making helps explain how perestroika was initiated. Having perceived the need for change, and having waited for the passing of the most influential members of the Old Guard, the Party power-brokers produced one of their number — a middle-aged male manager — to articulate and implement a programme of industrial and political reform. In Gorbachev's own words, 'Something strange was taking place: the huge fly-wheel of a powerful machine was revolving, while either transmission from it to work places was skidding or drive belts were too loose'.[13] The growth rate (as far as could be ascertained) in the country's income had halved in fifteen years and was stagnating. In terms of productive efficiency, product quality and the capacity to innovate, the Soviet Union seemed to be lagging further and further behind, so from the centre of this vast socioeconomic mechanism Gorbachev set about tightening the drive belts. How did he think he could stop the skidding?

His strategy, eschewing ready-made formulas, was to instigate change, which became progressively more radical as his original policies failed to have the desired effects. Some changes were largely technocratic and aimed at reforming the productive process. Others were designed to allow a political environment in which such reforms might work. Among the former were specific measures meant to encourage joint ventures with foreign firms; the self-financing of factories and collective farms; individual enterprise in small-scale production and trade; and the closure of non-paying plants operating at a loss. Among the latter were the introduction of secret ballots and multiple candidacy for elections; and fewer restrictions on press criticism of party policy.[14]

Clearly, given the integrated nature of the Soviet system, reform could not proceed far without a modicum of political and administrative decentralisation, and the relinquishing of some of the direct controls that characterise a command economy. At the same time democratisation was potentially political suicide for many of those who were supposed to carry through the reforms. In many cases, parasites were being asked to solve the problem of parasitism. Demagogues were being asked to accept diminished powers by other demagogues who showed no signs of relinquishing theirs. Not everyone agreed that something had to be done.

For the Soviet state-makers, however, and particularly the senior Party members committed to change, the need for reform had become acute. They were keen to see the Soviet Union remain a great power. This meant keeping up with the USA in military terms, while not succumbing to United States attempts to exhaust the Soviet Union in an increasingly expensive arms race. There was a clear sense that the USA was shifting the grounds of super-power competition from the military to the market, where the Soviet Union was clearly on the periphery.[15] By building a state within a state, with specialised research institutes and manufacturing centres designed to service military needs, Soviet state-makers had matched their United States rivals for decades. However, as Soviet society had become more urbanised and as people had become better educated, the distortions in the socioeconomic system had come to seem increasingly inequitable.

The choice facing Party leaders was to intensify domestic dualism, despite public dissensus, or to initiate radical reform (with no guarantee that the public would be satisfied this way either). They chose reform, with the 'social reorientation of the economy' as a major priority.

The rhetoric of reform showed how serious the question of public morale had become. The economic crisis was clearly social and cultural, to be confronted in those terms. The alienation of ordinary workers was a cause of direct concern, to be redressed by promoting greater public participation and by direct attacks on apathy and inefficiency.[16] The nineteenth All-Union Conference of the Communist Party of the Soviet Union, held in 1988, concluded that 'We must make people much more interested in the best end result, utterly overcome equalization tendencies, apply more boldly and everywhere the principle of payment according to the amount and, especially, the quality of the work done, and rule out a possibility of living a comfortable life while showing poor performance'.[17]

Modern-day state-making

The Soviet state is a recent invention. Over the space of one lifespan — three score years and ten — a succession of state-makers took a sprawling, still semi-feudal empire, and made it a world power providing for nearly 300 million people. They built a highly centralised political regime with the military might to project a global presence second to none and rivalled only by that of the USA.

How did their diverse practices further state sovereignty in the three aspects identified earlier, namely, formal territorial independence, singular authority and centralised institution-building, and popular participation?

Formal independence and equality

The modern Soviet state may be a recent invention, dating from 1917, but the history of Russia and of the Soviet Union is rich and complex. If it is told in terms of state-making alone then it began with the rise to prominence of Kiev, and the reign over the Eastern Slavs of Prince Svyatoslav in the tenth century. These early initiatives did not last, however, and the Mongol hordes of the thirteenth century found a region reduced to warring principalities. Tartar suzerainty lasted 200 years until the gathering of the Russian lands by Vasily II and the consolidation in the fifteenth century of Muscovite rule under his son, Ivan III (Ivan the Great). It was Ivan who first established diplomatic relations with Western Europe.

The first Muscovite emperor to visit Europe personally was Peter I. His reign was pivotal, and served to consolidate the Europeanisation of Russia that had been taking place throughout the seventeenth century. Catherine the Great in the eighteenth century, and Alexander I and II and Nicholas I and II in the nineteenth, extended and defended this process and the formal equality of the Soviet state in an emerging system of its peers. Thus the revolutionaries who took power in 1917, particularly the Bolshevik faction who came to dominate the revolutionary cause, did so as part of an organised international society with its own peculiar requirements and constraints. They were compelled to work within this framework, though their ideology did not accept its legitimacy. Indeed, their ideology prompted support for revolutionary movements wherever it seemed they would culminate in world socialist revolution.

One key difference between Bolshevism and the rule of the tsars, in other words, was a commitment to the end of the state system itself. This not only separated their leader and main ideologist, Lenin, from his reactionary predecessors, but alienated him from all his state-making confreres. Lenin had come to power despite the fact that Russia was not the place socialist revolution seemed most likely. His theoretical explanation for this anomaly posited a Communist Party acting in advance of the revolution's historic inevitability. This vanguard role was to be consummated and vindicated by international revolution. Lenin's analysis of the uneven development of world capitalism saw such a chain of events as imminent.

In terms of this theory, empire-building provided the profits needed to buy off the workers in the imperial countries. Given the tangible material rewards they received, they were much less likely to try to overthrow their rulers. It thus fell to the inhabitants of those lands ostensibly more backward in terms of capitalist development to instigate revolution. Needless to say, Lenin saw the Russians as prime movers in this regard. A socialist revolution in Russia was meant to lead to others in the more industrialised countries. The conditions in such countries had earlier seemed to favour such an outcome, but they ultimately did not do so. The Russian example was supposed to make workers elsewhere more aware of their false consciousness. Once enlightened by the Soviet example, workers elsewhere were supposed to revolt, and world socialism would ensue.

From this perspective a socialist world would not have international relations, as conventionally understood, since it would not need them. The fundamental conflict between the workers and those for whom they worked having being resolved, and class antagonisms having disappeared with the abolition of classes (as Marx had defined them), peace and global harmony were supposed to prevail.

Lenin came to power, in other words, committed to world revolution. In principle he rejected the state system as an artefact of international capitalism. He saw states as everywhere subordinate to the owners of the means of production. In practice, however, he was having to win a civil war and consolidate one-party rule and the integrity of the Soviet state.

Here Marx was of little help. Marx had not been very specific about how a socialist state might co-exist with non-socialist ones. It had been unnecessary since the question had little meaning in the light of his prediction that socialist revolution in the advanced capitalist countries would initiate global socialism. The fact of global socialism would have made the idea of co-existence academic. Socialism in one country was a contradiction in terms.

European nationalism made the question far from academic. The contradictions were acute. The Second International of the world's wage-labourers had broken up in 1914, for example, when European workers chose to identify with the capital-owning classes of their respective nations rather than with each other. Furthermore, the Russian revolution was not followed by others in the advanced capitalist world, which left Lenin without his original rationale.

In practice, Lenin tacitly accepted the formal equality of sovereign statehood, and the advent of conventional alliance diplomacy. This also meant accepting the need, forced by an unresponsive world system, to rank Soviet state-making over international revolution as a foreign policy priority. It meant a foreign policy, and the beginnings of a policy of socialism in one country only.

Lenin's successor, Stalin, made socialism in one country into one-man, one-party rule, alternately isolationist and diplomatically accessible by turns as international circumstances dictated. One such circumstance was the onset of Hitler's war on the West. Stalin had done little to impede Hitler's coming to power, since the expectation lingered that a proletariat revolution might still take place in Germany and that Hitler would expedite it. Hitler's expansionism forced a conventional geopolitical rereading of events, however, as did the rise of an intensely nationalistic Japanese state in the East, and the Japanese invasion of Manchuria.

The final Congress of the Communist International, held in 1935, was used by Stalin to popularise the notion of an alliance against fascism on the part of communists and non-communists alike. The Soviet Union joined the League of Nations, and though Stalin still gave support to worthy causes like the socialist side in the Spanish Civil War, he actively supported the concept of collective security, which was the notion that any state-makers within the interstate system who became aggressive would meet the combined opposition of their peers. The doctrine asserted that this should happen as a matter of course, with any ideological concerns and differences a secondary consideration.

When the leaders of Britain and France decided to appease Hitler at Munich in 1938, in the hope of avoiding war, collective security was clearly at an end and Stalin set about appeasing Hitler himself. After invading Austria and Czechoslovakia Hitler was set to strike further east. Rather than join the British and the French in a declaration of war on Germany, Stalin agreed with Hitler to keep the Russians apart, and to divide Poland between Russia and Germany. In geopolitical terms this left the Soviet Union in an enviable position, with the prospect of the European powers decimating each other in war, and Soviet state-makers then well-placed to arbitrate the ultimate outcome. A neutrality pact with the Japanese leadership seemed to strengthen this possibility.

In the event Hitler was not to be appeased and he marched on Leningrad, Moscow, Kiev and the Crimea. This pushed Stalin into a defensive alliance with the West, and a long and bitterly contested war with Germany he had not wanted and had tried hard to avoid, but had been forced to fight. Fighting this war required a prodigious productive effort, and a systematic appeal to national patriotism and pride. Communist ideology could not provide an equivalent sense of collective purpose and was downplayed for the duration. Victory, however, saw patriotism recast in terms of anti-capitalism, and the resurrection of the Marxist–Leninist resolve to prevail globally.

The motives of all capitalist imperialists were thus deemed highly suspect. At the same time Stalin set about consolidating the territorial gains victory had provided, routinising Soviet hegemony over Eastern Europe, and partitioning Germany into Western and Eastern wings.

The outcome was mixed. A defiant Tito in Yugoslavia managed to frustrate Stalin's designs to build a solid buffer between the Soviet Union and Western Europe, while the advent of a less than collaborative communist regime in China, and a war between North and South in Korea, continued to remind Soviet state-makers of the significance of sovereign jurisdiction and the ever-precarious character of geopolitics.

The death of Stalin and the ascension of Khruschev led to an accommodation with Tito, but relations with China did not improve. National interests proved more powerful than socialist solidarity, incidentally helping affirm for a more general audience the contemporary significance of the ideology of statism. Despite initial economic assistance to the Chinese, Soviet state-makers had no desire to help them actively prosecute their claim to control Taiwan, where the anti-communist regime from the mainland sat in defiant defeat, declaring its sovereign right to mainland rule.

The more general audience mentioned above included the post-war crop of newly independent third world countries. Khruschev saw there great potential for Soviet influence, given the plight of third world residents. Rather than providing active support for local communist parties, however, Khruschev took the anti-imperialist rhetoric of many third world state-makers as evidence of potential pro-Sovietism and set about offering assistance to a number of nationalist regimes who looked like they might bypass capitalism, as the Soviet Union was alleged to have done, to build socialism by statist means. He saw them as possible allies against the West.

As a general framework for these activities, Khruschev resuscitated the formula of peaceful coexistence between East and West. With the advent of nuclear weapons some such formula had become a necessity. The permanent acquisition of nuclear weapons suggested an equally permanent need for a strategy of live and let live. This did not seem to apply, however, to ideological competition with the capitalist world. Neither did it prevent Khruschev pushing the limits of United States resolve to the point of confrontation, as he did in trying to remove the Western presence from Berlin, or by putting Soviet missiles into Cuba. Within two years, however, by 1963, he had signed a nuclear test ban treaty with the USA and the UK, and relations with the West were generally much more relaxed. To the Chinese leaders, of course, this merely demonstrated further Soviet failure to prosecute the world communist cause.

A desire for compromise came not only from an awareness of the dangers of nuclear war. The post-war Soviet economy remained highly militarised, and thus unable to deliver more than the most basic of foodstuffs, clothing or housing to ordinary people. The attempt to provide a better standard of living for Soviet citizens required more attention to agriculture and the production of consumer goods. This in turn required a more amenable international strategic climate, since without such a climate the diversion of resources from heavy industry and the production of military hardware to light industry and agriculture was hardly feasible.

Khruschev's removal and the rise of Brezhnev marked a return to a more conservative Soviet regime. Nevertheless Brezhnev continued actively to pursue detente with Western Europe, while resisting (in Czechoslovakia by force of arms) any seemingly decisive East European moves out from under the Soviet umbrella of influence. Agreements with state-makers in the USA to slow down the nuclear arms race accompanied consistent attempts, in the Middle East for example, to counter United States influence.

After Brezhnev's death came two caretaker leaders, Andropov and Chernenko. Their deaths in turn opened the way for a younger, more technocratic leader, Mikhail Gorbachev.

Under Gorbachev all the familiar themes remained in evidence, namely, the parlous condition of the Soviet economy, doctrinal unease with a state-made world and with the major capitalist regimes in it, and an overarching awareness of the balance of nuclear terror. These themes were

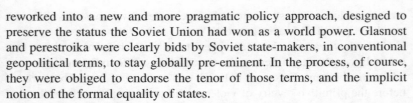

reworked into a new and more pragmatic policy approach, designed to preserve the status the Soviet Union had won as a world power. Glasnost and perestroika were clearly bids by Soviet state-makers, in conventional geopolitical terms, to stay globally pre-eminent. In the process, of course, they were obliged to endorse the tenor of those terms, and the implicit notion of the formal equality of states.

Part of Gorbachev's strategy was to sharpen the focus of Soviet foreign policy on Europe:

> Some in the West are trying to 'exclude' the Soviet Union from Europe ... Such ploys, however, cannot change the geographic and historical realities. Russia's trade, cultural and political links with other European nations and states have deep roots in history. We are Europeans ... The history of Russia is an organic part of the great European history ... Europe is ... [our] common home.[18]

Elaborating the metaphor, he went on to say that while 'the home is common ... each family has its own apartment'. This is probably the clearest possible image of the concept of formal equality that state sovereignty represents.[19]

In a world of sovereign domains the security dilemma is never far from state-makers' minds. As Gorbachev said:

> In speaking with foreign leaders I sometimes ask directly:'Do you believe that the Soviet Union intends to attack your country and Western Europe in general?' Almost all of them answer:'No, we do not'. But some of them immediately make a reservation, saying that the very fact of the USSR's immense military might creates a potential threat.[20]

Gorbachev's claim to understand such reasoning was a direct endorsement of it, and further evidence of his (nominal) acceptance of the geopolitical logic of interstate affairs. As he concluded: 'Every apartment ... has the right to protect itself against burglars.'[21]

Gorbachev's motives were unambiguous. He followed his paean to a common European heritage with the observation that: 'The building of the "European home" requires a material foundation ... We, in the Soviet Union, are prepared for this, including the search for new forms of cooperation, such as the launching of joint ventures, the implementation of joint projects in third countries, etc.'[22] Not only were they prepared for such initiatives, it could be argued that the Soviet state-makers (rather, wealth-makers) actively solicited them, seeking simultaneously to reassure European capitalists of the seriousness of their intent and the safety of any investments the said capitalists might care to make. 'It is high time to put an end to the lies about the Soviet Union's aggressiveness', Gorbachev concluded. 'Never, under any circumstances, will our country begin military operations against Western Europe unless we and our allies are attacked by NATO! I repeat, never!'[23]

Gorbachev was not above an appeal to cultural chauvinism either. One can only wonder, he mused, at the way a 'deep, profoundly intelligent and inherently humane European culture' was 'retreating to the background before the primitive revelry of violence and pornography and the flood of cheap feelings and low thoughts'.[24] This was a not-so-subtle jibe at the prodigious export trade of the cultural commodifiers of the USA in a bid, presumably, to elicit European sympathies, and to interest their investors.

The story of Soviet state-making, up to and including Gorbachev's glasnost and perestroika, bears witness to the capacity of the world's state-makers to discipline any potential wreckers of their system. Soviet state-makers, despite their ideological commitment to international socialism and to a non-state system of global relations, have never looked remotely like achieving these ends. They have not opted out. They have played the conventional game. They have usually had little choice. Whether they have seen this as opportunism on their part, while awaiting the inevitable triumph of socialism, hardly matters. They have contributed significantly, in practice, to the concept of the formal equality of all states in a world-wide state system.

Singular authority

Modern state-making means a commitment to sole control over all that happens within recognisable borders, and centralised institution-building. Where the border lines should run may still be in dispute. Central organisation and control may be partial or spasmodic, for constitutional reasons as in the case of a federal or confederal state, or because of an extraconstitutional challenge to the state-makers themselves (an insurrection, for example). The ideology of the state asserts the desirability of territorial integrity and of political cohesion. Thus constitutionally fragmented countries also have centralised arrangements that allow the presentation of a singular face to the world. Thus local insurgents or any other competing domestic force, such as a crime syndicate, will be suppressed wherever possible, and by military means if need be.

For Soviet state-makers, sustaining singular authority meant maintaining intact what was in effect the last of the European empires. The Soviet republics, in Gorbachevian parlance, constituted a 'unique union', a multi-nation nation. The diversity of the groups involved was enormous — over 100 discrete social entities, mostly with their own languages and with cultural histories extending well beyond the establishment of the pre-modern Soviet state — so the task was always difficult at best, and at worst constituted internal colonialism. It meant the continued frustration of long-standing claims for self-determination.

The Soviet Union was not alone in this. The corralling of disparate peoples into one-state formats has been a large part of the story of all contemporary political regimes. The process of integration is rarely complete either, as even the oldest state-made domains testify. The UK, for example, remains a patchwork of regional differences, and despite its name the nationalist sentiments of the Scots, the Welsh and the Northern Irish remain strong. Soviet state-makers have faced an inordinately large task in keeping singular authority over the component national parts of their land. The advent of glasnost and perestroika hardly helped.

In introducing these policies Gorbachev pointed first to the achievements of his predecessors, generally describing the Union as a success.

> Tsarist Russia was called a prison of nations ... [t]he Revolution and socialism have done away with national oppression and inequality, and ensured economic, intellectual and cultural progress for all nations and nationalities ... Our state would not have survived if the republics had not formed a community based on brotherhood and cooperation, respect and mutual assistance.[25]

If anything, he thought, previous policies had been too successful. They had fostered not only economic and cultural progress but the self-awareness of national groups as well. Hence the desire they often expressed for greater autonomy. How did his own approach fare in the face of this continuing desire?

To answer this question it is necessary to note that establishing and maintaining singular authority in the Soviet Union has been a multi-layered process. There were first those states not formally within the borders of the Soviet Union, but which had come at one time or another under its more or less direct influence, like the Eastern European states of Poland, Czechoslovakia, Rumania, Bulgaria, East Germany (the German Democratic Republic), and Hungary, as well as Yugoslavia and Finland. Each of these countries had its own complex political history. Some have spent long periods over the last few hundred years within the territorial domain of the emerging Soviet state. Their status as 'buffer states' between Western Europe and Russia has historically placed them in a precarious geopolitical position. All the Eastern European countries have had Soviet troops stationed within them, intermittently or continuously, for much of the last forty years.

The effect of Soviet proximity or of Soviet occupation was to prevent the state-makers concerned using their sovereign independence in anti-Soviet ways. The Eastern European response to glasnost and perestroika was initially mixed, though ultimately it paved the way for radical changes throughout the region. Soviet state-makers did not stop these changes, since their own initiatives had allowed them to happen. It was a measure of Soviet concern with the need for reform in the first place that they were prepared to step back from a major sphere of influence in the bid to open all socialist systems, their own included, to new wealth-making initiatives.

Secondly, there were the captive countries of Latvia, Estonia and Lithuania. These states lost their independence at the beginning of the last European war as part of a secret agreement between Soviet and German state-makers, and ended the war under Soviet domination. They never regained their sovereignty in this primary sense. Indeed, their formal independence could only be had at the expense of the singular authority of the Soviet state, a situation the nationalists involved deeply resented. They continued as a consequence to look for any and every opportunity to reclaim their lost autonomy.

Baltic nationalism remained strong throughout the post-war period despite Stalin's systematic oppression of it, and large-scale and intensive programmes of Russification. Glasnost and perestroika, by allowing greater criticism of central Soviet policies, and by legitimising decentralisation and democratisation, gave these subject citizenries new hope for greater economic, cultural and political independence. It made it possible for the leaders of the Baltic states to articulate clearly their case for the un-making of the Soviet state.

The articulation occurred in many forms. The Estonians, to take just one example, quickly imposed under local law a charge of 16 000 roubles for each newly arrived Russian worker (internal colonisation meant that 40 per cent of the Estonian population was non-Estonian). They gave public and private property equal status. They also granted permission for a number of new associations to operate openly, including the environmentally-conscious Greens, the Boy Scouts and, more importantly, the Estonian Popular Front (for the 'promotion of perestroika').

How could the state-makers in Moscow object to such a loyal demonstration of support for Gorbachev's decrees? A rhetorical question: Moscow newspapers began accusing Estonians of being neo-fascist, anti-Semitic, and anti-Russian. Local Russian workers, originally brought in to run industries established in Estonia by Soviet planners, set up their own organisation, the International Front (allegedly run and funded by the Soviet internal security police) to protest. Over half a million Russians resented the threat of possible eviction from their local jobs. Many were long-term residents, and many were indignant at Estonian ingratitude. Had not Russia brought progress and world culture to a backward and underdeveloped neighbour? Who owed what to whom?

Glasnost and perestroika certainly made it much harder for Soviet state-makers to justify their control over the Baltic states. Local leaders were keen to exploit Gorbachev's policies for whatever concessions they could win in the short term. These concessions were used in turn to keep alive the resolve to win independence in the long term, highlighting how dynamic state-making is and how a state must be constantly maintained if it is not to be un-made by those with other agendas.

The third part of the process of establishing and maintaining singular authority in the Soviet Union entailed the nationalities; that patchwork of ethnic groups that made up the polyglot and highly diverse Soviet populace. The dominant part of this patchwork, culturally and linguistically, was Russian, though the Russian Republic itself, one of the fifteen that made up the Soviet Union, contained sixty discrete nations (its land mass was three-quarters of the Soviet whole, that is, two times the size of the USA or China).

When Lenin came to power in 1917 he was faced with the problem of how to establish and sustain Communist Party power over such a mixed domain. His policy was two-handed. He was integrationist but at the same time supportive of minority cultures. He encouraged ethnic diversity while consolidating the new Soviet state. With his death, however, and with Stalin's single-minded drive to collectivise agriculture and develop Soviet industry, the integrationist trend dominated. Local cultures were overwhelmed by a new set of national, cultural and administrative practices that extolled the virtues of modernity and the importance of industrial productivity. This meant, in practice, intensive Russification by terror, with Russian language mandatory and Russian officialdom.

Under Khruschev and Brezhnev the pressure to integrate was eased somewhat, though the commitment to Russification was kept. Allowance was made for unity in diversity, rather than assimilation and integration only. Without the iron hand of repression, however, the balance between unity and diversity had to be struck in much more creative ways. This meant a combination of carrot-and-stick policies, designed to co-opt the collaborative and coerce the recalcitrant. Co-option meant giving local nationalist leaders a greater political stake in the system, while offering them material incentives to comply with state-making requests and to contain anti-Sovietism. It meant actively developing those national domains where living standards were low, and allowing at least some expression of nationalist sentiment as long as it remained non-political. Prominent and not-so-prominent dissenters were imprisoned or exiled.

Gorbachev's glasnost and perestroika meant a new turn again. Glasnost allowed an uncommon amount of organised protest, which in turn encouraged much greater nationalist dissent. Old antagonisms began to surface with new intensity. More open election processes produced candidates identified by national not Party allegiance, and such candidates began to win office. Civil disturbances sparked by ethnic issues became commonplace. Azerbaijan and Armenia became regular place-names in the Western press as public unrest spread.

Gorbachev argued a neo-Leninist line, espousing greater regional independence within the common framework of the Soviet state. The resolutions of the nineteenth All-Union Conference of the Communist Party of the Soviet Union proclaimed that:

> radical economic reform and democratization offer wide scope for the optimum combination of the interests of the national-state entities, on the one hand, and the country as a whole, on the other ... People must learn to distinguish between true national interests and their nationalistic perversion. Any claims to national exclusiveness are intolerable and insulting, and this also goes for the nation in whose name they are voiced.[26]

If they didn't learn their true interests, then presumably they could always be taught them. That is what singular authority means. No Soviet regime could allow the state to fragment as that would mean accepting its own demise. As the splintering intensified, therefore, so did the prospect of the use of force to maintain domestic integration. Gorbachev tried to allow enough rope for the Soviet political economy to become more free and productive, without having to hold so tight as to end up pre-empting his aims or hanging the state (or, presumably, himself). The necessity to solve the economic crisis and to match the technology and productivity of the West always had to be weighed against the perceived need for authoritarian rule, and the maintenance of the integrity of the Soviet Union itself.[27] The problem was hardly a new one. It had characterised Soviet affairs for four hundred years or more.

Because the Soviet Union was such a patchwork of national domains, and because its state-makers had built such a centralised and totalitarian political system, the dilemmas involved in letting the 'ethnic genie ... out of its bottle' were acute.[28] They were certainly heightened by glasnost and perestroika. The nationalities question, never resolved in the 1920s, resurfaced with a vengeance in the 1980s. That it should have done so suggests something of the power of regional national sentiment. It also indicates how the state has to be made from one moment to the next if its singular authority is not to be lost.

Popular participation

The Soviet Union is, by its own lights, an egalitarian state. Soviet state-makers are expressly committed to providing for the well-being of all the people who live within the borders of the Union. Popular participation in this vast human project has been very extensive. It has been actively discouraged, however, with regard to government. The long-term result seems to have been a profound sense of alienation, so profound as to have created a crisis in the country's productive capacity.

The response on Gorbachev's part, and that of his supporters, was on the one hand a liberalising one. Consider the following extract from the resolutions of the nineteenth All-Union Conference of the Communist Party of the Soviet Union:

> The Soviet state was born as a tool of the dictatorship of the proletariat and, at a later stage of social development, evolved into a state of the whole people. The task now is to bring the Soviet state system into full conformity with this concept, with all matters to be decided by the people and their plenipotentiary representatives and to be handled under full and effective control ... Our prime task is to fully restore the Leninist vision of democratic centralism.[29]

The resolutions confirmed the 'full authority of the Soviets of People's Deputies as the basis of the socialist state system and self-government' and the intention to conduct Party policy 'primarily via the bodies of people's representatives ... This makes it imperative above all to abandon the practice of Party committees acting in place of government or economic bodies ... [and] to completely abandon the command-style methods of work used by Party bodies'. At the same time the resolutions expressed the belief that 'the success of the reform of the political system decisively depends on the work of the Party ... as the political vanguard of the working class and all working people'. [30]

On the other hand the risks of a liberal political regime were self-evident, particularly in terms of a loss of the sort of singular authority felt necessary to stem domestic dissent and continue the programme of reform. Gorbachev consequently argued for and won extensive personal power. As President his authority rivalled that of Stalin's.

This was the rub. The Soviet government had been run in practice by the Communist Party. It had been a one-party state, and no amount of democratic rhetoric could disguise the centralised and dictatorial nature of one-party rule. With perestroika and glasnost, however, there was an attempt to shift this ruling role from a patrimonial to a caretaking one. The resolutions above were passed as part of those policies. They pointed towards a Soviet government run along more liberal lines. They suggested a serious retreat from, if not actual negation of, the key organising principle on which that government had been built. They suggested, in short, the eventual denial of Party control.

Much of a procedural nature was possible, of course, before talk of negation and denial was justified. Several resolutions addressed these procedural questions. One condemned admission to the Party according to quotas. Another recommended the right to recall elected Party members mid-term if they failed to fulfil their duties or if they disgraced themselves. Another recommended limits to terms of office. Others recommended the right to have freedom of discussion for Party election candidates, voting by secret ballot, and the nomination of more candidates than seats to be filled.

Many of these reforms were subsequently implemented. The result was an upsurge in political activity and public discussion, but no notable increase in productivity.

In highlighting the structural constraints on change, glasnost and perestroika laid bare the problem of state-making for the people, but not by them. It also, in a backhanded way, endorsed the concept of consensus as a key part of the modern ideology of the state.

Notes

1 R. Kaiser, 'The U.S.S.R. in Decline', *Foreign Affairs,* Fall 1988, p. 98.
2 G. Allison, 'Testing Gorbachev', *Foreign Affairs*, Fall 1988, pp. 19, 30, 31.
3 C. Castoriadis, 'The Gorbachev Interlude', *Thesis Eleven* 20, 1988, pp. 5-6.
4 M. Gorbachev, *Perestroika,* Fontana, London, 1988, p. 10.
5 R. Kaiser, op. cit., pp. 99, 100.
6 F. Feher, 'Crisis and Crisis-Solving in the Soviet System under Gorbachev's New Course', *Thesis Eleven* 21, 1988, p. 8.
7 P. Dibb, *The Soviet Union: the incomplete superpower*, Macmillan, London, 1986, p. 91.
8 F. Feher, op. cit., p. 8.
9 ibid., p. 9.
10 G. Hosking, 'A Great Power in Crisis: the first 1988 Reith Lecture', *The Listener*, 10 November 1988, p. 17.
11 ibid., p. 18.
12 ibid., p. 19.
13 M. Gorbachev, op. cit., p. 19.
14 ibid., p. 66.
15 V. Zhurkin et al., 'Challenges of Security — Old and New' (trans. G. Jukes), *Kommunist* no. 1 January 1988, pp. 42-50.
16 J. Battle, 'Uskorenie, Glasnost and Perestroika: the pattern of reform under Gorbachev', *Soviet Studies* vol. 40 no. 3, July 1988, pp. 370, 373.
17 M. Gorbachev, op. cit., p. 275.
18 ibid., pp. 191, 195.
19 ibid., p. 195.
20 ibid., p. 202.
21 ibid., p. 204.
22 loc. cit.
23 ibid., pp. 202-3.
24 ibid., p. 208.

25 ibid., p. 118.
26 ibid., pp. 298, 300.
27 On the equation of economic reform, technological backwardness and defence, see J. Hough, *Russia and the West: Gorbachev and the politics of reform*, Simon & Schuster, New York, 1988, ch. 9, 'Towards a Multipolar Policy'.
28 R. Kaiser, op. cit., p. 111.
29 M. Gorbachev, op. cit., pp. 281, 287.
30 ibid., p. 282, 287.

2

APPENDIX

Third world debt

What caused the third world debt crisis of the 1980s? What light does an analysis of these causes throw on wealth-making in the modern world?

The first appendix looked at the Soviet policies of glasnost and perestroika. It did so mostly in state-making terms, though the reform program of Mikhail Gorbachev was generally acknowledged to have had more than 'high political' significance. It also involved 'low political' issues and indeed, the political economy of perestroika was arguably its most important dimension.

Glasnost and perestroika also had social/ideological aspects, as the whole question of liberalising the Soviet political system and the Soviet market revealed. There were, furthermore, important social movements involved in the reform process, most notably those articulating demands for more autonomy for the captive nations of the Baltic, for example, or the diverse Soviet nationalities.

This second appendix looks at the issue of third world indebtedness, which is clearly of 'low political' concern. Though predominantly an economic problem, it too has other dimensions — state-making and social/ideological ones. However, I will be concentrating on the political–economy of the so-called crisis to explore not only why it should have arisen, but how this question might be answered from the three main approaches to political economy outlined above, namely, neo-mercantilism, liberalism and Marxism.

As a development problem debt repayment must be seen in context, since even if all the debts involved were paid, the debtor countries would be most unlikely to prosper (though some people within them would, as

they do now). The debt crisis does, however, show the world's wealth-making processes at work in a relatively unambiguous way. Any number of cases could have been chosen to show how the three main approaches to the world political–economy apply in practice. The growing significance of finance capital in general makes debt, however, an issue of more than passing interest.

More than Hiroshima every two days

The world capitalist system grew in a highly opportunistic and unplanned way. Progress was not smooth. It was highly troubled. Periods of dramatic growth alternated with equally dramatic slumps. Within the larger cycles of boom and bust, furthermore, there were lesser ones of inflation and stagnation (and sometimes both together). In the last two hundred years, for example, though industrial expansion and the increase in capitalist productivity were clearly dramatic, there were forty recessions. In the last twenty years alone there were four. 'Economic policy did not significantly modify — let alone prevent — any of these recessions', Andre Gunder Frank observes, 'but all of the[m] ... did significantly affect if not determine economic policy'.[1]

The effects of large slumps and smaller recessions were very uneven, in other words. They were intensely political. In the last century, for example, interstate indebtedness was one excuse creditors used to invade and occupy the territory of their debtors. Thus when the Egyptian state-makers of the late 1870s found themselves having to use more than half their country's income to pay for their loans (when they got into financial difficulties meeting their interest repayments) European creditors (the French and the British) moved in to manage their financial affairs. The British ultimately used this as part of their rationale for establishing an Egyptian protectorate. In short, they annexed the place.[2]

Such a move would not be feasible today, at least, not in a comprehensive way. The ideology of sovereignty and of non-intervention is too strong. Nor is annexation usually necessary. Territorial imperialism has been superseded for the most part by the seemingly more remote though no less intense relationships of political–economic dependence and interdependence.

The intensity of these relationships is marked. They juxtapose the most 'powerful, hierarchical, elitist institutions in rich countries ... and the poorest, most obscure, hungriest peasants or slum-dwellers in poor countries'.[3] Consequently the decisions made by bankers, rich-world state-makers, and the representatives of such international financial institutions as the World Bank and the International Monetary Fund have an immediate impact on ordinary people. The impact is not negligible. Indeed, it can kill, for example, by raising food prices. [4]

The remoteness of these relationships is equally marked. The juxta-position does not bring those involved face-to-face. The policy-makers whose decisions have such an 'explosive impact' on the lives of the lowly have been likened to bomber pilots 'for whom the shattered bodies 50,000 feet below are simply not there'. [5] They live in the world of the well-to-do, directly responsible for but largely insulated from the conditions under which the poor and the marginalised must live. Theirs is a comfortable world of privilege and plenty. The statistics that are the basis of the policies they shape or make are suitably dispassionate. State-makers, wealth-makers and international bureaucrats do not starve. Nor do they run with the dispossessed when they riot and are shot at for protesting about their plight.

This is worth bearing in mind when discussing third world debt since it can be difficult to retain a sense of the lived experience of it once the abstract analysis of cause and effect begins. The practices that make such indebtedness a problem are symptomatic of a larger developmental crisis that Susan George estimates costs more than 15 to 20 million lives a year; more, that is, than the 'equivalent of a Hiroshima every two days'. [6] The casualties are not so obvious because they are not all in one place, and they are not killed with a bang. They still die, though, and the debt crisis is one thing that kills them.

What is third world debt?

Debt is a familiar concept in commercial cultures. I borrow money; I buy what I want or need; I pay back whoever I borrowed the money from with other money I have garnered, plus extra for the privilege of having rented somebody else's savings for a while. The extra is the interest the lender gets for allowing me to use his or her funds in this way.

The system works as long as people keep making their payments. Indeed, capitalism could be said largely to be about the creative use of credit (debt). Most people, including companies and countries, get their credit from banks. They have been doing so in Europe since the sixteenth century when the Medicis and the Fuggers first made (and lost) fortunes financing the wars of the Holy Roman Emperors or the kings of Spain and France. Banks are basically profit-making enterprises that make money by lending money. They make a profit out of the difference between the interest they charge on a loan they might make to Morocco or General Motors or me, and the interest they pay to people who leave money with them for this purpose.

Anyone earning interest on money in the bank is making money and doing nothing for it other than making it available to be used by someone else. In this way money can make more money. The saver isn't working for the rent he or she gets for his or her savings. Other people have to do that. It is other people's productive use of the funds they have borrowed that allows them to repay their loans and to pay interest on them, thereby augmenting the accounts of the savers and supplying the bank with its share for providing this service. Presumably the profit that borrowers make by being productive includes something for themselves too, otherwise there would be no incentive to be productive or to borrow.

Banks are basically conveniences. They aggregate money and make it readily accessible to borrowers. They also speed the way money, as symbolic of productive value, moves around in the market. Most of it hardly touches the ground. Banks lend out much more than they actually have available in their vaults in the form of people's cash deposits. As a consequence most of the money in a capitalist economy is not paper cash and coin at all. It is made up of figures in bank computers. Furthermore, banks have only a fraction of what they say they have. They rely on the fact that depositors won't all want to draw out their deposits at once, so the cash reserves they carry to cover such withdrawals are relatively small.

The whole system runs as long as there is economic growth and profits flow in, old debt can be paid off and new debts can be undertaken. If confidence flags, however, and too many savers try to withdraw their deposits, the bank's cash reserves will not be enough. Bankers will start calling in loans, bankrupting many of those who have borrowed from them. If people panic and there is a run on savings, banks themselves can collapse. Businesses which want to borrow then can't, and can fail in turn. Indeed, banking relies on a 'gigantic confidence trick — the pretence that deposits which have been lent out are really still there, capable of being withdrawn at any time'.[7] It is a very creative trick, but it leaves banks very vulnerable.

Short of this sort of crisis, banks are very robust. They can decide when to stop backing a capitalist who is failing to produce; when, that is, to cease sanctioning his or her activities. They can continue to support someone they believe will trade his or her way out of a liquidity or productivity crisis. This applies particularly to national debtors.

> So long as bankers maintain confidence in a country's ability to pay interest on its debt, they can afford to be magnanimous where principal is concerned. Banks, like other commercial enterprises, care about profits. They care about receiving regular payments for the use of their money, and the longer this money is outstanding, the higher the profit. [8]

So what is important is not debt as such but the capacity to make

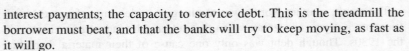

interest payments; the capacity to service debt. This is the treadmill the borrower must beat, and that the banks will try to keep moving, as fast as it will go.

Third world debt is more than one trillion US dollars. This is an enormous amount but it is only half the debt carried by the USA, only one-third the annual turnover of the world's top 200 corporations, and only one-tenth the amount of the world's annual economic activity. [9] The debt itself is not problematic. It is the capacity to service the debt that has become so, and the consequences this has for the third world's capacity to share in world production.

Many of the financially poorer countries are so deep in debt that new loans must be devoted almost entirely to paying the interest on old ones, with the bizarre result that not only can there be little productive use of any new money borrowed, but that a bank may make a loan only to find most of the money coming straight back again. Such a bank is in effect lending to itself, with only the granting process, the collecting service and the paperwork in between.

However bizarre it may seem this result is still preferred to having state-makers default since, unlike a person's property, or even the assets of a corporation, states can't be repossessed as Britain once repossessed Egypt. A national debt that is not rescheduled in some way is likely to be lost absolutely. As profit-making entrepreneurs, bankers abhor this possibility. Not only does it involve material damage to them and their banks, it can undermine confidence in the financial system as a whole, which in turn affects productivity and trade. It could even induce global economic depression.

Though long in the making, and arguably inevitable, third world debt did not emerge as a critical issue in world affairs until the early 1980s. The trigger was the decision in August 1982 by Mexican state-makers to suspend the country's debt repayments and to ask for debt rescheduling. The response was swift and set a precedent for the fifty other national debt-carriers who, within twelve months or so, had followed Mexico's lead. Bridging finance was organised and repayments were rescheduled as quickly as possible to stabilise the system as a whole.

The result was co-operation without reform. Rich-world state-makers, bankers, international financial institutions and the debt-carriers themselves worked closely not only to sustain the status quo, but also, it seems, to reinforce the plight of the poor. Rather than have bankers make provision for bad debt in their accounting ledgers, for example, debts were restructured to keep the system intact. Furthermore, the terms on which debts were restructured were traditional ones that secured the profits of the banks and conspicuously failed to effect any systemic reform.

The result, in other words, was to plunge a wide range of poorer countries into a depression greater than that suffered by industrialised states in the 1930s. Though debt was only one cause of their material hardship, often a relatively minor one, most people living in sub-Saharan Africa had living standards no better and often worse than the ones their parents had a generation previously, when many of the countries concerned first became sovereign states. Ordinary living standards likewise declined in Latin America where real wages, in a country such as Mexico, fell to half what they were ten years previously.

Why third world debt: neo-mercantilism?

We do not live in a neo-mercantilist world, despite its having certain neo-mercantilist features. In a neo-mercantilist world there would be national self-sufficiency on a wide scale, minimal international trade and minimal debt. This is not characteristic of the current world political–economy, however, and neo-mercantilism has not therefore been a cause of third world debt.

Ecological factors may yet move the world political–economy in a neo-mercantilist direction. A major planetary ecological crisis, for example, could well encourage the widespread adoption of doctrines of sustainable development. The autarchy of countries like Albania and Myanmar (formerly Burma) do not provide very positive examples, however, of what such self-sufficiency might mean. The command socialist regimes common to both sought to limit imports and to encourage domestic agricultural and industrial production. The result was subsistence living for all but a small minority, as well as (and not coincidentally) authoritarian rule and cultural isolation.

In practice neo-mercantilism abounds in selective and less generalised ways. Protectionist measures are used by many state-makers, for example, to bolster particular industries. These measures may be specific to particular sectors but their neo-mercantilist intention is clear. While espousing free market principles, capitalist industrialists can be as keen as command-economy ones to impose such self-serving restrictions, thus controlling imports and ostensibly securing some degree of commercial or political advantage. None of this has much relevance, however, when we come to consider the scale and scope of the debt burden poor countries currently bear.

Why third world debt: liberalism?

In principle, autarchic self-denial is anathema to radical liberals. Entrepreneurial activity in a free world market is the liberal way to get economic growth and development. In line with this view, economics and politics are seen as separate realms, and the debt crisis is considered primarily an economic issue, though it may have political ramifications. As an economic issue it is explained either as a result of macroeconomic shock, market imperfections, or the failure to adjust. [10]

The 'macroeconomic shock' approach highlights the way the enormous increase in the price of oil in 1973-74 and later in 1978-79 upset the global balance of payments. Before 1973-74 industrialised countries ran a moderate balance of payments surplus, while the non-industrialised countries, most of whom were oil-importing, ran deficits. Those with a surplus expected those with deficits to take their money and use it in productive ways. Through investment, foreign aid and non-concessional lending, the overall global balance was maintained.

After 1973-74 the industrialised countries had to pay much higher oil bills which meant they also began running deficits. The non-oil producing developing countries ran much larger ones. There was still money to finance these deficits, however, since the oil-exporting countries had a large surplus, which they recycled through commercial banks at rates that in real terms (once inflation was accounted for) were reasonably low; even negative in some cases.

After the second oil price-hike in 1978-79 policy-makers in the USA tightened the country's monetary policies (raising interest rates, increasing the value of the dollar, and decreasing the cost of oil and labour). This was part of a longer term effort to deal with the country's declining position in the world economy, relative to Japan, Europe and the newly industrialised countries of East and Southeast Asia. Because the effect, particularly of the higher interest rates, was to make corporate borrowing more expensive, United States businesses were given tax relief and huge defence contracts. The result was a 'triple debt crisis', [11] and a deep world recession for four years.

The dramatic change in the world market, from high growth to recession, had disastrous effects for many developing countries. As state-makers in the richer countries moved, in neo-mercantilist fashion, to protect their domestic markets from foreign competitors, they began making it harder for debtor-states to sell in their markets and therefore to earn the money needed to pay the interest on their debts. The debtor-state share of world trade declined.

As productivity slowed generally so too did the industrialised world's demand for commodities, which in turn drove down commodity prices. This also affected what poor-state debtors could earn abroad to pay interest bills. With both the volume and value of their exports cut, the squeeze on debtor-state economies (with notable exceptions like South Korea) was severe.

In addition, the high United States interest rates were attractive to capitalists in debtor countries who saw more profits to be made in the USA than in production at home. This effect was exacerbated by the flexible rates on most of the loans that the developing countries carried. Higher interest rates meant bigger repayment bills. Old loans became harder to service and new loans became much more expensive.

What was to be done? Macroeconomic shock analysts saw the debt crisis as manageable if growth in the industrialised countries could be sustained at about 3 per cent a year, and real interest rates could be brought down. Under these conditions the benefits of growth might be expected, in good liberal fashion, to trickle down, to open new markets, and to generate demand for developing-world commodities, thus driving up the price for their exports and stimulating new lending by the commercial banks. Kahler states that:

> Needless to say this explanation of the debt crisis is favored by the commercial banks and the debtor countries ... It awards primary responsibility to economic policy shifts beyond their control, not to their own actions or to imperfections in financial markets. Equally clear is the discomfort this reading of the debt crisis causes for Northern elites. Though they (and the international organizations that tend to reflect their point of view) may accept that the change in economic conditions was swift, they also emphasize that the disinflationary change was essential to longer-term growth and that the new environment is permanent; hence adjustment, however painful, is required.[12]

A second, less doctrinaire, version of liberal thinking highlights the financial market alone and the way, in a system that has no lender of last resort '[c]ontagion effects and herd behavior produce "feast or famine".'[13] The system is ungoverned. Banks have the opportunity, where they can, to do what they want. Their pursuit of short-term profit, however, can, and in many cases has, proved detrimental both to themselves and to their clients in the longer term. Bankers become less willing as a result to lend to poorer countries because of the risk of debt repudiation. (State-makers have not used repudiation because of their fear of alienating major creditors in what is now a financially highly interdependent world. Reprisals, while short of repossession, would still be severe.)

The notion that there might be market imperfections of this sort suggests the need for controls over both lending and borrowing behaviour. Classical liberalism would never countenance such a response. Political intervention is ideologically unacceptable, but of course it happens, and there was a good deal of it in managing the third world debt crisis. The whole saga involved colluding bankers, with state-makers stepping in to back them up, and the administrators of the major international financial institutions (dominated by creditor-country members like the USA) imposing liberalising market conditions.

A third strand in the liberal approach highlights the policies of debtor-state policy-makers and their failure to adjust. From this perspective local decision-makers are largely to blame. The difference between and within particular regions, like Latin America and Africa, shows that more than market imperfections and macroeconomics are involved. This being the case, the obvious response is to look at what state-making developers have been doing and how they have been doing it.

The remedy recommended here is close control of local development policies. Close control means curbing debtor government spending, reducing real wages, reducing tariffs, and floating currencies. It means even more in some cases — a fundamental reorientation of the pattern of development undertaken by the major debtors during the period of easy finance.[14]

Again this has a distinctly illiberal ring. It would hardly seem to be the way to let the free market sort the matter out. Yet the use of the International Monetary Fund to make bridging loans conditional on local policy adjustments, for example, seems to have had as much to do with policing creditor-state interests as promoting debtor-state ones. This prompts the question of who is this sort of development for? Those waiting for the benefits to trickle down? Or those who want access to third world markets and cheaper labour? Or both?

It also raises the more general question of what model of development debtors and creditors prefer. Susan George argues that the most common model in this regard assumes that all rich countries are the same, and that poor ones get to be rich by copying what the rich have done. This in turn has fostered an emphasis on economic growth, on industrialisation as being more important than food security, on the precedence large capital works ought to take over small-scale enterprises using ordinary people's practical skills, and on the need to orient poor-state economies out towards the world market.

This sort of imitative development also fosters conspicuous consumption. This can be as simple as the demonstration effect that prompts a Solomon Islands villager, for example, to sell his labour on a part-time basis (to a copra plantation owned by a multinational corporation perhaps) so he can earn enough to buy and run an outboard motor for his canoe. At the other extreme it can involve the entire state-making and wealth-making class of a developing country in pursuing a material lifestyle well beyond the national (but not their own class-specific) means.

More generally it can mean investment in inappropriate projects that involve large amounts of capital to little collective benefit. This is another example of the demonstration effect, though at the governmental level. State-makers buy costly, sophisticated concepts and equipment that are inappropriate but attractive because of their very modernity. They are attractive because they are contemporary and technologically complex. Policy-makers feel pleased to prefer such material or mental products, despite the fact that more modest and practical alternatives exist that would be more suitable for the society at large.

Imitative development also fosters corruption. State-makers and wealth-makers want to be able to copy the lifestyle of their peers in richer countries. Indeed, they often seek to outdo those peers in very expensive ways. Because they are the conduits through which state resources run, they are well placed to divert some of the stream towards themselves. Though these resources are typically paltry in terms of the collective need, they are vast as personal fortunes. Vivid accounts abound of monumental greed in this respect. The cost of corruption at all levels, but particularly that of comprador elites, is incalculable.

One of the most costly forms of such corruption is capital flight. State-makers and wealth-makers with access to funds in hard currencies may remit as much of them as they can to personal accounts in more developed economies. Capital flight can be a legitimate exercise in liberal-style profit maximisation. State-makers or wealth-makers in a poorer country who receive a bank loan, for example, may decide to invest the money back with the lending bank itself because of the high interest rates the bank offers to its depositors. As long as those state-makers and wealth-makers can get money from other sources they can repay what they borrow using new money from other loans. This gives them more interest on what they deposit than what they must repay, for the moment at least. They make a profit, and presumably more so than they could get investing at home. This leaves the bank short, but it relends the money returned on deposit to someone else at a rate high enough to exceed the shortfall between the interest it is paying and the interest it is receiving, so it makes a profit too.

Summarising this sort of behaviour Cheryl Payer notes how it has 'nothing to do with real investment or growth; it is a "Ponzi scheme", a chain letter-type con game in which there are bound to be losers at the point where new suckers cannot be found to participate in the game. On Main Street, a scheme like this could land its promoter in prison'. [15] The line between liberalism and unalloyed greed is often hard to find, and never more so than here.

Corruption comes at a social and political cost, namely, repression. Keeping access to and control over the conduits of state wealth can mean actively intimidating those who object. It is not surprising, therefore, that the state-makers involved spend heavily on security forces, where they are not already constituted as a military government themselves. Popular resistance is made progressively more radical as a result.

Money spent on arms purchases (as opposed to arms production, which rather ironically provides export earnings for debtor countries like Brazil and Egypt, who got into debt in the first place in part because of large arms purchases) is economically wasteful. Arms purchases generate no surplus that can be used to pay back the loans taken out to make them. They have to be paid for, in other words, from elsewhere in the economy, and welfare sectors typically suffer first. Popular resentment can always be dealt with using the purchased arms, justifying incidentally the security need for such arms in the first place.

Poor countries are not the only ones to spend heavily on defence. As noted earlier, part of the Reagan strategy for lifting from United States business the burden of the country's relative economic decline was to spend heavily on arms. This was a decision more to do with the strategic balance with the USSR, however, and the decision to pay for the local arms industry from the public purse, than any need to repress domestic dissent.

Why third world debt: Marxism?

George talks of the debt crisis as an error of judgement. Under boom conditions reckless lenders and improvident borrowers do deals which, come the bust, come unstuck. With regard to third world indebtedness '[n]ever before have so few been so wrong with such a devastating effect on so many'. [16]

She also talks of the debt crisis as a windfall which placed the bankers involved and the state-makers who backed them up in a very strong position to continue exploiting third world weakness to their own pecuniary gain. Capital transfers from poorer states to richer ones in the form of debt repayments now exceed those from richer states to poorer ones, whether in the form of aid or investment. The poor of the poorer countries subsidise in this way the living standards of the rich in both the poorer and richer ones. All, George concludes, in the name of development.

Judgements like these, that emphasise the greed of those who got the poor into their plight, bankers and borrowers alike, are radical versions of the liberal 'failure to adjust' and 'market imperfection' theses. From a Marxist perspective they are superficial. The point is not corruption, conspicuous consumption, or capital flight. The point is exploitation. Capitalists are profit-predators. Their behaviour is entirely predictable. It would be unrealistic to expect them to behave otherwise. But what about the consequences of that behaviour, and more particularly, the political consequences?

Radical liberals argue that this is ultimately not within their jurisdiction. Thus we find Holley concluding that '[w]hether reverse transfers of the order of 3 per cent a year or more of GDP will in practice prove tolerable to the heavily indebted countries is one of the imponderables and is essentially a political question'.[17] To a Marxist, however, the question is emphatically not so. Rather it is the heart of the matter. It is the basic reason why exploitation is inevitable.

Classical Marxists focus upon capitalism and its basically competitive character.[18] To them the crisis is not so much to do with the international financial arrangements that govern orderly credit use and debt repayment, since that crisis is only symptomatic of a larger, more profound crisis in the capitalist system as a whole. They see capitalism as moving in a cyclical fashion that spirals down, not up. Capitalists accumulate profits, some of which they reinvest in further production. Driven by competition they look for ways to make more money, or, in Marxist terms, to generate more surplus-value. The process is problematic, however, since '[a]ccumulation tends to undermine itself ... it cuts into the rate of profit, the flame which lures it forward'. The tendency for the rate of profit to fall, in other words, means 'deeper and more prolonged crises' as capitalism proceeds. [19]

Marx himself considered the use of credit by capitalists as both an example of the system at its most extreme and a harbinger of things to come.

> The two characteristics immanent in the credit system are on the one hand, to develop the incentive of capitalist production, enrichment through exploitation of the labour of others, to the purest and most colossal form of gambling and swindling, and ... on the other hand, to constitute the form of transition to a new mode of production. It is this ambiguous nature, which endows the principal spokesmen of credit ... with the pleasant character mixture of swindler and prophet. [20]

The capitalism of Marx's time was not the capitalism of today. Those who practised it were less organised and their efforts were on a smaller scale. Crises helped clean out the system, removing the less efficient and the less ruthless entrepreneurs. The growing aggregration of capital since his day, however, particularly by bankers, has made crises more dangerous. The productive parts of the system are now larger, and the prospect of their failure is potentially much more serious for the system as a whole. State-making has become, from this perspective, a matter of ensuring capitalism does not collapse. Finance capital has thus become state capital, 'not just in Russia but throughout the capitalist world'.[21] Furthermore, systemic irrationalities are sustained because it becomes too costly to contemplate the sort of bankruptcies that rationalisation would involve.

So 'the contradictions persist, the system staggers from slump to weak recovery, back into slump — and the debts have just grown and grown'.[22] The real crisis is never dealt with, which, in classical Marxist terms, means 'too much investment — too much to generate the rate of return necessary to satisfy investors or meet the interest payments on borrowed money'. This means that in a time of economic downturn the real crisis is 'not too little productive capacity but too much — too much for stagnant world markets in particular industries ... and too much to generate a rate of profit sufficient to meet the demands for interest repayment on borrowed funds'. [23] (South Korea may be an exception, but in a time of economic downturn exceptions like this can be very few.)

The real question, to a classical Marxist, then becomes how long the proletariat can suffer in those countries most affected before they revolt. Their emiseration cannot go on indefinitely. Or can it?

Less orthodox Marxists are not so sure. The debt crisis, in their view, has been a sustained and largely successful attempt by the world's capitalists to reassert their control over the political economies of the periphery. As countries develop they tend to become more independent. Their markets become harder to penetrate, their resources become more costly, and the investment opportunities they present become less profitable. It thus becomes necessary to cripple them again if capitalists are to maximise their profitability. How is this done?

Harry Magdoff gives one account of this process, drawing a picture of neo-imperial ebb and flow, peripheral countries borne high on the tide of international finance when it is up, and stranded and helpless when it is down.[24] Those countries able to industrialise have been able historically to use the markets, the resources and the economic surplus of others to get rich. The others — typically ex-colonies whose class structures and international relationships have been radically distorted by their subordinate status — have remained dependent, their local wealth-makers and state-makers collaborating with the capitalists of the industrialised countries to keep their countries tied into the political economy of the developed metropoles. One symptom of this dependency, and a continuing cause of it in turn, has been 'debt peonage',[25] manifest in contemporary times as the debt crisis.

The obvious alternative to dependency is neo-mercantilist self-reliance. If economic hardship, political instability and social distress are the consequences of staying in the system, quitting it is an obvious option. Do debtors quit, however, only to find nowhere to go?[26]

Cheryl Payer thinks not. She queries whether poorer countries have ever actually needed imported capital. The best solution, she believes, is for debtor countries to default and for their creditors to accept the fact. There might be no more loans, but debtor countries would then have their own capital to use instead of losing it in interest repayments. The world trade system could then be reconstructed on a 'pay-as-you-go basis', she concludes. It would be 'slower but healthier', and the most positive outcome would be 'enhanced autonomy for the previous debtor countries, in place of the slavish, but insincere, subjection to finance capital which still rules the Third World'.[27]

Classical Marxists would disagree. Like the liberals they would not see default, autarchy and trade by barter as a feasible option in the contemporary political economy. The loss of lines of credit, of trading opportunities and of any assets left outside, would make self-reliance too costly. More importantly, it would not stop local workers being exploited. It would 'merely [mean] that the local ruling class would receive a larger share of the surplus-value'. [28]

Unlike radical liberals, however, classical Marxists would see the problem as caused by world capitalism. The bankers and state-makers of the creditor countries may have prevented the debtors declaring themselves bankrupt, but 'whilst they have rescued the banks, they have not rescued the debtor economies'.[29]

Classical Marxists would see the rich as living on borrowed time. The intolerable pressures on those who have been marginalised by the normalisation strategies of the world's capitalists will be what ultimately wrecks the system. The underlying accounts are ones that can only be paid in terms of a new and non-capitalist mode of production.

While less orthodox neo-Marxists may sympathise with this sentiment, they have seen capitalism mount its own rescue more than once, and are less optimistic than their more conventional peers that in the last instance the laws of history as Marx discerned them will prevail. The hour of the last instance is a lonely one, they feel, and it is proving to be very late indeed.

Notes

1 A. Frank, 'Can The Debt Bomb Be Defused?,' *World Policy Journal* vol. 1 no. 4, Summer 1984, p. 739. See also C. Kindleberger, *Manias, Panics and Crashes*, Macmillan, London, 1978.

2 H. Magdoff, 'Third World Debt: Past and Present', *Monthly Review* vol. 37 no. 9, February 1986, p. 1.

3 S. George, *A Fate Worse Than Debt*, Penguin, Harmondsworth, 1988, p. 6.

4 loc. cit.

5 ibid., p. 7.

6 ibid., p. 262.

7 P. Green, 'Debt, the Banks and Latin America', *International Socialism* no. 21, Autumn 1983, p. 8. For a liberal view see H.Holley, *Developing Country*

Debt: the role of the commercial banks, Chatham House Papers no. 35, The Royal Institute of International Affairs, Routledge & Kegan Paul, London, 1987, particularly ch. 5, 'Creditor and Debtor Interests'.

8 S. George, op. cit., p. 13.

9 ibid., pp. 12–13.

10 M. Kahler (ed.), *The Politics of International Debt*, Cornell University Press, Ithaca, 1986, p. 12.

11 G. Epstein, 'The Triple Debt Crisis', *World Policy Journal* vol. 2 no. 4, Fall 1985, p. 626.

12 M. Kahler, op. cit., pp. 12–13.

13 ibid., p. 14.

14 ibid., p. 13.

15 C. Payer, 'Causes of the Debt Crisis' in R. Cherry et al. (eds), *The Imperial Economy* vol. 1, Union for Radical Political Economics, New York, 1987, p. 198.

16 S. George, op. cit., p. 44.

17 S. Holley, op. cit., p. 76.

18 P. Green, op. cit., p. 3.

19 ibid., p. 10.

20 K. Marx, *Capital: a critique of political economy* vol. 3, Progress Publishers, Moscow, 1966, p. 441.

21 P. Green, op. cit., p. 18.

22 ibid., p. 16.

23 ibid., pp. 33, 32.

24 H. Magdoff, op. cit., p. 4.

25 ibid., pp. 5, 8.

26 A. Frank, op. cit., p. 739.

27 C. Payer, op. cit., p. 204.

28 P. Green, op. cit., p. 52.

29 loc. cit.

3

Indigenous peoples

APPENDIX

What is an indigenous people? What claims do they make? How do they make them?

The first appendix looked at contemporary Soviet state-making and state unmaking. It discussed the economic and social dimensions of glasnost and perestroika, but it was primarily concerned with the polity, as far as this can be dissociated from the material premises on which it is based.

The second appendix examined the question of third world debt. Though it glanced at the social/ideological aspects of this issue, it concentrated on the political economy of it, as this might be construed from a neo-mercantilist perspective, or a radically liberal perspective (which talks of economy only, confounding it as little as possible with the concept of the polity), or a materialist perspective (which talks of modes and relations of production).

The following case study briefly explores the attempts made to mitigate the problems indigenous peoples face because of the state-bound nature of the world in which they live. It is a social study, and for the purposes of this appendix the focus will be on social affairs. It will examine the nature of the claims made by indigenous peoples to win greater autonomy in the states where they are located, and in world society as a whole.

It will be immediately apparent, however, that the concerns of indigenous peoples have economic and political consequences as well. They have important implications, in other words, for 'high' and 'low' politics. Again, many social movements could have been chosen to exemplify this dimension, though the plight of indigenous peoples seemed particularly apt.

What is an indigenous people?

The problems indigenous peoples face are as old as modern state-making. As state-makers progressively increase the scope and intensity of their practices, so they magnify the concerns of all the minority peoples caught within them, including those of the so-called indigenous peoples. These concerns have most clearly included the collective desire not to be killed. They have also included, however, a specific sense of the kind of survival such peoples prefer, namely, one where their cultural identity can be maintained, and where the onslaughts of those who would destroy minorities as identifiable peoples can be prevented indefinitely.

Lists made of those indigenous peoples still extant today usually cite the Central and South American Indians, the Inuit Eskimos, the Australian Aborigines, New Zealand's Maoris, the Saami of Scandinavia, the Ainu of Japan, and diverse tribal groups in Africa, India, the Soviet Union and Papua New Guinea. All these groups have found themselves struggling to defend their right to occupy the areas they have traditionally inhabited, as well as having to cope with state-makers administering their affairs, and undermining their capacity to maintain their distinctive traditions and traits. Few have fared well. Most have found themselves 'politically weak, economically marginal, and culturally stigmatized'.[1]

The indigenous peoples listed are the descendants of the original inhabitants of lands that today form the territories of nation-states. Many of these lands were taken and settled by force. This usually involved the suppression of the nations already there or, where the nationals proved too strong to eliminate or assimilate, the superimposition of a state-specific national identity. Some local peoples with distinctive cultures managed to resist this superimposition, and those that did so successfully are those that have lived to tell the tale. Current definitions of indigenous peoples consequently highlight their status not only as aboriginal and culturally distinct, but as colonised too.

This definitional shift is part of the process of taking the key conceptual questions out of the hands of the state-makers — the colonisers — and putting it into those of the colonised; or rather, the reclaiming of control over the political language involved by those victimised by it. The whole question of just who is what in this context is much more widely recognised now to be politically loaded; to be a reflection of the state of political play at whatever place and time a particular definition has been made. Thus '[t]he right of indigenous peoples to self-definition and self-identification, as well as to determine membership', as Rodolfo Stavenhagen points out, 'has ... become a major issue in recent debates and in negotiations between the indigenous and the State, both at the national and international levels'.[2]

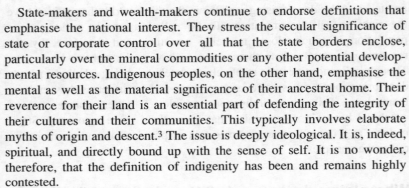

State-makers and wealth-makers continue to endorse definitions that emphasise the national interest. They stress the secular significance of state or corporate control over all that the state borders enclose, particularly over the mineral commodities or any other potential developmental resources. Indigenous peoples, on the other hand, emphasise the mental as well as the material significance of their ancestral home. Their reverence for their land is an essential part of defending the integrity of their cultures and their communities. This typically involves elaborate myths of origin and descent.[3] The issue is deeply ideological. It is, indeed, spiritual, and directly bound up with the sense of self. It is no wonder, therefore, that the definition of indigenity has been and remains highly contested.

With this in mind, the line between the concept of the nation and that of indigenous peoples is particularly hard to draw. Nation, as argued above, refers to a people who (with the exception of the gypsies) associate themselves with a particular geographic area, and who share a common heritage. What is the difference between this and the idea of indigenous peoples? They too are culturally distinct and attached to the land. In principle, then, the two are the same. There is one important difference, however, which is the notion that indigenous peoples have aboriginal status. They were the first inhabitants of part or all of the country in question, and being the first confers, in international law, prior claim to possession.

State-makers have exaggerated the difference between nation and indigenity in their bid to associate nation with state, and to marginalise the indigenous. State-makers will usually construct a hierarchy that has the national culture (whether synthetic, or the culture of a component people writ large) at the top. All other nationalities are made subordinate. They are either eliminated or tolerated depending on the size and significance of the indigenous group or groups, and the state-makers' political style.

Indigenous peoples generally realise that they have little chance of winning recognition as sovereign states in the modern sense. They may use 'nation' for the propaganda advantage it provides, and to highlight the persistence of internal colonialism, or they may eschew it as part of their oppressors' vocabulary and therefore as alien to them. The tactical advantage of the former lies in reminding state-makers of the right of indigenous peoples to self-determination. The advantage of the latter is the way it reminds indigenous peoples themselves of their exclusivity. They rarely claim 'statehood', however, despite the validity the claim may have, because of the futility of doing so in a state-bound world.

There is also a definitional battle over whether to use 'people' or 'population'. It is part of the ideology of the state, as developed in Europe and taken up by decolonising regimes in the third world, that nations have the right to self-determination. To be called a people rather than a population is much closer to being a nation, and therefore, by the reckoning of state-makers themselves, to having the right to be a state. Though indigenous peoples rarely claim statehood, being labelled a people does bring moral pressure to bear on state-makers in terms they endorse themselves. This gives indigenous peoples a better chance, not of statehood but of a compromise that gives them more autonomy. State-makers, as a consequence, prefer to talk of populations and communities rather than peoples.

What claims do they make? How do they make them?

For most indigenous peoples, their key claim is land. This claim is typically part of a long-standing attempt to win greater control over any territory they retain and, where possible, to get more back. State-makers typically discount such attempts as opportunistic, inappropriate or ill-timed. They assert that there should be only one category of citizenship within the border of the state. They see state sovereignty as indivisible. Indigenous peoples, however, see land and autonomy as essential prerequisites to their survival as separate communities. Their claims directly subvert, however, the principle of undivided rule.

Land

Land claims have intensified as state-makers and wealth-makers have sought to exploit areas that were once considered marginal, and therefore fit only for marginalised populations (like those of the indigenous peoples) to live in. With nowhere uncoveted to go, and no desire to relinquish their ancestral home-lands, those local communities of indigenes hardest pressed in this way have sought to stall the process or, at very least, to get compensation for what they have lost. [4]

Indigenous peoples have few formal channels through which to make land claims. They can appeal to the courts, but these administer alien laws, usually in ways partial to the dominant culture. They can seek, where the system permits it, political representation, but indigenous peoples are usually too small or too divided among themselves to make a difference in this regard or to sustain the necessary campaigns. They can also withdraw their labour, but the economic threat this represents is likely to be limited.

Their major weapon in practice is embarrassment, that is, the soliciting of sympathy for their plight among the rest of the populace 'at home', and among the morally moved abroad. This way they can attempt to shame the

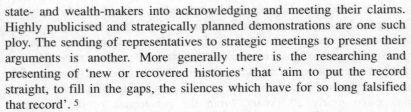

state- and wealth-makers into acknowledging and meeting their claims. Highly publicised and strategically planned demonstrations are one such ploy. The sending of representatives to strategic meetings to present their arguments is another. More generally there is the researching and presenting of 'new or recovered histories' that 'aim to put the record straight, to fill in the gaps, the silences which have for so long falsified that record'. [5]

These new and recovered readings of the past provide very different versions of the present. They can go 'some way [at least] towards representing the experiences and perspectives of powerless groups. They are part of the political struggle, for they represent ways of analysing and better understanding the unequal, often racist, distribution of power, and contest the terms and the outcomes of political action'. [6]

In the case of Australia, for example, the official account of the country's story has always said very little about the fate of the indigenous Aboriginal population. Formal histories have given, until very recently, a heavily censored account of what happened to this people, an account that has been used in turn to justify the status quo and affirm white dominance. As Jan Pettman points out:

> 'Australian' history was — and often still is — a series of myths which rationalise white colonisation and white privilege. It renders Aboriginal people, and the history of violence, dispossession, incarceration and continued racism, invisible — or, when noticed, blames them for their own oppression. Aboriginal people have other histories; they have resisted and rejected much white knowledge about themselves, their history and what needs to be done.[7]

How whites have perceived Aborigines over the 200 years since their occupation of the country is a revealing story in itself. Aborigines were first seen as animals. This legitimised the notion that the continent was uninhabited (terra nullius) and hence open for settlement without treaty. Certainly the Aborigines were largely treated as less than human, as savages. They were hunted, shot, poisoned and, where useful, exploited as nothing better than one example among many of the local fauna. Indeed, the last (formal) massacre of indigenous peoples in Australia was only fifty years ago.

Over time, as whites consolidated their control, their general perception of Aborigines began to shift and they came to be accorded child status, which in practice meant protection, reserves, and conversion to Christianity. Where fathered by whites, the young could be taken away to be trained ('for their own good') as domestics for white households. The male adults were used as a source of cheap labour on cattle stations. The female adults were used sexually, or taken into domestic service.

By the 1930s they began to achieve (in white perceptions) the status of stroppy adolescents. As their familiarity with white institutions grew, Aborigines began petitioning the federal parliament and using forms of protest familiar to those of whites. The struggle was protracted, but in 1967 Aboriginal men and women were finally accorded formal adult status as Australian citizens, and given voting rights. In all, the process had taken nearly 200 years. From the perspective of the European invader/settlers it was one of 'growing Aborigines up' in their own minds. Aborigines, of course, had always considered themselves grown up. The problem was exclusively a white one.

For many whites the process is far from complete, of course. Many still distinguish, for example, between 'real' Aborigines and 'part' Aborigines, distinctions which are not only personally and socially offensive and hurtful but that also have 'powerful political functions in challenging many Aborigines' right to speak for, or even about, Aboriginal claims'. [8]

Furthermore, distinctions like these, it is argued:

> change the name of the game, from indigenous status, colonisation and racism to culture of poverty explanations, by suggesting that Aborigines are culturally deprived or have 'lost' their culture; that their 'disadvantage' flows from poverty, social damage, the matriarchal family. Colonisation and dispossession, if remembered at all, are seen as distant causes; welfarism, not liberation, is the required response ... [This not only hinders] critical reflection on current social relations and cultural processes ... [it] deflects attention and energy ... [from whites]'. [9]

It promotes prescriptions which may well provide more money for Aboriginal affairs but does so at the cost of greater Aboriginal dependence, the maintenance of white control, and what has been called welfare colonialism.

Land rights claims remain central to the Australian Aboriginal cause. The lack of an original treaty like New Zealand's Waitangi Treaty has made their legal arguments difficult to sustain. On the other hand, the lack of a treaty suggests that Aborigines still own the whole country, whether or not they control it. This moral argument does not carry far in practical terms, but it does remind others of the magnitude of the original European landgrab, and the immoral manner of it. Pettman concludes that:

> Nothing in traditional Aboriginal society, its wisdom or organisation prepared it for invasion by late eighteenth-century or nineteenth-century Britishers — restless, materialistic, competitive — highly dangerous people, technologically and ideologically. In almost every regard, the two societies could hardly have been more different ... conflict was inevitable. But it wasn't only misunderstanding, or difference. The real conflicts were over power and control — over resources ... The two modes of production were incompatible. The two forms of land use could not coexist. [10]

This story is not unique to Australia. European imperialists created recognisable versions of the same narrative around the globe. Given the equally universal resistance to the claims of indigenes by those who inherited the imperial legacy — the leaders of the new states — that is, it is no surprise to find groups like the Australian Aborigines seeking solidarity with peers elsewhere. They now use such international links to try to shame concessions out of the state-makers involved, though it is an inevitably tenuous ploy, and the moral pressure is limited.

Despite similarities in the story of their subjugation around the globe, the histories of indigenous peoples are not the same. They are also divided in many ways among themselves. It is a measure of their determination and their desperation, therefore, that any such links should have been forged.

Indigenous peoples are not, after all, multinational corporations with portable business interests. They are not state-sanctioned diplomats or international civil servants with the resources of the whole system upon which to draw. They are highly parochial peoples distinguished by their commitment to particular localities and ways of life. They are as diverse as human beings can be, yet in the last decade they have become sufficiently active at the global level to form bodies such as the World Council of Indigenous Peoples. They have attended conferences together. They have brought cases before international tribunals. They have sought allies in the wider international community who might support their aspirations and help them to hold up to critical scrutiny the actions of state-makers and wealth-makers.

The extent to which international activity is a useful political strategy depends to some extent on the country within which any particular indigenous people is located. Embarrassing Australian state-makers, for example, is not easy. Despite living in a liberal democracy, with a large social welfare programme and a commitment to decolonisation, Aboriginal Australians still suffer badly on every political, social and economic scale. Whites live on average twenty years longer than Aborigines. Their children have one-third the chance of dying in infancy. The numbers of whites employed, not in prison, graduating from schools, earning good incomes and living under decent conditions, are all proportionately higher.

Embarrassing Australian state-makers is easier than embarrassing Soviet, Chinese, Brazilian or Filipino ones, though some state-makers are vulnerable in ways less easily dismissed. The World Bank, for example, has made loan grants to Brazil for developing the Amazon basin conditional on the settling of the land claims of some of the indigenous peoples living there. How useful this lever has been, however, and the extent to which it is a public relations gesture to distract attention from the genocide and ethnocide taking place in practice, are important questions yet to be answered to the satisfaction of the indigenes. Non-economic sanctions are typically ignored outright.

Language

Land, and its attendant development prospects, are not the only claims indigenous peoples make. They have persistently expressed concern about preserving their cultures, particularly the languages that allow the transmission of cultural codes and symbols. An indigenous people that is losing its language is one that, culturally speaking, is condemned to death.

To define the language of discourse is to have power of a peculiarly pervasive sort. The French, for example, have fought a long (and losing) battle to have their language retained as that of interstate diplomacy. The more widely French is spoken, the more French culture is understood and appreciated (and the more influence France has and the more money it makes). It was arrogance of a similarly self-serving sort that prompted the European imperialists to denigrate wherever they could the languages of their subject peoples as dialects.

The attempt to control the human tongue has meant that in most of the countries concerned 'indigenous languages are not given legal recognition, are not used in official administrative and judicial dealings, are not taught in schools, and the people who do use them are discriminated against and treated by the non-indigenous as outsiders, foreigners, barbarians, primitives'. [11]

To recognise the legitimacy of the language of indigenes is to recognise the existence of such people as a people, with state un-making potential. As a consequence most state-makers choose the assimilationist option, prohibiting or discouraging the practice of indigenous religions, the wearing of traditional costumes, the use of indigenous names, the protection of exploitable land sites because of their sacred significance, or any attempt to restrict tourism.

Those state-makers who do not opt for assimilation usually come to regret it. Cultural pluralism not only tends to undermine the centralising trend of modern state-making, but also raises other issues. Particular cultural practices of particular indigenous peoples, for example, may actively offend the mores of the state-made majority. Respect for indigenous culture can mean sanctioning behaviour state-makers hold abhorrent. Only vigorously pluralistic countries are likely to be able to sustain a non-assimilationist option for any length of time with any degree of success.

Customary law

The issue of language affects all others. The preservation of indigenous social and political institutions is not possible without the distinctiveness that separate speech confers. Nowhere is this more evident than in the area of customary law.

One of the most effective ways of forcing indigenous peoples to assimilate is to prohibit the use of their own language in their law-making, law-enforcing and law-adjudication procedures. This is the first step toward subjecting them to the alien forms and rules of the dominant culture. Through customary law indigenous mores are shown respect and taught to the young. Indigenous society itself is protected and promoted in the process. The non-recognition or the active denial of customary law amounts to ethnocide.

Customary law cannot be detached, however, from the larger political plight of indigenous peoples. This leads back to self-determination and questions about ownership of the land. Sovereign state-making conflicts with the independence that indigenous peoples see as their birthright. The latter must be made subordinate if state-makers are to exercise overall authority. This means that state-makers, to remain sovereign, can allow only limited self-government on the part of subject peoples. 'From time immemorial', however, 'indigenous and tribal peoples have been jealous of their sovereignty and independence. Most of them were incorporated against their will, through military and political pressures, into administrative systems not of their own choosing. They were reduced to minority status'. [12]

There is nothing new or unusual about this. State-making has been used to crush uncounted cultures. The efficiency of state-making in this regard does not, however, negate the arguments used by captive and colonised peoples for self-determination. They continue to be made, by minority groups in general and by indigenous peoples in particular, in their bid for more autonomy.

The claims of indigenous peoples are often the same as those of minority groups. The Minority Rights Group in London has for some years publicised the plight of marginalised peoples like the gypsies in Europe or the Tamils in Sri Lanka, and it becomes conceptually quite difficult deciding where such groups end and where indigenous peoples begin. Indigenous peoples have resisted being categorised as ethnic minorities, however, presumably to heighten the sense of their special aboriginal status.

Claims as rights

All such groups use the language of rights, particularly internationally, to further their claims. This language is now quite highly developed. In 1957, for example, the International Labour Organization (ILO) adopted a Convention (number 107) on the Protection of Indigenous and Tribal Populations. Revised in 1989, this set out in some detail a comprehensive wishlist of internationally applicable standards pertaining to control of their political, economic and social practices. In 1981 the UN set up a Working Group to draft a Universal Declaration of Indigenous Rights. Both documents cast the claims of indigenous peoples in terms of the doctrine of human rights.

Rights talk necessarily raises the whole question of the doctrine itself: who is it for, and what does it say? Rights are moral entitlements. As indicated earlier, they are the needs and wants that people feel most strongly they ought to have. As there is no external authority to sanction such claims, they stand only on the strength of the arguments for them. The stronger the claim, the better the argument has to be that backs it up. The doctrine is therefore a rationalist one, though it draws upon a value commitment to such moral concepts as justice, freedom, equality and individual and communal well-being, and the sense of compassion ostensibly common to all.

To appreciate what is involved we have first to define for ourselves what we think our most fundamental entitlements might be, by virtue of our singular status as human beings. It is useful at this point to remind ourselves of the reciprocal character of human rights. Rights have cognate duties, and one way of checking how fundamental our claims feel is by asking ourselves whether we can envisage granting the same claim if it were made on us by others.

There is a classic thought experiment, originally suggested by John Rawls,[13] we can perform here. A contemporary variant of it prompts us to imagine we are about to join a colony in space. The transport mechanism will get us there but with no guarantee what we will be like when we arrive; whether, that is, we will appear in the colony as a man or woman, young or old, black or white, gay or straight, disabled, Christian, Buddhist, Muslim, or Hindu. The question is: what rules would we write for such a colony, not knowing in advance what we might be like when we got there?

Under these conditions, unless radically conditioned otherwise, we would most likely devise very tolerant rules applicable regardless of such attributes as those listed above. In our own interests we would structure the society so that it paid most respect to our essential humanity, and least to secondary qualities like gender, race or age. (The assumptions built into the veil of ignorance used in this experiment give it an individualist bias, but that, though arguable, is still defensible.)

What, however, if in this colony there were a number of sovereign populations that contained discrete groups of people who happened to be there first, and who had been put at a well-nigh permanent disadvantage by the colonising process. We might also, in case we turned up as a member of one of these groups, want a separate bill of rights (and duties) that provided some protection against discrimination, oppression and exploitation by the community at large.

Of course, we live in such a colony already. It is our own planet. There are such sovereign populations — they are states. There are such discrete groups, some of whom we identify as indigenous peoples, who do not want to be assimilated or integrated into someone else's culture, or at least want to be able to choose which, if any, aspects of that culture they assimilate.

This desire brings them up against the political and legal systems of the state-makers. It can also bring them up against globally endorsed human rights practices that promote and protect the basic entitlements of the individual (though in other cases it may be the claims of the people as a whole that makes possible the enjoyment of basic rights by the individuals within it). The tension between the individualist and collectivist approach to rights claims can be acute.

On the one hand we have the individualist standards enshrined in the Universal Declaration of Human Rights, and the two Covenants that spell it out. These provide a specific and comprehensive list of human entitlements. They have received near-universal recognition, although their implementation has been limited and partial. Indigenous peoples, insofar as their members are considered human (and we saw with the Australian Aborigines how protracted and problematic extending the mantle of humanity can be), are entitled to all of them.

On the other hand:

> [t]here is a growing consensus ... that these international human rights instruments are not enough to guarantee the survival and protection of indigenous peoples around the world, particularly in the face of accelerated economic, social and cultural changes. Thus, the need for the definition of collective economic, social and cultural human rights ... Such collective rights are no substitute for the enjoyment of individual rights and do not supersede them. Nor do they necessarily stand in contradiction to individual rights. Rather, collective rights (such as the right of peoples to self-determination) must be seen as a necessary condition for the full enjoyment of individual rights, and conversely, the rights of collectivities may be deemed human rights only when they in turn enhance the enjoyment of individual human rights, not when they crush them. [14]

Certain traditions or customs in particular indigenous cultures — the ritual sexual mutilation of children and adolescents, for example — violate human rights. So do those practices that promote the social, economic and political inferiority of women. What has priority — the collective right to cultural identity, or the universal individual human right to liberty or equality? There is no formulaic answer. Collective rights are necessary to protect indigenous peoples. However, collective rights are no substitute for the enjoyment of individual rights in the Western tradition and do not, in that tradition, supersede them.

As indicated above, collective rights can, of course, affirm individual rights; they can be a necessary condition for their full enjoyment (as in the right of peoples to self-determination). Where collective rights do conflict with individual rights, they are human rights only when they enhance the enjoyment of individual rights, not when they deny them. The rights doctrine walks on two legs, in other words, collectivist and individualist. Each without the other makes for a lopsided whole.

Revising the ILO Convention No. 107, and drafting a United Nations Declaration on Indigenous Rights, are part of the attempt to use international tactics to change the behaviour of state-makers. In a state-bound world, upholding such rights requires the collaboration and support of state-makers themselves. In this sense it is advantageous that both instruments be drafted by state-makers for state-makers in organisations set up and maintained by state-makers. Thus state-makers can feel that they own the outcome. They may, as a consequence, be more favourably disposed towards honouring the spirit, if not the letter, of these instruments.

Indigenous peoples were not formally included in the process of drafting or revising the ILO Convention and though it articulates most of the claims that indigenous peoples make, this lack of consultation has reinforced the feeling that the state itself is the main problem indigenous peoples face, however benevolent its makers seem to be. The process of drafting the United Nations document has been much more participative, which may satisfy indigenous peoples but makes state-makers less inclined to ratify and implement its provisions.

As moral claims, lists of the rights of indigenous peoples are readily ignored by state-makers and wealth-takers. They have the power to do so, and as Carr points out, the powerful will invariably create the morality convenient to their cause. State-makers and wealth-takers share interests that do not coincide with those of indigenous peoples. Many of the latter's claims could only succeed against the interests of the former. It is hardly surprising, then, that state-makers and wealth-takers are wont to dismiss the rights of indigenous peoples as moralistic.

Moral claims of any sort are readily dismissed as mere moralism; as nothing but the rationalisation of particular desires; as wants or needs dressed up in the language of rights, but as lesser concerns regardless. Indeed, it is easy to dismiss the whole business of ideals in international politics as utopian. This is in line with the realistic appreciation of an indifferent universe. 'The great world', as Bertrand Russell put it, '... is neither good nor bad, and is not concerned to make us happy or unhappy. All such philosophies spring from self-importance and are best corrected by a little astronomy'.[15]

Moral expectations are certainly disappointed in political practice, yet they persist, and it would be as dangerous to deny their importance as it would be to say that brute force doesn't matter. Brute force does matter; but then so do people's beliefs. They legitimise brute force, and they can de-legitimise it too.

Modern international society is not very hospitable to rights talk. The basic principle of the society of states is the mutual recognition of sovereign jurisdiction. The other side of this coin is the acceptance by state-makers of the obligation not to interfere in each other's internal affairs. In the sort of international society where order among states is the highest value, the very idea of human rights and duties is potentially disruptive. It potentially sanctions intervention. If human rights are being abused in a particular state, it provides a rationale and a justification for going in to help. Such a justification, however, breaks the basic rule of the society of states itself.

Occasionally most state-makers will agree, at least tacitly, that such an intervention is warranted, and there are expeditions like the Tanzanian invasion of Uganda to topple Obote, or the Vietnamese invasion of Cambodia to overthrow Pol Pot. Intervention is also easier where it involves, as in these two cases, state-makers with poor sovereign credentials. Usually, though, the whole idea is anathema.

The international society of states is inhospitable to rights talk. Human rights are nonetheless given lip-service everywhere. It is a curious kind of back-handed compliment to the doctrine that it has become so pervasive despite its being so ineffectual.

The emphasis differs between ideological domains. State-makers in liberal capitalist countries are inclined to think of human rights in terms of the civil and political rights of individuals. They are the countries where these rights were first achieved and where they are best enjoyed. Rights to economic security, education or racial equality are seen as having been established through, and dependent for continuance on, freedom from arbitrary arrest, freedom of speech, and the freedom of political association.

The formal ideology in command socialist countries has traditionally depicted human rights in economic, social and cultural terms. Glasnost and perestroika gave voice to popular sentiments in support of freedom of expression and representative government. Civil and political rights like these that were not built upon economic and social foundations were traditionally regarded as bourgeois affectations.

For the state-makers of the developing world, the most important human rights have been the collective ones — the right of subject peoples to be freed from colonialism; the right of subject states to be freed from the neo-colonialism of transnational corporations and rich-world banks; and the right of subject races to be freed from white domination.[16]

For the indigenous peoples at the bottom of the pile it has been a protracted struggle convincing liberals of the validity of rights other than those rationally attached to individuals. It has been equally difficult convincing Marxists that the sentiments underlying their claims are as legitimate as class awareness.

Indigenous peoples and the state

One reason the struggle has been so protracted is that, contrary to conventional expectations about modernisation, about changing modes of production (and their assimilationist effects), and despite the nation-building of ambitious state-makers, indigenous peoples have not disappeared. Instead, state-making has raised ethnic awareness to new heights as people have become aware of their collective identity and have attempted to secure it in the face of the nation they are being told to obey. Rapid economic change, and changes in modes of production, have caused large demographic shifts which have also influenced people's sense of themselves as culturally distinct. Both sets of processes have affected indigenous peoples, who have found, or have been forced to find, new ways of asserting their autonomy and integrity.

The ways they have found are mostly indirect and symbolic because of their weakness, their powerlessness. They have had to resort to Carroll's competences, which are not inconsiderable. Using the power of their powerlessness, indigenous peoples around the world have consolidated an impressive log of rights claims. They have offered indirect opposition in a number of other ways as well, including 'cultural conservatism, reinforced by passive resistance'.[17]

As a result, traditional realists have had to revise their ideas about the singular significance of the state; about state-making as nation-making (and how successful this has been); and about the difference between domestic and foreign affairs. [18] How far should such revision proceed?

Some say the importance of indigenous peoples as social movements is minimal. The state constraints upon them are too severe, it is said, to allow their cause to become significant. In Dyck's words, '[t]he demands involved in endeavouring to bridge the organizational and cultural gap between the indigenous communities and various levels of government are onerous and unrelenting',[19] and as a result they never get anywhere.

Where state-makers can't eliminate cultural differences altogether, and can't eliminate the internal 'others' entirely, they can always fetishise them by making them into curiosities, and seek to control them that way.

Other analysts are less pessimistic. While admitting the difficulties that indigenous peoples face, and the lack of conventional economic and political resources available to them, they see their very capacity to endure as likely to win in the long run. The use by indigenous peoples of a more 'patient approach, ... the persistence and ingenuity typical of hunter-gatherers in making the most of opportunities others might deem nonviable' gives them a historical advantage.[20] We do well not to under-estimate the 'complexity, resilience, and even [the] irrationality' of ethnic bonds.[21] By organising around their aboriginal status, indigenous peoples, though disadvantaged, are mobilised in ways that state-makers and wealth-takers find hard to match.

The range of human rights indigenous peoples can claim is extensive. It includes the right to exist physically, to determine their own affairs, to control their traditional lands, to exploit the resources on or under those lands, and to live as they choose.[22] The international laws that render these claims legitimate are administered by state-makers, who find them easy to ignore.[23] They have the might that allows them to be indifferent, but their right to do so is contested. It is these rights that indigenes use in their long-term attempts to erode radically the might of the state. These moral claims can be sustained over generations by dedicated indigenes determined to survive. It may well, in such cases, be the state that gives way.

Notes

1 N. Dyck (ed.), *Indigenous Peoples and the Nation-State: "Fourth World" Politics in Canada, Australia and Norway,* Social and Economic Papers no. 14, Institute of Social and Economic Research, Memorial University of Newfoundland, St Johns, 1985, p. 1.

2 R. Stavenhagen, 'Effective protection and comprehensive development of the social and economic sectors in indigenous communities through international standard-setting activities', UN Centre for Human Rights, Geneva, 16-20 January 1989, pp. 5-6.

3 A. Smith, 'Ethnic Identity and World Order', *Millenium: Journal of International Studies* vol. 12 no. 2, 1983, pp. 152–3.

4 Independent Commission on International Humanitarian Issues, *Indigenous Peoples: a global quest for justice,* Zed Books, London, 1987, p. 23.

5 J. Pettman, 'Learning about power and powerlessness: Aborigines and white Australia's Bicentenary', *Race and Class* vol. 29 no. 3, Winter 1988, p. 69. See also B. Morris, 'The politics of identity: from Aborigines to the first Australian' in J. Beckett (ed.), *Past and Present: Constructions of Aboriginality,* AIAS, Canberra, 1988.

6 J. Pettman, op. cit., p. 69.

7 ibid., p. 70.
8 ibid., p. 76.
9 loc. cit. Also B. Morris, op. cit., p. 65.
10 J. Pettman, op. cit., p. 73.
11 R. Stavenhagen, op. cit., pp. 8–9.
12 ibid., p. 14.
13 J. Rawls, 'Justice as Fairness', *Philosophical Review* vol. 67, 1958, pp. 64–94, and the rejoinder by Brian Barry, 'The liberal theory of justice: a critical examination of the principal doctrines' in J. Rawls, *A theory of justice*, Clarendon Press, Oxford, 1973.
14 R. Stavenhagen, op. cit., p. 17.
15 B. Russell, *The Basic Writings of Bertrand Russell*, George Allen & Unwin, London, 1961, p. 371.
16 R. Vincent, 'Race in International Relations' in R. Walker (ed.), *Culture, Ideology and World Order*, Westview Press, Boulder, 1984.
17 N. Dyck, op. cit., p. 10.
18 S. Ryan, 'Explaining ethnic conflict: the neglected international dimension', *Review of International Studies* vol. 14, 1988, pp. 162-4. Also J. Stack, 'The Challenge of Ethnonationalism' in S. Lamy (ed.), *Contemporary International Issues: contending perspectives,* Lynne Rienner Publishers, Boulder, 1988, pp. 229–45.
19 N. Dyck, op. cit., p. 12.
20 ibid., p. 17.
21 J. Stack, op. cit., p. 243.
22 E. Anderson, 'The Saskatchewan Indians and Canada's New Constitution', *Journal of International Affairs* vol. 36 no. 1, Spring/Summer 1982, pp. 125–48.
23 R. Pettman, *State and Class: a Sociology of International Affairs*, Croom Helm, London, 1979, ch. 7, 'The Sociology of International Law'.

Bibliography

1985 *Social Research* vol. 52 no. 4.

1988 *Millenium* vol. 17 no. 3.

1989 World Survey on the Role of Women in Development, United Nations, New York.

Alexandre, L. 1989, 'Genderizing International Studies: Revisioning Concepts and Curriculum', *International Studies Notes*, vol. 14 no. 1.

Alker, H. 1981, 'Dialectical Foundations of Global Disparities', *International Studies Quarterly*, vol. 25 no. 1.

Allison, G. 1989, 'Testing Gorbachev', *Foreign Affairs*.

Althusser, L. 1971, 'Ideology and Ideological State Apparatuses (notes towards an investigation)', in *Lenin and Philosophy and Other Essays*, L. Althusser, Monthly Review Press, New York.

Anderson, B. 1983, *Imagined Communities: reflections on the origin and spread of nationalism*, Verso, London.

Anderson, E. 1982, 'The Saskatchewan Indians and Canada's New Constitution', *Journal of International Affairs* vol. 36 no. 1.

Ashley, R. 1980, *The Political Economy of War and Peace*, Frances Pinter, London.

Ashley, R. 1981, 'Political Realism and Human Interests', *International Studies Quarterly*, vol. 25, no. 2.

Ashley, R. 1983, 'Three Modes of Economism', *International Studies Quarterly* vol. 27.

Ashley, R. 1984, 'The poverty of neo-realism', *International Organization* vol. 38, no. 2.

Ashley, R. 1987, 'The Geopolitics of Geopolitical Space: Toward a Critical Social Theory of International Politics', *Alternatives* vol. 12.

Ashley, R. 1989, 'The "State" of the Discipline: realism under challenge?', unpub. paper.

Bandarage, A. 1984, 'Women in Development: Liberalism, Marxism and Marxism-Feminism', *Development and Change* vol. 15.

Banks, M. 1984, 'The Evolution of International Relations Theory' in *Conflict in Society,* M. Banks (ed.), St Martin's Press, New York.

Banks, M. 1985, 'The Inter-Paradigm Debate' in *International Relations,* M. Light & A. Groom (eds), Frances Pinter, London.

Barnett, R. & Muller, R. 1984, *Global Reach: the power of the multinational corporations,* Simon & Schuster, New York.

Barry, B. 1973, 'The liberal theory of justice: a critical examination of the principal doctrines' in *A theory of justice,* John Rawls, Clarendon Press, Oxford.

Bassett, S. (ed.) 1989, *The Origins of Anglo-Saxon Kingdoms,* Leicester University Press, Leicester.

Battle, J. 1988, 'Uskorenie, Glasnost and Perestroika: the pattern of reform under Gorbachev', *Soviet Studies,* vol. 40 no. 3.

Berman, M. 1982, *All That Is Solid Melts Into Air: The Experience of Modernity,* Simon & Schuster, New York.

Bernard, J. 1987, *The Female World from a Global Perspective,* Indiana University Press, Bloomington.

Bernstein, R. 1983, *Beyond Objectivism and Relativism: science, hermeneutics and praxis,* Basil Blackwell, Oxford.

Boggs, C. 1986, *Social Movements and Political Power: emerging forms of radicalism in the West,* Temple University Press, Philadelphia.

Bozeman, A. 1960, *Politics and Culture in International History,* Princeton University Press, Princeton.

Brandt, K.-W. 1986, 'New Social Movements as a Metapolitical Challenge: the social and political impact of a new historical type of protest', *Thesis Eleven,* no. 15.

Brown, S. 1988, 'Feminism, International Theory, and International Relations of Gender Inequality', *Millenium* vol. 17 no. 3.

Bull, H. 1977, *The Anarchical Society,* Macmillan, London.

Bull, H. & Watson, A. (eds) 1984, *The Expansion of International Society,* Clarendon Press, Oxford.

Burstyn, V. 1983, 'Masculine Dominance and the State' in *The Socialist Register 1983,* R. Miliband & J. Saville (eds), Merlin Press, London.

Burton, J. 1968, *Systems, States, Diplomacy and Rules,* Cambridge University Press, Cambridge.

Caldicott, H. 1978, *Nuclear Madness,* Jacaranda, Brisbane.

Camilleri, J. 1984, 'The Advanced Capitalist State and the Contemporary World Crisis' in *Culture, Ideology and World Order,* R. Walker (ed.),

Westview Press, Boulder.

Caporaso, J. 1987, 'The International Division of Labor: a theoretical overview' and 'Labor in the Global Economy' in *A Changing International Division of Labor*, J. Caporaso (ed.), Lynne Rienner Publishers, Boulder.

Cardoso, F. 1979, *Dependency and Development in Latin America*, University of California Press, Berkeley.

Carr, E. 1962, *The Twenty Years' Crisis 1919-1939: an introduction to the study of international relations* (2nd edn), Macmillan, London.

Carroll, B. 1972, 'Peace Research: The Cult of Power', *Journal of Conflict Resolution* vol. 16 no. 4.

Carse, J. 1986, *Finite and Infinite Games*, Penguin, Harmondsworth.

Castoriadis, C. 1988, 'The Gorbachev Interlude', *Thesis Eleven*, no. 20.

Chase-Dunn, C. 1981, 'Interstate System and Capitalist World-Economy' in *World System Structure*, W. Hollist & J. Rosenau (eds), Sage, Beverly Hills.

Chilton, P. (ed.) 1985, *Language and the Nuclear Arms Debate*, Frances Pinter, London.

Claude, I. 1962, *Power and International Relations*, Random House, New York.

Cohn, C. 1987, 'Sex and Death in the Rational World of Defense Intellectuals', *Signs* vol. 12 no. 4.

Connell, R. 1983, 'Class Formation on a World Scale' in *Which way is up? Essays on sex, class and culture*, R. Connell (ed.), George Allen & Unwin, Sydney.

Connell, R. 1987, *Gender and Power: society, the person and sexual politics,* Polity Press, Cambridge.

Corrigan, P. & Sayer, D. 1985, *The Great Arch: English State Formation as Cultural Revolution*, Basil Blackwell, Oxford.

Cox, R. 1987, *Production, Power, and World Order: social forces in the making of history*, Columbia University Press, New York.

Der Derian, J. 1987, *On Diplomacy: a genealogy of Western estrangement*, Basil Blackwell, Oxford.

Deutsch, K. 1963, *The Nerves of Government*, The Free Press, New York.

Dibb, P. 1986, *The Soviet Union: the incomplete superpower*, Macmillan, London.

Dore, R. 1969, 'The Japanese Personality' in *Asia Handbook* (rev. edn), G. Wint (ed.), Penguin, Harmondsworth.

Dyck, N. (ed.) 1985, *Indigenous Peoples and the Nation-State: 'Fourth World' Politics in Canada, Australia and Norway*, Social and Eonomic Papers no. 14, Institute of Social and Economic Research, Memorial University of Newfoundland, St Johns.

Dyer, J. 1986, 'The Psychopathology of Nuclear War', *Bulletin of the Royal College of Psychiatrists*, vol. 10.

Edelman, M. 1971, *Politics as Symbolic Vision*, Markham Publishing Co., Chicago.

Engels, F. 1952, *Origin of the family, private property and the state in the light of the researches of Lewis H. Morgan*, Foreign Languages Publishing House, Moscow.

Enloe, C. 1987, 'Feminists Thinking About War, Militarism, and Peace' in *Analysing Gender: a handbook of social science research*, B. Hess & M. Feree (eds), Sage, Newbury Park.

Enloe, C. 1989, *Bananas, Beaches and Bases: making feminist sense of international politics*, Pandora, London.

Epstein, G. 1985, 'The Triple Debt Crisis', *World Policy Journal* vol. 2 no. 4.

Feher, F. 1988, 'Crisis and Crisis-Solving in the Soviet System under Gorbachev's New Course', *Thesis Eleven*, no. 21.

Foucault, M. 1982, 'The Subject and Power', *Critical Inquiry* vol. 8.

Frank, A. 1966, 'The Development of Underdevelopment', *Monthly Review*, vol. 18 no. 4.

Frank, A. 1984, 'Can The Debt Bomb Be Defused?', *World Policy Journal* vol. 1 no. 4.

Frank, A. & Fuentes, M. 1987-88, 'Nine Theses on Social Movements', *Thesis Eleven* nos 18-19.

French, M. 1985, *Beyond Power: on women, men, and morals*, Jonathon Cape, London.

Frost, M. 1986, *Towards a Normative Theory of International Relations*, Cambridge University Press, Cambridge.

Geertz, C. 1980, *Negara: the theatre state in nineteenth-century Bali*, Princeton University Press, Princeton.

Geertz, C. 1987, ' "From the Native's Point of View": On the Nature of Anthropological Understanding' in *Interpreting Politics*, M. Gibbons (ed.), Basil Blackwell, Oxford.

George, J. 1989, 'International Relations and the Search for Thinking Space: another view of the third debate', *International Studies Quarterly*, vol. 33 no. 3.

George, S. 1988, *A Fate Worse Than Debt*, Penguin, Harmondsworth.

Gilpin, R. 1987, *The Political Economy of International Relations*, Princeton University Press, Princeton.

Gorbachev, M. 1988, *Perestroika*, Fontana, London.

Green, P. 1983, 'Debt, the Banks and Latin America', *International Socialism* no. 21.

Grotius, H. 1925, *De Jure Belli ac Pacis*, Clarendon Press, Oxford.

Gurtov, M. 1988, *Global Politics in the Human Interest*, Lynne Rienner Publishers, Boulder.

Haas, E. 1953, 'The Balance of Power: prescription, concept or propaganda?', *World Politics* vol. 5 no. 4.

Hartsock, N. 1983, *Money, Sex and Power*, Longman, New York.

Healey, D. 1988, 'Japanese Private and Public Capital Outflows and Asian Economic Development in the 1980's', OECD Development Centre, Paris, Doc. No. CD/R(88)34.

Heller, A. 1984, 'Marx and Modernity', *Thesis Eleven* no. 8.

Herbert, N. 1988, *Quantum Reality*, Rider, London.

Hobbes, T. 1914, *Leviathan*, J.M. Dent, London.

Hobsbawm, E. & Ranger, T. (eds) 1983, *The Invention of Tradition*, Cambridge University Press, Cambridge.

Hoffman, S. 1967, 'Perceptions, Reality and the Franco-American Conflict' in *Image and Reality*, J. Farrell & A. Smith (eds), Columbia University Press, New York.

Holley, H. 1987, *Developing Country Debt: the role of the commercial banks*, Chatham House Papers no. 35, The Royal Institute of International Affairs, Routledge & Kegan Paul, London.

Holzgrefe, J. 1989, 'The Origins of Modern International Relations Theory', *Review of International Studies* vol. 15.

Hoogvelt, A. 1982, *The Third World in Global Development*, Macmillan, London.

Hosking, G. 1988, 'A Great Power in Crisis: the first 1988 Reith Lecture', *The Listener*.

Hough, J. 1988, *Russia and the West: Gorbachev and the politics of reform*, Simon & Schuster, New York.

Howard, M. 1989, 'Ideology and international relations', *Review of International Studies* vol. 15 no. 1.

Hume, D. 1951, 'The Balance of Power' in *Hume: Theory of Politics*, F. Watkins (ed.), Nelson, Edinburgh.

Huntington, S. 1988-89, 'The U.S. — Decline or Renewal?', *Foreign Affairs* vol. 67 no. 2.

Hymer, S. 1972, 'The Internationalization of Capital', *Journal of Economic Issues* vol. 6 no. 1.

Ichiyo, M. 1987, *Class Struggle and Technological Innovation in Japan Since 1945*, International Institute for Research and Education, Amsterdam.

Independent Commission on International Humanitarian Issues 1987, *Indigenous Peoples: a global quest for justice*, Zed Books, London.

Jones, A. 1987, 'The violence of materialism in advanced industrial society: an eco-sociological approach', *Sociological Review* vol. 35 no. 1.

Kahler, M. (ed.) 1986, *The Politics of International Debt*, Cornell University Press, Ithaca.

Kaiser, R. 1988, 'The U.S.S.R. in Decline', *Foreign Affairs*.

Kay, G. 1975, *Development and Underdevelopment: a Marxist analysis*, Macmillan, London.

Kegley, C. et al. 1988, 'The Multinational Corporation: Curse or Cure?' in *The Global Agenda* (2nd edn), C. Kegley & E. Wittkopf, Random House, New York.

Keynes, J. 1933, 'National Self-Sufficiency', *The New Statesman and Nation*.

Kidron, M. & Segal, R. 1987, *The New State of the World Atlas*, Pan Books, London.

Kindleberger, C. 1970, *Power and Money: the economics of international politics and the politics of international economics*, Basic Books, New York.

Kindleberger, C. 1978, *Manias, Panics and Crashes*, Macmillan, London.

Kitto, H. 1951, *The Greeks*, Penguin, Harmondsworth.

Knorr, K. 1973, *Power and Wealth: the political economy of international power*, Macmillan, London.

Krasner, S. (ed.) 1983, *International Regimes*, Cornell University Press, Ithaca.

Kubalkova, V. & Cruikshank, A. 1985, *Marxism and International Relations*, Clarendon Press, Oxford.

Kuhn, T. 1979, *The Structure of Scientific Revolutions* (2nd edn), University of Chicago Press, Chicago.

Kunzle, D. 1984, 'Introduction to the English Edition' in *How to Read Donald Duck: imperialist ideology in the Disney comic*, A. Dorfman & A. Mattelart, International General, New York.

Langmore, J. & Peertz, D. (eds) 1983, *Wealth, Poverty and Survival*, George Allen & Unwin, Sydney.

Leaver, R. 1989, 'Restructuring in the Global Economy: from Pax Americana to Pax Nipponica', Working Paper No. 61, Peace Research Centre, The Australian National University, Canberra.

Lenin, V. 1973, *Imperialism, The Highest Stage of Capitalism*, Foreign Languages Press, Peking.

Lerner, G. 1986, *The Creation of Patriarchy*, Oxford University Press, Oxford.

Lukes, S. (ed.) 1986, *Power*, Basil Blackwell, Oxford.

Luxemburg, R. & Bukharin, N. 1972, *Imperialism and the Accumulation of Capital*, Allen Lane, London.

Mabbot, J. 1958, *The State and the Citizen*, Arrow Books, London.

Magdoff, H. 1986, 'Third World Debt: Past and Present', *Monthly Review* vol. 37 no. 9.

Mann, M. 1986, *The Sources of Social Power* vol. 1, Cambridge University Press, Cambridge.

Marcuse, H. 1968, *One-Dimensional Man: the Ideology of Industrial Society,* Sphere, London.

Marx, K. 1964, 'Estranged Labor' in *Economic and Philosophic Manuscripts of 1844*, K. Marx, International Publishers, New York.

Marx, K. 1966, *Capital: a critique of political economy* vol. 3, Progress Publishers, Moscow.

Marx, K. & Engels, F. 1975, *Manifesto of the Communist Party*, Foreign Languages Press, Peking.

Marx, K. & Engels, F. 1977, *The German Ideology*, Lawrence & Wishart, London.

Mattelart, A. 1979, *Multinational Corporations and the Control of Culture: the ideological apparatuses of imperialism*, Harvester Press, Sussex.

McLaughlin, B. (ed.) 1969, *Studies in Social Movements*, The Free Press, New York.

Mies, M. 1986, *Patriarchy and Accumulation on a World Scale: women in the international division of labour*, Zed Books, London.

Mies, M. et al. 1988, *Women: the last colony*, Zed Books, London.

Mill, J. 1975, *Subjection of Women*, Massachusetts Institute of Technology Press, Cambridge.

Miller, J. 1981, *The World of States*, St Martin's Press, New York.

Modelski, G. (ed.) 1987, *Exploring Long Cycles*, Lynne Rienner Publishers, Boulder.

Moore, B. 1966, *Social Origins of Dictatorship and Democracy*, Penguin, Harmondsworth.

Morgenthau, H. 1978, *Politics Among Nations* (5th edn rev.), Alfred A. Knopf, New York.

Morris, B. 1988, 'The politics of identity: from Aborigines to the first Australian' in *Past and Present: Constructions of Aboriginality*, J. Beckett (ed.), AIAS, Canberra.

Mowlana, H. 1986, *Global Information and World Communication*, Longman, New York.

Mumford, L. 1934, *Technics and Civilisation*, George Routledge & Sons, London.

Niebuhr, R. 1936, *Moral Man and Immoral Society: a study in ethics and politics*, Charles Scribners' Sons, New York.

Orwell, G. 1960, 'Politics and the English Language' in *Identity and Anxiety*, M. Stein et al. (eds), The Free Press, Glencoe.

Page, J. 1975, *Psychopathology*, Aldine, Chicago.

Pakulski, J. 1990, *Social Movements: the politics of moral protest*, Longman Cheshire, Melbourne.

Pateman, C. 1988, *The Sexual Contract*, Polity Press, Cambridge.

Payer, C. 1987, 'Causes of the Debt Crisis' in *The Imperial Economy* vol. 1, R. Cherry et al. (eds), Union for Radical Political Economics, New York.

Pettman, J. 1988, 'Learning about power and powerlessness: Aborigines and white Australia's Bicentenary', *Race and Class* vol. 29 no. 3.

Pettman, R. 1979, *State and Class: a Sociology of International Affairs*, Croom Helm, London.

Pettman, R. 1989, 'The Psychopathology of Nuclear Deterrence' in *Beyond Deterrence,* G. Rodley (ed.), Centre for Peace and Conflict Studies, University of Sydney.

Pope, A. 1974, 'The Balance of Europe' in *Collected Poems*, A. Pope, Everyman's Library, London.

Randall, V. 1987, *Women and Politics: an international perspective* (2nd edn), Macmillan, London.

Rapoport, A. 1984, 'Preparation for Nuclear War: the final madness', *Journal of Orthopsychiatry* vol. 54 no. 4.

Rawls, J. 1958, 'Justice as Fairness', *Philosophical Review* vol. 67.

Reardon, B. 1983, *Sexism and the War System*, Teachers College Columbia University, New York.

Righter, R. 1978, *Whose News?: politics, the press and the third world*, Burnett Books, London.

Rorty, R. 1987, 'Method, Social Science and Social Hope' in *Interpreting Politics*, M. Gibbons (ed.), Basil Blackwell, Oxford.

Rudolph, L. & Rudolph, S. 1967, *The Modernity of Tradition: political development in India*, University of Chicago Press, Chicago.

Russell, B. 1961, *The Basic Writings of Bertrand Russell*, George Allen & Unwin, London.

Ryan, S. 1988, 'Explaining ethnic conflict: the neglected international dimension', *Review of International Studies* vol. 14.

Rytting, R. 1989, 'Class Struggles in Japan', *Restructuring and Labor* no. 19.

Sampson, A. 1973, *Sovereign State: the secret history of ITT*, Hodder & Stoughton, London.

Schmitt, H. 1979, 'Mercantilism: a modern argument', *The Manchester School of Economic and Social Studies* vol. 47.

Schuman, F. 1958, *International Politics: The Western State System and the World Community* (6th edn), McGraw Hill, New York.

Seager, J. & Olson, A. 1986, *Women in the World: an international atlas*, Simon & Schuster, New York.

Sen, G. & Grown, C. 1987, *Development, Crises and Alternative Visions: Third World Women's Perspectives*, Monthly Review Press, New York.

Shultz, A. 1973, *A Theory of Consciousness*, Philosophical Library, New York.

Sinha, R. 1988, 'U.S. Hegemony and the Japanese Challenge', *Coexistence* vol. 25.

Sivard, R. 1985, *Women: a world survey*, World Priorities, Washington.

Smith, A. 1983, 'Ethnic Identity and World Order', *Millenium: Journal of International Studies* vol. 12 no. 2.

Spengler, O. 1961, *The Decline of the West*, Knopf, New York.

Stack, J. 1988, 'The Challenge of Ethnonationalism' in *Contemporary International Issues: contending perspectives*, S. Lamy (ed.), Lynne Rienner Publishers, Boulder.

Stavenhagen, R. 1989, 'Effective protection and comprehensive development of the social and economic sectors in indigenous communities through international standard-setting activities', UN Centre for Human Rights, Geneva.

Stephen, J. 1967, *Liberty, Equality, Fraternity*, Cambridge University Press, Cambridge.

Strange, S. 1986, *Casino Capitalism*, Basil Blackwell, Oxford.

Tawney, R. 1930, 'Foreword' in *The Protestant Ethic and the Spirit of Capitalism*, M. Weber, Unwin, London.

Taylor, T. 1978, 'Power Politics' in *Approaches and Theory in International Relations*, T. Taylor (ed.), Longman, London.

The Harvard University Nuclear Study Group 1983, *Living with Nuclear Weapons*, Harvard University Press, Cambridge.

The Military Balance, annual, The International Institute for Strategic Studies, London.

Thomas, L. 1983, *Late Night Thoughts on Listening to Mahler's Ninth Symphony*, Bantam, New York.

Thompson, E. 1982, *Zero Option*, Merlin Press, London.

Thompson, S. & Schneider, H. 1986, 'Nuclear Winter Reappraised', *Foreign Affairs*.

Thorndike, T. 1978, 'The revolutionary approach: the Marxist perspective' in *Approaches and Theory in International Relations*, T. Taylor (ed.), Longman, London.

Tilly, C. (ed.) 1975, *The Formation of National States in Western Europe*, Princeton University Press, Princeton.

Tilly, C. 1985, 'War Making and State Making as Organized Crime' in *Bringing the State Back In*, P. Evans et al. (eds), Cambridge University Press, Cambridge.

Touraine, A. 1982, 'Triumph or downfall of civil society', *Humanities Review* vol. 1.

Toynbee, A. 1946 and 1957, *A Study of History* (Somervell abridgement), Oxford University Press, Oxford.

Van Duijn, J. 1983, *The Long Wave in Economic Life*, George Allen & Unwin, London.

Vincent, A. 1987, *Theories of the State*, Basil Blackwell, Oxford.

Vincent, R. 1984, 'Race in International Relations' in *Culture, Ideology and World Order*, R. Walker (ed.), Westview Press, Boulder.

Viner, J. 1948, 'Power Versus Plenty as Objectives of Foreign Policy in the Seventeenth and Eighteenth Centuries', *World Politics* vol. 1 no. 1.

Vogler, C. 1985, *The Nation State: the neglected dimension of class*, Gower, Aldershot.

Walker, R. 1984, 'World Politics and Western Reason: Universalism, Pluralism, Hegemony' in *Culture, Ideology and World Order*, R. Walker (ed.), Westview Press, Boulder.

Walker, R. 1988, *One World/Many Worlds: struggles for a just world peace*, Lynne Rienner Publishers, Boulder.

Walker, R. 1989, 'Ethics, Modernity and the Theory of International Relations', unpub. paper.

Walker, R. 1989, 'The Concept of Culture in the Theory of International Relations' in *Culture and International Relations*, J. Chay (ed.), Praeger, New York.

Wallerstein, I. 1974, *The Modern World-system: capitalist agriculture and the origins of the European world-economy in the sixteenth century*, Academic Press, New York.

Wallerstein, I. 1979, *The Capitalist World-economy*, Cambridge University Press, Cambridge.

Waltz, K. 1979, *Theory of International Politics,* Addison-Wesley, Reading.

Warren, B. 1973, 'Imperialism and Capitalist Development', *New Left Review* no. 81.

Wight, M. 1967, 'Western Values in International Relations' in *Diplomatic Investigations,* H. Butterfield & M. Wight (eds), Allen & Unwin, London.

Wight, M. 1978, 'The Pattern of Power' and 'The Balance of Power' in *Power Politics*, H. Bull & C. Holbraad (eds), Leicester University Press, Leicester.

Williams, R. 1983, *Keywords* (rev. edn), Fontana, London.

Wollstonecraft, M. 1975, *Vindication of the Rights of Women*, Penguin, Harmondsworth.

Wood, G. 1985, 'The Politics of Development Policy Labelling', *Development and Change* vol. 16.

Yuval-Davis, Y. & Anthias, F. (eds) 1988, *Woman-Nation-State*, Macmillan, London.

Zhurkin, V. et al. 1988, 'Challenges of Security — Old and New' (trans. G. Jukes), *Kommunist* no. 1.

Index